Freud Rediscovered

Also by Lucy Freeman

Fight Against Fears
Before I Kill More
The Dream
The Psychiatrist Says Murder
The Case on Cloud Nine
The Cry for Love
The Story of Anna O.
Betrayal (with Julie Roy)
The Sorrow and the Fury
Who Is Sylvia?

Freud
Rediscovered

by Lucy Freeman

 ARBOR HOUSE NEW YORK

Acknowledgments

My thanks to Donald I. Fine, president of Arbor House, whose idea this book was, and to Joan Marlow, editor, whose artful skill helped shape it, Eden Collinsworth, director of publicity, and Mary Yost, my literary agent.

Also to the following psychoanalysts for the help they have given: Dr. Ralph Crowley, Dr. Charles Fisher, Dr. Gerald V. Freiman, Dr. Lawrence J. Friedman, Dr. Martin Grotjahn, Dr. Henriette Klein, Dr. Robert Langs, Dr. Karl Menninger, Dr. Burness Moore, Dr. George Pollock, Dr. Lewis Robbins and Dr. Walter A. Stewart, as well as a few psychoanalysts who described cases, which I have used to illustrate various points, without identifying either analyst or patient.

And to Helen Fischer, administrative director of the American Psychoanalytic Association; Ron McMillen, of the public information office, American Psychiatric Association, and David Schroedel, psychotherapist.

Thanks too to Katherine Wolpe, librarian, and Jeanette Taylor and Ruth M. Reynolds of the New York Psychoanalytic Institute library.

"What this world needs are men of strong passions who have the ability to control them."

—Sigmund Freud, in a conversation with Theodor Reik

Contents

I

Freud Is Alive and Well

Nearly twenty-one centuries have passed since Plato wrote, "The life that is unexamined is not worth living," and advised man to "Know thyself."

It was easy to *say* "Know thyself." But how was man to *do* it?

By what alchemy could he reach into his mind and release imprisoned thoughts and memories?

Interpret the meaning of dreams that puzzled his intellect and tormented his soul?

Explain why he often acted against his better judgment and why "will power" did not enable him to change?

For close to two millenniums Plato's celebrated dictum seemed to pose an impossible challenge to mankind. Then, at the dawn of the twentieth century, a lone doctor in Vienna, Sigmund Freud, conducted what Alexander Pope, in 1733, called "the proper study of mankind." Freud made startling discoveries that were to revolutionize the thinking of the world about the mind of man. Five centuries before Christ, Heraclitus had said, "The soul of man is a far country, which cannot be approached or explored." But one man, Sigmund Freud, not only crossed the frontier of that far country but penetrated its heartland, and through his writings and personal influence made the inner landscape available to all who dared follow.

This is the century of Freud. As Auden wrote:

> To us he is no more a person
> Now but a whole climate of opinion.

Freud's discovery of psychoanalysis is the most important force exerted by an individual in our century on all areas of society, according to Dr. Alan Stone, president of the American Psychiatric Association, whose 25,000 members represent eighty percent of the nation's psychiatrists. In his acceptance speech at the May 1979 meeting in Chicago, Dr. Stone declared:

"The genius, the Daedalus, who gave psychiatry its wings was, in my opinion, Sigmund Freud. The power of the Freudian vision of mankind transformed the twentieth-century mind in its 'everyday' conception of the human situation. The palpable power of Freud's ideas elevated our profession. Ironically, even those of us who loudly repudiated his ideas were raised on his shoulders."

Freud has been called the "Darwin of the mind." Freud and Darwin were *the* seminal thinkers, the foundation-layers for twentieth-century thought on human evolution and behavior. Darwin dealt with the physical evolution of *homo sapiens,* Freud discovered the origins and development of his psyche.

Darwin's *Origin of the Species* came out when Freud was three years old. After graduating from high school at seventeen, Freud decided to study medicine, in large part, he said, because the new theories of Darwin, theories that were stimulating thought all over the world, "strongly attracted me."

Freud later equated the psychic and emotional development of civilization with that of the individual. He considered nations and mankind as a whole as prisoners of the past—prisoners who attempted, most of the time unsuccessfully, to break free of destructive behavior.

Freud saw the history of man as the process of a slow awakening to consciousness and civilization from a primitive, prehistoric state. The caveman was intent on mere survival in a world of preying monsters, foraging for food and guarding himself against savage enemies who struck in the dark. It took millions of years for the human intellect to start functioning beyond this primitive instinctual level.

At first Freud was rejected by his colleagues in Vienna, who ridiculed his theories and treated him with contempt. Gradually he became accepted in Switzerland, France, Germany, England and the United States, where in the 1940s and 1950s, psychoanalysis became fashionable among intellectuals. Hundreds of thousands read about Freud and the more intrepid bought his books, including *A General Introduction to Psychoanalysis*. The analyst's couch became the refuge of the affluent who sought self-knowledge and relief from inner anguish.

Even those who had never been to a psychoanalyst nor read Freud's works became familiar with Freudian ideas. It became popular to speak sophisticatedly of "id" and "ego," "defense" and "projection." Psychoanalysts were caricatured in cartoon, joke, book and film. Psychotherapy was "in"—feared, but granted power and a grudging respect.

Psychoanalysts served in the armed forces in World War II, helping emotionally disturbed fighting men overcome the trauma of war, and the growing belief in the new science of the mind rose higher. But it appeared by the 1960s that the magical expectations were not to be fulfilled. Not everyone who underwent psychoanalytic treatment was promptly "cured." Not every psychoanalyst proved to be God. Psychoanalysis was labeled passé.

"Psychoanalysis is dead," a belligerent reporter said recently to Helen Fischer, administrative director of the American Psychoanalytic Association.

"The reports of our demise are greatly exaggerated," she replied quietly.

Ms. Fischer has watched the membership of the Association double in the past fifteen years, and like the psychoanalysts themselves has paid little attention to the recurring "obituary" of psychoanalysis. Such obituaries have appeared intermittently ever since Freud delivered his lecture "On Male Hysteria" before the

Vienna Medical Society on October 15, 1886, asserting hysteria could be found in men as well as women. Up to then doctors believed only women were subject to hysterical attacks—in fact, the word "hysteria" was derived from the Greek *hystera* meaning uterus or womb.

Psychoanalysis has been attacked regularly. As Freud said, ". . . it is the inevitable fate of psychoanalysis to arouse opposition and to embitter people." It has been criticized as "the opiate of the upper classes," the rich and the bored. Replying to this, Dr. Leston L. Havens, author of *Approaches to the Mind*, stated, "Since I have always carried on my work both at a public hospital and in private practice, for me the rich and the poor have sat side by side. It is hard to judge who is the unhappier." Studies show "appalling rates of psychiatric illness in all classes, so the reason for treating the poor is not that the rich are well," he pointed out.

Psychoanalysis, like any complicated medical technique such as kidney dialysis and heart transplants, defies broad application, he asserted. But the psychoanalytic technique, by easing inner suffering, provides the knowledge that may make possible the discovery of other methods more broadly applicable, such as psychotherapy based on Freudian theories.

Because Freud discovered psychoanalysis, the term "Freudian analysis" is redundant, inaccurate. Other kinds of therapy cannot be termed psychoanalysis in the strict sense of the word. Many do not realize this and refer to a Jungian or Adlerian therapist or a behavioral psychologist as "my analyst."

It is interesting how almost everyone gives his opinion as an expert on psychoanalysis. Some jeer at Freud's theories even as they reveal they have unconsciously accepted them. One woman vehemently denounced psychoanalysis after her twenty-two-year-old son went into treatment and moved away to his own apartment. She said angrily, "I don't believe this Freudian nonsense—that unhappiness is rooted in childhood."

Ten minutes later she announced, just as angrily, "My husband grew up dominated by his selfish, man-eating mother, so no wonder he has problems!"

Freud was aware of such "resistance," which he knew led many to condemn or ignore his discoveries. He understood that the process of socialization involved repressing powerful sexual and aggressive drives, and that the human psyche built strong defenses against the recognition of these primitive instinctual desires—to become angry when one is asked to face feelings and thoughts believed damaging to the self-image.

Such "resistance" against the acceptance of psychological truths, Freud said, had to be overcome in every personal analysis. He defined resistance as the operation of the unconscious part of the ego to block awareness of the anxiety that serves as a warning signal that erotic or aggressive impulses are emerging.

Resistance is one of the primary reasons why psychoanalysis is a long and gradual process. The patient has to overcome the barriers to self-awareness before he can begin to understand his own neurotic patterns and how to break them. Resistance was a formidable obstacle to the acceptance of psychoanalysis as a science. It was the resistance of Viennese physicians that caused Freud to stand alone as he established psychic precedent, facing the contempt and envy of medical colleagues threatened by a new approach to mental illness, an approach most neither understood nor wished to understand.

Pasteur pointed out that the only way to deny the existence of microbes was to refuse to look into the microscope. Those who scorned Freud's findings were refusing to turn their mind's eye inward, to face the facts of psychic life.

As in ancient times the bearer of evil tidings was killed, so Freud —and psychoanalysis—were figuratively annihilated. Freud knew he had "wounded mankind"—his words—by showing that man was not master of his fate, but controlled by mental forces of which he was often unaware. It was a deep blow to man's pride.

One of the first charges brought against psychoanalysis—and still prevalent in spite of the new sexual freedom—was that psychoanalysis advocated licentiousness. To say this is to misunderstand Freud's theories. He discovered what he called the psychosexual development of man, from the cradle to the grave, and showed how it could be crippled by emotional traumas in infancy. Freud advocated sexual *liberation*—the gratification of the sexual impulse divorced from the compulsiveness of promiscuity as well as the inhibition of frigidity and impotence. But this was far different from sexual *license,* a sign of *not* being sexually free. A person sexually free can live in harmony and intimacy with someone and has no need to "prove" his or her sexuality through sheer numbers of sexual encounters or "conquests."

Today Freud is attacked by some of the leaders of the women's liberation movement who view him as a male chauvinist, claiming that he perpetuated the exploitation of woman. Let Freud defend himself in his own words, written in 1933 in his paper "Femininity":

"But we must beware . . . of underestimating the influence of social customs, which . . . force women into passive situations . . . the suppression of women's aggressiveness which is proscribed for them constitutionally and imposed on them socially favors the development of powerful masochistic impulses. . . ."

When Freud asked Princess Marie Bonaparte, "What does a woman want?", this was not an accusatory inclusive observation but a casual comment, possibly a natural query about some of his neurotic women patients who brought him complaints based in part on the prudish times in which they lived.

In his personal life Freud never discriminated against women. Among his close friends were several sensitive, brilliant women, including Bonaparte and Lou Andreas-Salomé, who became psychoanalysts, and his wife's sister, Minna. He confided to them his deeper thoughts, treated them as equals.

In fact, Freud's first patients were women, to whose emotional liberation he was dedicated. For ten years before he became a psychoanalyst, he repeatedly recalled, as though enraptured, the words of a young woman (the famous "Anna O.") who referred to her experience with Dr. Josef Breuer as "the talking cure." Freud later said that this woman helped lead him to psychoanalysis.

Were it not for Freud's discovery of the crippling effects of repressed sexuality in women, in all likelihood the sexual revolution would not have occurred as soon as it did, and the women's liberation movement might be a thing of the future rather than a current social force. By recognizing the powerful role of repressed sexuality in the life of both men and women, Freud contributed in large part to the end of the puritanical era.

Some feminists criticize Freud for pronouncing women inferior when he wrote, "Anatomy is destiny." What he meant was merely that women seemed destined to bring up the children and take care of the home and that men were destined to be breadwinners, seekers of power and adventurers. And in the days before the birth control revolution and before the existence of daycare facilities and maternity leave, these destinies were more usually than not fulfilled.

"Anatomy is not destiny but the attitudes associated with anatomy influence destiny." These are the words of Dr. Rebecca Z. Solomon, president of the American Psychoanalytic Association. She points out that though Freud's views on female psychology have been severely criticized by some, "we must remember that the women he analyzed brought to his couch the views about femininity prevalent at the time, and that these views also influenced Freud's interpretation of what he heard and observed."

She cites the end of his article on femininity, in which "Freud reminds us that his views are tentative, that they are based on observations of troubled women, and that we need to learn much more about the matter. We *have* learned some more about the matter and there have been modifications of Freud's views."

Freud was never satisfied with equating femininity with passivity, submissiveness and masochism, and masculinity with activity and assertiveness, Solomon maintained. His formulation of femininity suffered "because he did not emphasize sufficiently the importance of pre-Oedipal experience and sociological expectations. But he noted these limitations and advised further investigators to pay more attention to them."

Freud has also been attacked by certain feminists for his belief that the vaginal orgasm was superior to the clitoral, that is, of climax achieved through intercourse rather than by masturbation or manual manipulation by another. But rather than taking Freud to task for daring to place a value judgment on the mechanics of female sexuality, the women's liberation movement might better applaud him for bringing to light the fact that there was such a thing as female sexuality. Freud lived in the Victorian era, when British wives were urged to "think of England" during the presumably distasteful act of sex. Were it not for Freud—who not only had a great influence on later sexologists but also changed the general and particularly the paternal outlook on sex—it is probable that many fewer women today would be experiencing orgasms of any kind.

Who knows what Freud would have said about woman today? Times have changed drastically since those "romantic," sexually inhibited days of the early twentieth century. Two-thirds of the women in the United States have sexual intercourse by the age of nineteen, almost all before marriage, according to a recent study at the Johns Hopkins School of Hygiene and Public Health. One in five has sexual intercourse at the age of sixteen and one in ten becomes pregnant before seventeen. We can hardly condemn Freud for failing to respond to a situation that did not exist in his lifetime.

The very date and circumstances of his birth have been held against Freud. Critics charge that he was "a nineteenth-century Viennese," as though this negated his theories. They grant that he was a genius but then add that, like all geniuses, he was limited by his era—one might say the same about Darwin or Einstein. Referring to Freud, Dr. Karen Horney wrote, "Not even a genius can entirely step out of his time." And Dr. Clara Thompson: "Although a genius, Freud was in many respects limited by the thinking of his time as even a genius must be."

According to Dr. Joseph Wortis, who went to Freud for analysis, Freud once told him, "Calling me a genius is the latest way people have of starting their criticism of me. First they call me a genius and then they proceed to reject all my views." (Itself a Freudian reaction—killing the totem father figure.)

It has also been fashionable to charge that Freud was dogmatic and unyielding in his beliefs. The facts show the opposite. "The essence of Freud's work and thinking, with very few exceptions, was open to change, and he never hesitated to alter his own views in the light of his broader understanding of the human condition," says Dr. Francis McLaughlin, a past president of the American Psychoanalytic Association.

Freud continually revised, changed, added to his discoveries. Which is why it is relevant to know the exact date he stated a theory. For more than twenty years he believed the conflicts caused by the sexual instinct formed the basis of neurosis and that its core was the Oedipus complex. Then, in the 1920s, he discovered the aggressive instinct, said he had been wrong about the Oedipus complex as the core of neurosis and that the pre-Oedipal years, from birth to age four, set the stage for neurosis.

Originally he described the mind as composed of conscious and unconscious. Then, in 1921, he came up with a new "structure of the mind." He divided it into the id, ego and superego, stating both ego and superego had unconscious aspects. He defined the ego as that sphere of the mind that mediated between the raw emotions of the id and the outside world, and also mediated within the individual, trying to keep peace between the demands of the id and those of the superego, or conscience.

In a letter to Freud sent three days before his seventieth birthday Andreas-Salomé praised his discovery of psychoanalysis, saying, "It is not only a 'young science', but a science for the young at heart!" Freud remained young at heart, which enabled him to be open-minded and flexible as he established the psychic blueprint for the years ahead. Seven days after his seventieth birthday, on May 13, 1926, he responded to Andreas-Salomé's letter:

". . . we have not yet earned the right to dogmatic rigidity . . . we must be ready to till the vineyard again and again."

Which he did until the day he died, thirteen years later. And throughout his life he continually urged other psychoanalysts to extend the boundaries of his discoveries.

Today emphasis is on the earliest years of life, which Freud found the important ones in psychosexual development. He said in 1925 that it was "only by examining the first manifestations of the patient's innate instinctual constitution and the effects of his earliest experiences that we can accurately gauge the motive forces that have led to his neurosis and can be secure against the errors into which we might be tempted by the degree to which things have become remodeled and overlaid in adult life."

Analysis of early childhood is "tedious and laborious and makes demands both upon the physician and upon the patient which cannot always be met," he warned. "Moreover, it leads us into the dark regions where there are as yet no signposts." He added a characteristic wry note: "Indeed, analysts may feel reassured, I think, that there is no risk of their work becoming mechanical, and so of losing its interest, during the next few decades."

He was leading right into the future when he said it seemed to him analysts concentrated too much upon symptoms and concerned themselves too little with the causes: "In bringing up children we aim only at being left in peace and having no difficulties, in short, at training up a model child, and we pay very little attention to whether such a course of development is for the child's good as well."

As early as January 16, 1899, Freud wrote his friend Dr. Wilhelm Fliess, a Berlin nose and throat surgeon who had attended Freud's lectures in Vienna at the suggestion of Breuer, about a woman patient suffering from depression. Freud said, "I always thought that in early childhood she must have seen her mother in a similar state, in an attack of real melancholia." He was saying the depressive mood of a mother had a deep and lasting effect on her child—a subject current psychoanalysts are studying extensively.

Freud was aware, as no other man before him, that emotional and sexual development in a child was influenced by his everyday experiences with a mother and father. He left it to later psychoanalysts to observe the extent and the ways in which a child's emotional life was shaped by his parents—especially in regard to the parents' expressed or repressed hatred.

After discovering the nature of and the ways to reach the unconscious part of the mind, Freud painstakingly outlined the theory of psychosexual development—a major achievement for one man's lifetime. But he did not stop there. He added contribution after contribution to the understanding of the human mind.

There are those who demand omniscience from Freud, who would reject him wholesale for ever having had a mistaken idea, an erroneous thought—the magical demand of childhood that the parent be perfect.

Was it not enough he was the first to construct a "scaffolding of the mind," as he called it?

That he paved the way for a more humane understanding of all mankind, the emotionally crippled as well as the "normal"?

That he gave us understanding of the nature of hate and prejudice?

That he enabled thousands upon thousands of troubled men and women to gain a second chance in life through the treatment he called psychoanalysis?

But even if one has never been near a psychoanalyst's office or read a word *of* Freud or *about* him, one's life has been changed in myriad ways because of him.

He established that mental health is not merely the absence of illness but the ability to use potentials to a far greater degree. He showed the way to the prevention of mental illness by unearthing most of its causes, and discovered a technique of giving help.

He observed that mental illness could arise from psychological conflicts that started in childhood. The child psychology movement—1979 was the international Year of the Child—is an extension of Freud's emphasis on the importance of experiences, emotions and fantasies of early life.

He added a new "right" to human rights—the right to mental health, which starts with the parent's ability to bring up a child. The belief a parent may consider a child his possession, to abuse physically and psychically, is no longer sacrosanct, or even tolerable. Child abuse is a crime. Carrying this a step further, a psychiatrist and two other therapists, writing in the *News* bulletin of the Southern California Psychiatric Society, have formulated the concept of "parental bankruptcy," calling on "society to provide an alternative to the biologic nuclear family when it has failed repeatedly."

Freud changed the doctor-patient relationship as it applied to the easing of mental pain. He did not treat his patients in the way the autocratic, despotic doctors of his day did. He thought of the patient as a troubled human being, entitled to respect and understanding. He was the second physician—Breuer was the first—with the capacity to sit quietly for hours and listen to the patient's every word, honoring his silences, noting his every gesture. Diagnosis was not his goal. He wanted to ease the pain. He asked only that the patient try to speak spontaneously and freely.

What Freud observed in his patients and in himself he saw as universal human processes that apply "to all professions that deal with the effects produced by the human mind," as Dr. Ives Hendrick, author of *Facts and Theories of Psychoanalysis,* summed up. There is probably no aspect of our society psychoanalysis has not touched. Its theories permeate medicine, psychiatry, psychology, social work, sociology, anthropology, the law, the courts, penology, education, literature, the arts, politics, religion.

Even the sports world. "Two hours before the Yankees' game with the Red Sox yesterday, George Steinbrunner was in his Freudian seat," wrote Dave Anderson in the New York *Times* on July 2, 1979, explaining, "The principal owner and principal voice of the Yankees was in the swivel chair behind Billy Martin's desk in the manager's office," waiting to see Martin.

Perhaps the greatest tribute to Freud is the large numbers of troubled men and women who seek, through therapy, to ease their unhappiness, realizing they no longer have to suffer emotional agony. Even those who settle for the latest fad therapy are trying to become better acquainted with the self.

Not in spite of, but *because of* the questionable new "therapies" and their inadequacies, psychoanalysis today is even more firmly entrenched as the basic science of human behavior. Many have rushed to the pseudo-therapist who promises "quick change," "freedom from hangups," a "more fulfilling sex life." Some patients have achieved temporary release of anxiety or inhibition. But when the weekend "encounter" or "marathon" was over, they often felt even more depressed, realizing that another false hope had collapsed.

We would all welcome simple solutions to our not-so-simple problems, but little of value ever comes easy. Unlike the fad therapies, psychoanalysis requires an investment of time, work and dedication on the part of both patient and analyst. The failure of the quick-fix therapies has helped swing the pendulum back to psychoanalysis, back to the ground-breaking pioneer work accomplished by Sigmund Freud.

Yes, Freud is very much alive and well and living in and around all of us. He discovered fundamental mental processes reflected in the activities of everyone. He discovered an approach to stop what he called "internal bleeding"—the hurt, the grief, the rage, the loneliness.

Freud gave us the weapon of understanding with which to deal with ignorance, deceit, greed, tyranny, unreason and savagery— in our own hearts and in the hearts of others. He helped give us a belief in the dignity of every man, woman and child, as well as their right to emotional freedom.

Man has yet to take the next step "which will lead from having been an animal to becoming a truly human person," says Dr. Martin Grotjahn: "At the present time man behaves as if he is the missing link between the ape of yesterday and the human of tomorrow. Before he can develop appropriate and effective controls he must survive by hope for the future when the voice of reason and love may be heard by all and not only by a few."

By tracing human unrest and destructive behavior to their sources in the psyche, Freud may have made peace at least a possibility—both for the individual and nations. But he had no illusion peace would come swiftly either to one man's soul or to the warring nations of the world. He wrote to a young writer, Bruno Goetz:

> My purpose is to help as well as I can the many people who today live internally in hell. My scientific findings, my theories and methods, aim at making them conscious of this hell so that they will be able to free themselves from it.

When Freud was proposed for the Nobel Prize in Literature (which he was not awarded) in October 1916, he wrote to his friend and colleague Sandor Ferenczi that "it would be absurd to expect a sign of recognition, when one has ⅞ of the world against one." Today, as more come to acknowledge the value of Freud's discoveries, the founder of psychoanalysis has been awarded many a belated token of recognition, if not a Nobel prize.

Freud offered us more than we still know how to use.

2

The Mental Underground

Freud made it possible for man to gain conscious control of his passions rather than repress them or act them out in destructive fashion. He shone the light of reason on our inner world of unreason—a world more powerful in our lives than the external, reasonable one.

He studied what other men considered "crazy" or "illogical," made psychic sense of it. Even the non-sense of the psychotic became more understandable as the expression of caged emotions. He wrote Fleiss that the meaningless jabbering of the psychotic often contains symbols that, to his unconscious, hold specific meanings. "Have you ever seen a foreign newspaper after it has passed the censorship at the Russian frontier?" he said. "Words, sentences and whole paragraphs are blacked out, with the result that the remainder is unintelligible. A 'Russian censorship' occurs in the psychoses, and results in the apparently meaningless deliria."

Freud discovered the nature of the unconscious, its effect on mental functioning and how to reach hidden fantasies that had been repressed so they would lose their destructive power. He was the first to formulate a science based on the unconscious and to make the world of fantasy and dreams accessible to treat neurosis.

Prior to Freud, the concept of the unconscious belonged to the literary, rather than the scientific, domain. For centuries poets, philosophers and playwrights had recognized "another part of the mind." The term "unconscious" had been used as early as 1837, when Thomas Carlyle wrote: "The uttered part of a man's life bears to the unuttered, unconscious part, a small unknown proportion. He himself never knows it, much less do others."

The very use of the couch for therapy had an early precedent. In his play *The Clouds*, Aristophanes portrays Socrates at the Dionysium, an open-air theater on the southeast slope of the Acropolis, playing psychoanalyst to the Attic farmer Strepsiades. Socrates asks Strepsiades to use the couch and unburden his soul:

Socrates: Come, lie down here.
Strepsiades: What for?
Socrates: Ponder awhile over matters that interest you.
Strepsiades: Oh, I pray not there.
Socrates: Come, on the couch.
Strepsiades: What a cruel fate.
Socrates: Ponder and examine closely, gather your thoughts together, let your mind turn to every side of things. If you meet with difficulty, spring quickly to some other idea: keep away from sleep.

Under the guidance of Socrates, the farmer eventually admits he wishes to control the waxing and waning of the moon so the months would cease and his bills never come due.

Aristophanes intuitively foretold some of the insights of psychoanalysis. For one: a repressed wish underlies conflict causing emotional turmoil. For another: the importance of the couch and the recumbent position, similar to that of sleep, where thoughts freely emerge in dreams.

When Strepsiades says, at the idea of lying on the couch, "What a cruel fate," he echoes the fear of most patients as they first face the couch. And when Socrates tells Strepsiades to "gather your thoughts together, let your mind turn to every side of things," and suggests that if this is difficult, "spring quickly to some other idea," he anticipates the process of free association which Freud later introduced as a psychoanalytic technique.

As Freud said, "The concept of the unconscious has long been knocking at the gates of psychology and asking to be let in. Philosophy and literature have often toyed with it, but science could find no use for it. Psychoanalysis has seized upon the concept, has taken it seriously, and has given it fresh content."

Before it becomes possible to form any "correct view" of the origin of what is mental, Freud asserted, "it is essential to abandon the overvaluation of the property of being conscious." He described the unconscious as "the larger sphere, which includes within it the smaller sphere of the conscious."

Freud delighted in telling jokes to illustrate his concepts. He described the unconscious with the anecdote of Itzig, a "Sunday" horseback rider, who was galloping through the park when a friend saw him and called out, "Itzig, where are you going?"

"Don't ask me," he said. "Ask the horse."

Freud said he first became aware of the power of the unconscious on November 18, 1882. He was a young scientist, twenty-six years old, a teaching assistant in the research laboratory of the Institute of Physiology at the University of Vienna, the oldest German university in existence. Its director, Dr. Ernest von Brücke, was one of the great physiologists of the century. Freud was studying histology, the branch of biology concerned with the microscopic study of tissue.

On that autumn day in 1882, Freud's close friend Josef Breuer, a famous Viennese physician fourteen years older than Freud, confided details of his treatment of a young woman suffering from hysteria. For centuries physicians had been trying to discover the cause of this ailment that afflicted so many women. Doctors were usually unsympathetic to the suffering women, blamed them for "pretending" to be ill, since there was no organic cause for the headache, or paralyzed leg or arm, or nervous tic or hallucination.

Breuer was known as "the doctor with the golden touch" because he often healed where other physicians failed. He had a gentle, compassionate manner plus extraordinary patience and a willingness to explore new ways of treatment. For hysteria he had been using hypnotism, as other physicians did, following in the footsteps of Mesmer, who had been forced a century earlier to flee Vienna for the more liberal Paris when the medical profession charged him with charlatanism. But by the 1880s Viennese physicians were using hypnotism, putting hysterical women into a trance and urging them to "give up" their illness.

The young woman Breuer had treated was named Bertha Pappenheim, as Dr. Ernest Jones later revealed in his biography of Freud. Breuer and Freud were to call her "Anna O." when they wrote of her treatment ten years later.

Breuer first saw Bertha Pappenheim on December 11, 1880. He had been called to her home by her mother, Mrs. Siegmund Pappenheim, a wealthy woman related to the Warburgs of Germany. Mrs. Pappenheim was distraught because her twenty-one-year-old daughter lay on her bed day after day, mute and motionless as a corpse much of the time, refusing to eat. Breuer found the young woman living, as he said, "in two states of consciousness." In the early evenings she fell into a self-hypnotic state, or *absence* (a French term), in which she felt confused or suffered terrifying hallucinations, seeing "black snakes" or "death's heads" in the room. She also had many physical symptoms—paralysis of her right arm and both legs, inability, at times, to hear or speak, searing headaches, a wracking nervous cough and difficulty seeing. She ate only oranges, fed to her by a nurse.

Down the hall, the young woman's father, whom she had nursed through the night for five months, sharing these duties with her mother, lay dying of an abscess on his lung, the result of tuberculosis. Breuer observed that Bertha was "passionately fond" of her father.

Breuer told Freud that at first, under hypnosis, his young patient talked slowly, forcing words out, but speaking unintelligibly, mixing several languages. Then she began to restrict herself to her native German, and at last he was able to understand her. She complained that something was "tormenting" her, repeating the word, "tormenting, tormenting."

To his surprise, Breuer found that as she recalled experiences that had frightened, embarrassed or disgusted her, one by one her physical symptoms vanished. Each scene she remembered under hypnosis was related to a specific physical illness. When she described the event and expressed emotion she felt at the time, the symptom disappeared.

For instance, she could drink no water during a hot spell of six weeks, took in liquids by eating fruit. She told Breuer under hypnosis that she suffered "a tormenting thirst." Then she said she hated the new nurse her mother had hired to take care of her because the nurse had a "horrid little dog." She had seen him lapping water out of a glass the nurse had placed on the floor. As she said this, anger and disgust distorted her face. When she came out of the hypnotic trance, she turned to Breuer and asked, "May I have a glass of water, please?"

She mentioned taking care of her dying father night after night, hour after hour, with only a dim light burning. One night she heard an orchestra playing dance music next door. Neighbors were giving a party and she wished she could go—she loved to dance. But as she looked at her father, pale and wan on the bed, she felt ashamed for being so selfish. Overcome by guilt, she started to cough violently. When Breuer appeared the next day, he realized the persistent cough that had plagued her had disappeared.

Another time under hypnosis, referring to the hallucination of the "death's head" she sometimes saw, she told Breuer that just after her father fell ill she had gone to visit an aunt, though she was very tired because she never got enough sleep during the day. The maid asked her to wait in the parlor. As she opened the door, she expected, as usual, to see her face reflected in the mirror on the opposite wall. Instead, she saw the face of her father, twisted in pain, and then the face turned into a skull, a death's head. She fell to the floor in a faint. After she told him about this experience, Breuer noted she never again mentioned the hallucination, as though no longer haunted by it.

One morning, when Bertha was under hypnosis, he asked about the "snakes" she said she occasionally saw in her room. She brought up a summer night at her family's country home, when she was so exhausted she could not keep her eyes open even though her father had a high fever. Her mother had gone to Vienna for a few days. She tried to stay awake, knowing how sick her father was, but dozed off. She woke with a start, feeling guilty. Looking at her father, she saw a black snake slithering out of the wall toward him. She tried to raise her right arm to drive the snake away but found it paralyzed. She looked at her hand to see what was wrong. Each finger had turned into a little snake. Her arm had remained paralyzed ever since. . . .

The next time Breuer saw her the arm was once again normal and remained so. He said this "constituted the root of her whole illness." Thereafter she was "free from the innumerable disturbances which she had previously exhibited." He had been successful in asking her to concentrate her thoughts on the symptom they were treating at the moment, and to tell him the occasions on which it had appeared.

After eighteen months Breuer abruptly broke off Bertha's treatment, and for a long time he did not tell Freud why. Actually, he had become frightened by what he sensed of her erotic involvement with him, as well as by his own attraction to her. His wife complained he "talked too much" at home about his young patient. Frau Breuer became jealous, there were even rumors that she threatened suicide if he did not give up the patient.

When Breuer told Bertha of his decision to stop seeing her, she threw herself on the floor in a fantasized pregnancy. She claimed she was about to give birth to his baby. He hypnotized her to calm her, then left, and never saw her again.

Freud, who was three years older than Bertha Pappenheim, was fascinated by the case, though he knew little of the treatment of hysteria; he received his medical degree on March 31, 1881, the day after Bertha first stepped out of the bed in which she had lain paralyzed since the previous December 11. And in the summer of 1881, when Breuer was visiting his young patient at her country home, Freud was studying the nerve cells of the crayfish under a microscope, reaching the conclusion the axis cylinders of the nerve fibers were fibrillary in structure. (He was the first to demonstrate this fundamental feature, which helped pave the way to the neurone theory.)

Freud believed Breuer had made an important discovery in the treatment of hysteria and urged him to report it to the medical world. Breuer refused, saying he had enough of hysterical women, they were an ordeal and he was giving them up as patients.

As Bertha Pappenheim ended her treatment, in the spring of 1882, Freud came home from medical school one evening in April to find an attractive young woman, five years his junior, visiting one of his sisters. Her name was Martha Bernays. They fell in love and became engaged in June. Six months later, Freud's sister Anna was engaged to Martha's brother Eli. Martha and Freud had a courtship that lasted four and a quarter years, three of which they were separated when she went with her mother to live in Hamburg. Freud wrote Martha 900 letters during this period, all of which she saved.

In one letter, written July 13, 1883 at two in the morning, Freud made a reference to Bertha, telling Martha that he had visited Breuer that evening and Breuer had mentioned "your friend Bertha Pappenheim." Both young women were members of the small German-Jewish community in Vienna, where Martha Bernays had arrived from Hamburg in 1869 at the age of thirteen. They may even have been distantly related. Martha's grandfather, Isaac Bernays, Chief Rabbi of Hamburg, was related to Heinrich Heine, as was Bertha Pappenheim through her mother.

Seventeen days after Martha married Freud, on September 13, 1886, she wrote to her mother that Bertha Pappenheim had come to see her "more than once" at her apartment in the *Suehnhaus*. Martha said Bertha Pappenheim seemed fairly well during the day but still suffered hallucinatory states when evening approached, as she had done at first during her treatment with Breuer.

If Freud ever met Bertha Pappenheim, he guarded this secret well. In a letter dated July 8, 1915, to Dr. James J. Putnam, professor of neurology at Harvard University, whom Freud had met on his trip to America in 1909, Freud wrote: " . . . I never saw his [Breuer's] famous first case and only learned of it years later from Breuer's report." Freud may have used "saw" in a professional, rather than personal sense, since Martha wrote of Bertha Pappenheim visiting their home a number of times.

When Brücke advised Freud to give up research as financially unrewarding and prepare for general practice, Freud became an intern at the Viennese General Hospital, then one of the famous teaching centers of the world. As a junior resident physician, in

May, 1883, he transferred from the department of medicine to the psychiatric clinic run by Dr. Theodor Meynart, who had impressed Freud in medical school as the most brilliant man he had ever met. As a result of Freud's study of the mental disorder then known as "Meynart's Amentia"—acute hallucinatory psychosis— he believed the hallucinations might be related to thoughts not consciously experienced by the patient.

Though, as Freud said, he had become a physician "quite reluctantly," he now was "impelled by a strong motive to help nervous patients, or at least to understand something of their conditions." There were few neurological specialists in Vienna. But in the distance "glimmered the great name of Charcot," and he went to Paris on October 11, 1885, to study under the famous professor of pathological anatomy at the Salpêtrière, an institution housing thousands of the chronically ill, aged and insane, and which because of Charcot was known as "the Mecca of the neurologist."

Watching Charcot prove hypnotism could *induce* hysteria, Freud realized how powerful mental suggestion was on the subterranean recesses of the mind. Charcot, a tall, impressive man with a shock of black hair and a profile resembling Dante's, would walk out on the platform, a spotlight shining on his strong face. In a low but distinct voice, using simple, precise words, he would explain to the young doctors how hysteria could be produced under hypnosis.

He nodded to two assistants. They carried onstage a young woman, limp with depression and despair. They placed her in a chair where she sat, eyes half-closed. Charcot talked to the woman quietly for a moment. She sank into sleep, hypnotized.

She seemed not to feel the pinch he gave her arm, or the pin with which he pricked her skin. She obeyed his every command. When he asked her to do so, she went into convulsions, then arched her body in the *arc de cercle* assumed by many hysterics, head and heels touching the floor, carrying out movements later recognized by Freud as symbolic of the sexual act.

Charcot believed that in some people hypnosis could bring out an underlying existing hysteria and its symptoms. He was challenged by A. A. Liébeault and Hippolyte Bernheim, two physicians working in a private clinic at Nancy in southern France. They claimed almost anyone could be made hysterical if given suggestions under hypnosis. The hysterical symptoms, they said, were due to the orders of the hypnotist, who freed the suggestibility of the person. Freud later went to Nancy, observed the work of Liébeault and Bernheim and decided they were correct.

But Charcot had established one basic fact: under suggestion a hypnotized person could *produce* physical symptoms. He proved a physical symptom need not always be organic—it was also important to prove what something is *not* before it could be shown what it *is*. Charcot also used, in a primitive way, the technique Mesmer unwittingly discovered, what Freud later called *transference*.

Watching Charcot demonstrate time after time how hypnotism could induce hysterical symptoms, Freud concluded there was a part of the mind outside awareness and far more powerful than the conscious part. The unconscious had come alive before his very eyes. He speculated that unconscious mechanisms, as yet unknown, not only could explain hysteria but existed in *all* persons, and played a vital part in their lives even though they were unaware of it.

Freud was also impressed by Charcot's use of the word *trauma*. Charcot spoke of trauma as a sudden psychological injury or shock following a physical accident that, he believed, brought out the hidden symptoms of hysteria. Freud thought psychological trauma might exist by itself or be caused by emotional shocks as well as physical.

Charcot also referred to "memories forgotten" and stressed the importance of sexual feelings in hysteria. He once told a colleague, in Freud's presence, when the colleague asked Charcot's opinion about a nervous, invalid wife, that her husband was either impotent or "exceedingly awkward." The colleague expressed astonishment that this should have anything to do with the wife's condition. Charcot said, "In such instances, it is always a matter of sex —always, always, always." Charcot was characteristically less than equivocal. Nonetheless, his insight was a startling and significant one.

Freud spoke with warmth and gratitude of Charcot, calling him a truly great man and teacher who had encouraged him, an unknown stranger, by admitting him to an intimate circle and allowing him to translate some of Charcot's books into German.

After Freud left Salpêtrière in the autumn of 1886, he returned to Vienna, where, at the age of thirty, he married Martha. There he started private practice as a specialist in nervous diseases.

At first he treated his patients by the accepted medical methods of warm baths, rest cures and electrotherapy, though he realized no lasting cure was ever brought about by these treatments. In a short while he put aside his electrical apparatus, which gave the patients very mild shocks, remarking of W. Erb's classic book on electrotherapy, "The realization that the work of the greatest name in German neuropathology had no more relation to reality than some 'Egyptian' dream book, such as is sold in cheap book shops, was painful, but it helped to rid me of another shred of the innocent faith in authority from which I was not yet free."

He recalled Charcot's work, then that of Liébault and Bernheim, who would hypnotize a child suffering from muscular rheumatism in an arm, then tell the child his arm would feel no pain when he woke. The child, on waking, had lost the pain in his arm temporarily.

Freud remembered that Bernheim had said, "In truth, we are all potentially or actually hallucinating . . . during the greatest part of our lives." Freud also recalled how Bertha Pappenheim had been helped under hypnotism by Breuer to remember frightening memories connected to her physical symptoms. He later said he learned from Breuer not to "suggest" that patients feel better but to ask about a particular symptom or events in their lives that were traumatic—what Freud called "investigation under hypnosis" as contrasted to "suggestion." He said he found it "much more attractive than the monotonous and violent suggestive command which was devoid of every possibility of inquiry."

Now he asked his women patients to try to remember specific events connected with their paralyzed hands or splitting headaches or stuffy noses. The first patient he put under hypnosis, he referred to as Frau Emmy von N. She was a woman of forty whose symptoms and personality so interested Freud that he devoted a large part of his time trying to help her, as Breuer did Bertha Pappenheim.

The first time Freud saw Frau Emmy von N., at her home, she was lying on a sofa, her head resting on a leather cushion. She had finely fashioned features, looked much younger than her age. Her hysterical symptoms included a ticlike movement of her face, frequent interruption of her own remarks with a curious clacking of the mouth and the compulsion every so often to break into what she was saying, with the cry, "Keep still! Don't say anything! Don't touch me!"

She easily sank into a hypnotic trance, started to talk of her past. Freud found many of her fears related to events in childhood. She had a horror of worms, recalling that when she was a little girl someone had given her a pretty pincushion as a gift, but the next morning, to her disgust, she had found worms crawling out of it. The pincushion had been filled with bran that had not dried and had thus become infested. Ever since, Frau Von N. had, not surprisingly, been unable to bear the sight of a worm. (With the understanding Freud later contributed of the part that symbolism plays in the unconscious, the worm probably stood for "penis" and her compulsive cry "Keep still! Don't say anything! Don't touch me!" may have related to a very early traumatic sexual experience with a man.)

Freud discovered that when he suggested an idea to Frau Von N. while she was conscious, she did not act on it. He concluded that any suggestion made by the doctor and accepted by the patient on the sole basis of conscious, nonhypnotic obedience rarely if ever met with success. The conscious wish alone was not enough to bring about inner change.

Even during periods when Frau Emmy von N. felt most depressed, she was capable of managing a large, industrial business, kept an eye on the education of her children, carried on correspondence with prominent intellectuals. She had to leave Vienna but wrote asking Freud's permission to be hypnotized by another doctor.

Freud did not consider he had truly helped her. He believed one reason for his failure was the use of hypnosis. He did not like issuing assurances and commands to patients. He also had grave doubts as to the value of hypnosis in curing mental illness. He believed that even the most startling results were likely to disappear if his personal relation with the patient became disturbed. The relationship, he noted, could be re-established if a reconciliation were brought about. But this only proved the personal relation between patient and doctor was stronger than the suggestions given under hypnosis (which accounted for "Anna O's" relapses after Breuer left her). It was precisely this factor that had escaped the notice of other doctors.

How to bypass hypnotism and yet release imprisoned memories, as Breuer had often done with Bertha Pappenheim? The problem was, as Freud put it, to find out something from the patient the doctor did not know and the patient did not *consciously* know.

Following what he called "a dim presentiment," Freud asked his patients to tell him every thought that came to mind, no matter how insignificant they considered it to be, hoping this might cause hidden memories to surface.

"Fraulein Lucy R." was one of the first patients with whom Freud abandoned hypnosis and gave the instruction to "associate freely." She was a governess who sought help because of rhinitis, a severe inflammation of the sinus passages of the nose. She told Freud she felt depressed, fatigued and could not eat or do her job efficiently. She looked after the children of a widower, a man she admired.

One day Freud asked if it were possible she was hopelessly in love with this man.

She answered, "Yes, I think that's true."

Freud said in amazement, "But if you knew you loved your employer, why didn't you tell me?"

"I didn't know—or rather I didn't want to know," she said. "I wanted to drive it out of my head and not think of it again and I believed latterly I have succeeded."

Freud was struck by the fact she had tried to forget—to repress —the thought that she loved her employer, and also to forget her frustrated feelings. He reached another revolutionary conclusion —that the blocking out of an unpleasant idea from consciousness is an essential cause of hysteria, or what he later called neurosis. If the awareness of an emotion associated with a thought was too excruciating to be borne, the painful thought was banished from consciousness. Freud named this process of exclusion *repression*.

He later described his theory of repression as "the foundation-stone on which the whole structure of psychoanalysis rests, the most essential part of it." A thought may be repressed, Freud said, when it was considered dangerous to self-esteem. But the repressed thought does not remained buried. In seeking an outlet it produces some form of disturbance, either physical or psychological. Freud gave the name *conversion* to the converting of a repressed thought and its concomitant emotion into physical symptoms.

His theory of psychosomatic illness crystallized in his discussion of the treatment of Fraulein Elisabeth R. She came to Freud so crippled she could hardly walk. Freud wrote of the case: "We may ask: What *is* it that turns into physical pain here? A cautious reply would be: something that might have become, and should have become, *mental* pain."

Elisabeth R. told Freud that her sister had died recently. At the funeral, as Elisabeth stared at the face of her dead sister in the coffin, then at her sister's husband, whom she loved, she thought, "Now he is free again and I can be his wife." Then she quickly dismissed the idea as evil. The next day she could hardly move her legs. As she talked of the traumatic experience and what she believed to be her shameful feelings—her sexual desire for her brother-in-law—she regained her ability to walk.

Freud now used the Greek word *trauma*, literally meaning wound, to describe a psychic wound. He gave an example of a woman of forty-five who suffered at times a penetrating pain in her forehead, between her eyes, which lasted for weeks. During her analysis with Freud, the patient recalled that one day when she was fifteen and lying in bed, her grandmother had given her a look "so piercing she felt it had gone right into her brain." She said she thought the old woman was "viewing her with suspicion" (perhaps accusing her silently of masturbating, for which she then felt guilty). After remembering this painful moment, she laughed. The pain in her forehead did not appear from then on.

Another patient, a married woman, suffered neuralgia in her cheek. One day while mentioning a remark of her husband's she had felt as a bitter insult, she put her hand to her cheek, gave a loud cry of pain and said, "It was like a slap in the face." Her neuralgia disappeared.

In treating another woman, Frau Cäcilie M., who suffered pain in her legs, Freud learned that the first time her feet hurt had been when she walked into a room full of strangers. She confessed at that moment she was afraid she might not find herself "on the right footing." Freud made an observation from this about the literalness of language as it applied to the unconscious, and its dramatic effect on the body: "In taking a verbal expression literally and in feeling the 'stab in the heart' or 'the slap in the face' after some slighting remark as a real event, the hysteric is not taking liberties with words, but is simply reviving once more the sensations to which the verbal expression owes its justification."

Between 1892 and 1895 Freud developed the process of free association as a technique and used it regularly to reach hidden emotions and forgotten experiences. He compared the new process to "excavating a buried city." He urged patients not to think about what they would say, but to spontaneously utter any thoughts that came to mind. He concluded that the longer the pause, "the more it is to be feared the patient is rearranging what has occurred to him and is mutilating it."

He was now on the way to deeper exploration of what he called "the mental underground." When he gave up hypnosis, he was able to understand something that had long eluded him. He had proved his premise that patients, while awake, could recall memories. But to do so took great trust in the doctor and, even then, only with difficulty could they speak of the traumatic past.

Freud wondered why many forgotten experiences could be recalled fairly easily under hypnosis. He noted that the buried memories all had something in common: they were painful, alarming, disagreeable or shameful. And so it occurred to him that precisely *because* the buried memory was painful, alarming, disagreeable or shameful it had been forgotten. If it could be remembered under hypnosis but not consciously, something was at work in the patient's conscious that fought against recalling the painful or shameful memory.

Believing the dangerous memory was always close to consciousness and could be reached eventually if the patient continued to free associate, Freud said, "It is merely a question of getting some obstacle out of the way."

What was the obstacle to conscious recollection? Freud called it *resistance*—a defense the patient used to protect himself against psychic pain. The same force was responsible for producing the physical and mental symptoms that were a compromise between conscience and passion.

Hypnosis did not do away with resistance but only bypassed it. This was why hypnosis could not succeed in helping someone feel better permanently. Breaking through the resistance had to be a conscious act, part of the patients' understanding of their own defenses.

Resistance made patients unwilling to speak of taboo thoughts or feelings and caused them to censor ideas. When this happened, it was evidently beyond their emotional strength to bring up the deeper thoughts. The psychoanalyst had to persist until the resistances were dissolved.

Freud spoke of the *overdetermination* of a symptom, inhibition or phobia. This was caused not by one memory or one emotion, but by a "succession of partial traumas and concatenations of pathogenic trains of thought." He also pointed out that some neurotics possessed brilliant intellect and strong character but appeared "weak-minded" because their mental capacity was "divided and only a part of its capacity is at the disposal of their conscious thought."

He defined *rationalization* as the intellectual distortion by which people justify an unconsciously motivated thought, act or symptom that has been repressed. If we do not want to go to a party because we dislike the hostess but keep this awareness from ourselves, we may refuse to go for a multitude of other reasons: the weather is bad, we have a headache, we have no proper outfit to wear.

What Freud called the *repetition-compulsion* was a psychic tendency to repeat over and over, in compulsive form, a childhood situation, what he called the attempt "to restore a previous state of affairs."

Freud changed the whole concept of mental illness by showing it was not the result of a weakening of intellect or a malfunction of the brain, but the impact of intense emotions on mental functioning. Even persons with genius I.Q.s, able to teach the most abstruse science or write a profound novel, could fall mentally ill.

The phrase uttered by Bertha Pappenheim, "the talking cure," haunted Freud. In 1886 he managed—after many a verbal battle—to persuade Breuer, who for four years had practiced only internal medicine, to resume treatment of hysterical women, and to co-author an article about "the talking cure" for the medical profession. This was ten years after Breuer had last seen his young patient. By then Freud had treated a number of hysterical patients and was formulating his own theories.

Breuer and Freud gave their article the formidable title, "On the Psychical Mechanism of Hysterical Phenomena, Preliminary Communication." In preparation for it, Freud wrote three memoranda. The first was a letter to Breuer dated June 29, 1892, saying, "I am tormented by the problem of how it will be possible to give a two-dimensional picture of anything that is so much of a solid as our theory of neurosis."

It is interesting he uses the word "tormented," the one Breuer's young patient first used to describe how she felt, the word that led Breuer to question her further, as a result of which he realized she lived in two worlds. In one she was coherent, able to express her thoughts, even the angry and fearful ones. In the other she was possessed by hallucinations and images so terrifying she could not think or speak logically. Her powers of perception and processes of thought broke down and she spoke what sounded like gibberish.

In this memoranda of 1892 Freud refers to "a second state of consciousness." This is believed to be the first time in his published scientific work that he refers to the unconscious.

The "Preliminary Communication" appeared in 1893 in two issues, January 1 and January 15, of the periodical *Neurologisches Centralblatt,* the leading German neurological journal published fortnightly in Berlin. The article was promptly reprinted in the *Vienna Medical Journal.*

The authors referred to the young patient Breuer had treated as "Anna O." After describing how her symptoms disappeared when she recalled the experiences relating to them and how she felt at the time, Freud and Breuer warned: "Recollection without affect [emotion] almost invariably produces no result." They were saying that the use of words—intellectualization—was of no value without what Breuer termed the "catharsis" of emotion.

Freud's classic line, "Hysterics suffer mainly from reminiscences," appears in this article. He explained that the reminiscences related to symptoms appearing when an impulse to act was "repressed." The symptoms appeared "in place of" the action. They represented a "strangulated" emotion. Both the traumatic incident and the emotion became lost to memory, as though they had never happened. But the symptom persisted and offered what Freud called "partial gratification" of the wish to act.

Anna O.'s emotional reactions to painful experiences as she nursed her dying father had been repressed, but the emotions remained attached to memories in the unconscious. They gained partial outlet through her symptoms—the paralyzed arm and legs, the headaches, the blindness. As the original experience, along with the emotions it produced, was brought to consciousness, the "imprisoned" emotions were discharged and the symptoms vanished. This treatment the authors called the "cathartic method." It was the forerunner of psychoanalysis.

Freud then persuaded Breuer to join him in the writing of a book, *Studies on Hysteria*, published in 1895 in Leipzig and Vienna. It was the first book on the infant science-art Freud named psychoanalysis. He actually used the word "psychoanalysis" for the first time in a paper published March 30, 1896, in French.

Studies on Hysteria contained four of Freud's own case studies and a fuller account of the treatment of Anna O., whose "remarkable case," Freud stated, led to the founding of psychoanalysis. In this book the basic concepts of psychoanalysis were formulated. Moreover, the authors gave a detailed description of the underlying cause of neurosis and of mental processes and concepts never before explained, including repression, psychic determination, unconscious mental activity, overdetermination, defense, resistance, psychic trauma, the sexual cause of neurosis, conflict, conversion, ambivalence (mixed feelings of love and hate) and transference.

Freud was later to describe transference as a living repetition of past relationships, together with the expression of emotions and wishes appropriate to these past situations, during which the symptoms of the patient's illness disappeared. His neurosis is replaced by what Freud called a "transference neurosis of which he can be cured by the therapeutic work. . . . The transference thus creates an intermediate region between illness and real life through which the transition from the one to the other is made."

With the analyst, the patient's responses were not random or haphazard but "recurring variations on the buried themes of his life."

One of Freud's classic lines is found in *Studies on Hysteria:* "Much is won if we succeed in transforming hysterical misery into common unhappiness." Or, as he later put it, "The goal of psychoanalysis is to turn neurotic suffering into normal human misery."

Freud was thirty-seven when *Studies on Hysteria* was written, Breuer fifty-one. In the latter's chapter on Anna O., he reported that when her treatment ended, she left Vienna and "traveled for a while, but it was a considerable time before she regained her mental balance entirely. Since then she has enjoyed complete health." Ernest Jones reported that Bertha Pappenheim had a relapse shortly after Breuer stopped seeing her and was taken to a private sanitarium in Gross Enzerdorff, where she "inflamed the heart of the psychiatrist in charge." At this point her mother, whom Jones describes as "somewhat of a dragon," rushed to Vienna from Frankfurt, her former home to which she had returned, and "took her daughter back to Frankfurt for good, at the end of the eighties."

Once in Frankfurt Bertha Pappenheim functioned well. She sought a new life, became a leader in volunteer social work. She founded the first Jewish institution, the home at Isenburg for delinquent girls and unwed mothers of the Jewish faith. She crusaded against the exploitation of poor Jewish girls by merchants who turned them into prostitutes. She never married, though she lived, as Breuer put it, with a normal "mental balance." He had given her just enough help at a crucial time so she substantially recovered from the psychotic episodes related to the illness and death of her father. In terms of Freud's further development of psychoanalysis, the help given by Breuer would have been only the start of treatment. Under Freud the analysis then would have extended into memories and feelings about Bertha's childhood with her "dragon" mother as well as with her father, and her early sexual fantasies.

Breuer ended his friendship with Freud soon after the appearance of their book because of what Freud called, in a letter to Andreas-Salomé dated October 4, 1918, "the 'red rag' of the sexual factor."

Freud's belief that hysteria was caused by sexual repression emerged in his chapter on the psychotherapy of hysteria with which *Studies on Hysteria* concluded. This was no new theory for Freud. In a previous paper, "The Neuro-psychoses of Defense," he had outlined ways in which he believed the defense of the conscious personality against disturbing or forbidden sexual feelings might produce hysteria, compulsive behavior and psychosis.

Breuer, in his chapter on theory, also mentioned the sexual drive, though he noted "a complete lack of sexuality" in Anna O., saying she never spoke of love. But he did say, "The sexual instinct is undoubtedly the most powerful source of persisting increases of excitation (and consequently of neurosis)." Traumatic experiences, he said, produced quantities of "excitation," or charges of energy, to the nerves, charges too large to be dealt with in the normal way, and thus created neuroses. But along with most of the Viennese medical profession—and the rest of the world—Breuer could not accept Freud's theory of the critical importance of sexuality or the idea that sexual impulses existed in children. Freud asserted "the innocence" of childhood was a myth, that children had sexual desires which "any attentive mother or nursemaid had always been able to see for themselves but which every adult later felt bound in conspiracy to reject or deny."

On November 21, 1907, Breuer wrote to psychiatrist Auguste Forel, "I confess that plunging into sexuality in theory and practice is not to my taste. But what have my taste and my feeling about what is seemly have to do with the question of what is true?" And so, twelve years after his rupture with Freud over the role of sexuality in neurosis, Breuer conceded that his colleague had been right. It was to take the rest of the world a good deal longer to acknowledge Freud's breakthrough discovery of the primacy of the sex drive.

In the years that followed, Freud continued to explore the shadowy secrets of the unconscious. His self-analysis after the death of his father, to whom he felt very close, helped open the gates to a more widespread understanding of the human mind. Freud applied to himself and his patients the words of Terence, the Roman playwright who lived from 185–159 B.C.: "Nothing that is human is alien to me."

He had already defied the medical bias of the day with his revolutionary idea that man was governed in large part by the unconscious, and by his belief that every word the patient uttered was important to the understanding of his illness. Freud commented, "I was one of those who 'disturbed the sleep of the world', as Hebbel says and . . . I could not reckon upon objectivity and tolerance."

He realized that his close friend Breuer had broken away from him because of Breuer's fear of sexuality. Breuer had not been aware of the nature of "transference"—he did not know Bertha Pappenheim was bestowing on him all the passion she had felt as a little girl for her father.

When Breuer died in Vienna, on June 20, 1925, at the age of eighty-four, Freud said in his obituary: "He had come up against something that is never absent—his patient's transference onto her physician—and he had not grasped the impersonal nature of the process." Breuer had not connected this "transference" to his patient's emotional illness. Instead, he felt "profoundly shocked," as he later told Freud, by his patient's seeming sexual advances (and no doubt by his own reciprocal desires) and "fled the house in a cold sweat."

Freud had first met Breuer at the Institute of Physiology in the 1870s. During his courtship of Martha, Freud wrote her that Breuer was "my friend and helper in my difficult circumstances," meaning that at one time he even loaned Freud money. Freud also wrote, "We grew accustomed to share all our scientific interests with each other. In this relationship the gain was naturally mine."

He referred to Breuer as "the ever-loyal Breuer," and seemed on the most intimate terms with him and his wife. Later their families were friendly, Freud named his eldest daughter after Breuer's wife Mathilde.

Despite their eventual rift, Freud never altered his belief that Breuer had made two fundamental discoveries out of which psychoanalysis developed: 1) A neurotic symptom results from emotions deprived of their normal outlet, 2) the symptom disappears when its unconscious causes are made conscious.

It is a long way from these simple but basic discoveries to the complicated theories Freud developed into a body of psychoanalytic knowledge and treatment. The nature of emotional illness, with its roots in the sexual and aggressive conflicts of childhood, was further illuminated by Freud in the years that followed his collaboration with Breuer, as he continued to see patients and to write until practically the day of his death at age eighty-two, on September 23, 1939, at 20 Maresfield Gardens, London.

From the year after his marriage, 1887, until 1902 came a period of extraordinary creativity in Freud's life. Scientists occasionally experience one explosive moment when "truth," so to speak, reveals itself. For Freud there was no one moment of truth but many moments of truth, just as in a personal psychoanalysis.

But if a moment were to be arbitrarily selected, it might be the discovery of what Freud himself called "the great secret." It did not spring full-blown to his mind, but slowly dawned on him as he sat listening to his women patients tell him of childhoods in which their fathers had raped them. He sensed something wrong, doubting that so many fathers could be sexual perverts.

Finally he realized that the unconscious part of the mind lacked a sense of reality. It did not distinguish between truth and what he called "emotionally charged fiction." This was the "great secret." Many, though perhaps not all of the seductions, represented the *unconscious wish* of the woman. Possibly as little girls they had been "seduced" to a certain degree by ardent hugs and kisses; however, the majority were not victims of incestuous attacks but of their own fantasies.

They were living partly in "psychical reality," as distinguished from the reality of the outer world. The inner reality did not distinguish between truth and the unconscious wish. In the world of psychic reality, fantasy reigns supreme. As Freud put it: "Reality—wish fulfillment: it is from this contrasting pair that our mental life springs."

If outer reality proved too harsh or frustrating, troubled persons might retreat more deeply into psychic reality. Some even lost sight of the boundaries between the inner and outer worlds—the way one sometimes feels on waking from a powerful dream.

Freud theorized that each instinctual urge was accompanied by a fantasy containing a wish. "Unconscious fantasies have either always been unconscious and formed in the unconscious, or more often they were once conscious fantasies, daydreams, and have been purposely forgotten and driven into the unconscious by 'repression'. Their content may then either have remained the same or may have been altered, so that the fantasies which are now unconscious are derivatives of fantasies that were once conscious."

Unconscious fantasies, or daydreams, are a constant feature of our mental life, an ever-present accompaniment of conscious experience, according to Dr. Jacob A. Arlow in his Abraham A. Brill Memorial Lecture presented in behalf of the New York Psychoanalytic Society in November, 1963. In his lecture, entitled "Unconscious Fantasy and Disturbance of Conscious Experience," Dr. Arlow said: "The private world of daydreams is characteristic for each individual, representing his secret rebellion against reality and against the need to renounce instinctual gratification. Fantasy reflects and contains the persistent pressure emanating from the drives."

Fantasies are grouped together around certain basic childhood wishes and experiences, primarily attached to erotic or hostile feelings. In these systems of fantasies one edition of the fantasy-wish may represent a later version or "defensive distortion" of an earlier fantasy, Arlow stated. Which fantasy version of the unconscious wish will contribute to conscious experience depends on a number of factors, including the integration of the personality, the state of ego-functioning and the ability to test reality, he added. The intrusion of fantasy upon conscious experience may at times be so overpowering as to seem relatively independent of the influence of reality. In a personal psychoanalysis the patient is helped to distinguish between reality and unconscious fantasy. The analysis becomes "the proving ground in which one can demonstrate to the patient how he confuses the past with the present, the daydream with reality."

No sharp line of distinction can be made between conscious and unconscious fantasies, Arlow went on, adding that it seems more appropriate to speak of "fantasies which are fended off to a greater or lesser extent, bearing in mind that the role of defense may change radically with circumstances."

Freud said that no mental process, even "pure" thought, is free from conscious or unconscious emotion and, therefore, without "some delicate influence" on the body. He made it clear that *mind* and *consciousness* were not identical, though mankind had always equated the two. He showed that we think on two levels—the conscious and unconscious. Unconscious thinking goes on day and night, even as we sleep. It emerges in disguised form in our dreams. The unconscious, whose functioning Freud named "the primary system," not only holds wishes and fears and hopes that stem from our primitive, savage self, which hates ferociously, is dangerously jealous and greedy, but also is the source of our imagination and creativity. It has no sense of time, it does not recognize a "no" or a doubt and it never takes external reality into account.

The conscious, whose functioning Freud named "the secondary system," since it developed out of the unconscious, controls the demands of our unconscious urges, chiefly sexual and aggressive, as they come up against the prohibitions of conscience. Conscious processes are marked by inhibition, restraint of action and use of reason.

Freud discovered that repressed fantasies may exert a powerful and continual influence on us as adults. As Robert Waelder put it: "Our infantile past has tremendous power over us. We only seem to live entirely in the present. Ghosts from the past walk in broad daylight. It is as if man brings his childhood along with him, like an invisible personal world which casts its shadow into the world of reality. Our reaction to the real world is partly determined by these ghosts."

A certain amount of repression improves the ability to be thoughtful by eliminating conflicts that would interfere with thought. But too much repression may cause creative thinking to become inhibited as a disproportionate amount of psychic energy becomes involved in holding down the repressions. Fundamental in Freud's thinking was the image of mental activity as energy expended in one form or another. He saw the mind in operation as a form of dynamic equilibrium between opposing forces, an equilibrium that was constantly being disturbed and restored to balance.

Freud's concept of what constituted "the energizing forces of the mind" went through many stages of development and change. At first he divided the mind into conscious and unconscious parts. He saw what he called the libidinal urges dominating the unconscious, while the ego, or self-preservative forces, curbed the dangerous, anti-social sexual wishes.

Freud used the word *libido* to refer to how sexual impulses are represented in the mind. We feel "libido" as sexual yearning and/or love. Freud described libido as the way love makes itself known to us, just as hunger or anger as a threat to life are the ways self-preservation makes itself known. He called libido "the motor force of sexual life," an energy directed to an "object."

Libido is bent on pleasure, on discharging sexual wishes. In the child the libido does not seek genital gratification because the child is not yet ready for this mature expression of sexual development. The child's libido seeks pleasure from such partial gratifications as the desire to look, to touch, to taste. After separation from his mother for an afternoon a child can obtain libidinal satisfaction merely on seeing her return. Any time a child feels delight, he presumably is satisfying his libidinal desires.

Freud compared libido that was unable to attain normal sexual gratification to a stream that "when it found its principal bed dammed, filled side roads which were empty until then." He described "the various channels along which the libido passes" as "related to each other from the very first like inter-communicating pipes," adding, "we must take the phenomena of collateral flow into account."

Libido, he said, goes through many phases. Originally it centers on the self when we are egotistical, interested only in the gratification of our own needs. As we become aware of the outside world, we transfer some of our libido to those nearest and/or most important to us—mothers, fathers, brothers and sisters, friends and teachers. If too much of our libido becomes centered on sexuality, our very thinking may become so eroticized that it is difficult to develop reason and judgment. We learn to sublimate our libido in work, creativity, athletics. Or we bestow libido on "things," such as antiques or stamp collections. Or on abstract ideas such as science, religion, politics.

As Freud expanded his treatment from the realm of neurosis

into psychosis he encountered mental processes that could not be correlated within his theoretical framework of "libidinal" versus "self-preservative" drives. These processes include the formation of delusions, megalomania and withdrawal from the world. He then theorized that psychoses could be understood as representing "surplus investments of libido in the self," as opposed to the outside world. He called the psychoses "the narcissistic neuroses," and the neuroses "the transference neuroses," meaning that they could be understood during the process of psychoanalysis which used "transference" to understand the patient's past.

Freud maintained that physical illness could be linked to the distribution of libido. He said if there is too much disturbance of the sexual drive during the first months of life, when a baby's world focuses on taking in things through the mouth, later illnesses may strike the gastric system. If the disturbances occur during the second developmental or anal period, as the child is being trained to control excretory functions, the later illnesses may be intestinal. And so, according to Freud, the distribution of body libido is the main factor in determining where physical illness appears. During childhood, the libido tries to get gratification through every sensory organ—mouth, tongue, hands, nose, ears, eyes. When a bodily organ, for one reason or another, becomes particularly charged with erotic feelings and thereby feared by the child, this is the organ that in later life has a predisposition to disease. Adults whose noses cause them suffering, for instance, may, when they were babies, have picked their noses, as most babies do in exploring their bodies, and were severely slapped or shouted at. For such people the nose would retain a special erotic quality, because it was an area they were forbidden to explore, whose very touch brought punishment. There is something both fascinating and dangerous about the nose, which is a protuberance and at the same time possesses an opening, so that for some it may symbolize the genitals of either man or woman.

When frustrated in later life, the libido may regress to this early stage, to which some portions of its energy have remained attached in memory, Freud said, and it does so through the fantasies that are directly linked to the repressed fixation. The libido travels from the fantasies, now subconscious, to their sources in the unconscious, and thus back to the fixation point. When we become physically ill, Freud said, we may be trying to cope with repressed sexual desires of childhood for which we feel guilty and so feel the need to be punished (in later years he added aggressive wishes).

One man with severe asthma, for example, went into psychoanalysis to see if it would help him overcome the asthma, since nothing else had succeeded. After months on the couch he recalled experiences in childhood connected to breathing. He held many distorted fantasies about the importance of his breath. He believed that success in sexual intercourse depended on his maintaining steady, regular breathing and tried to regulate both his own breathing and that of his partner. He told his analyst that he had slept in his parents' bedroom until he was four, and remembered hearing his father's heavy breathing when he had sex. He thought the heavy breathing was a sign something dreadful was happening to his father, and feared he might die. This man had tried to keep such terror from his own life by controlling his breathing, especially during the sex act. His breathing had become a very precious thing, associated with fantasies of sex and rage. There were other reasons too for his difficulty in breathing. He remembered that when he was a child his mother would sometimes hold him so tightly to her breast—her way of showing love—that he felt suffocated, wanted to scream. Once he could understand why he guarded his breathing so carefully, his asthma was relieved.

In discussing physical illness, Freud said: "In the last resort we must begin to love in order that we may not fall ill, and must fall ill if, in consequence of frustration, we cannot love."

It followed that one of the ways in which lonely people tell the world their libido has no place to go is through psychosomatic illnesses. Such illnesses contain a plea for love and also indicate that the person has repressed sexual desire and put his energy into suffering. As Freud said, "So long as he suffers, he ceases to love."

The symptom is directly related to fantasies that accompany and are related to the repressed impulse connected to that part of the body. The repression returns in the form of the physical symptom which may be anything from a bleeding ulcer to a persistent cough. For example, a boy may have experienced so deep a fear of castration that he may become unduly concerned with the function of any organ that symbolizes the male genitals, Freud said. He may react to his eye as though it were a penis and, if his fear is great enough, it may cause disorders of the eye, even blindness. The nose, the tongue, the toes, the hands—any projection of the body —may serve as substitute for the penis in fantasy. The symbol is the shorthand of the unconscious. "The symptoms represent the patient's sexual activity," in Freud's words.

Freud also spoke of the "deliria of the body," such as fainting spells and convulsive seizures, prevalent in the Viennese society of that day. Freud said they were associated in the sufferer's unconscious with sexual intercourse fantasized as an act of violence. He pointed out that St. Vitus' dance was a caricature of the sexual act, as did Paracelsus, a physician of the fourteenth century, who described the attacks as imitations of the motions of sexual intercourse.

It was through the symptoms of physical illness, as mentioned, that Freud first started to understand the psyche more fully. The symptoms of the women who complained of paralyzed limbs, headaches, facial tics, coughs, led to the fantasy—the repressed dangerous or embarrassing wish. Freud realized that a sexual desire had somehow been thwarted and that the symptom had formed as a substitute for the repressed desire. The symptom represented an attempt by the unconscious to cope with a conflict no longer recognized consciously. The symptom was relieved when its unconscious cause—the underlying wish—became conscious. The symptom served the purpose of partial gratification of the sexual wish, Freud discovered. It was a substitute for the sexual satisfaction that the person could not obtain in reality. When any one of the bodily organs serves an erotic as well as a physiological function, the intense erotic feelings may disturb its functioning— be it mouth, stomach, anus, skin, nose or what you will—unconsciously will, that is.

Through physical illness we not only inflict suffering on ourselves for what we believe to be evil wishes, but also take unconscious revenge on those we feel have hurt us—if we are sick we cannot work, or function sexually, and others must care for us.

By physical illness we also avoid any open expression of anger against those we supposedly love and instead play for their attention and sympathy. Symptoms mask the aggressive impulse when it becomes infused with anger. The impulse to murder, for instance, can be repressed and converted into physical illness: A leading psychiatrist told of a man who suffered a severe attack of arthritis during which he could not move his right arm. Doctors failed to help so he decided to go to a hypnotist who promised to cure the arthritis. Under hypnosis the man was assured there was nothing wrong with his arm. When he emerged from the hypnotic trance, he was able to move his arm freely, all paralysis gone. The next morning when he woke, he went to the kitchen, seized a large carving knife, walked into the bedroom and slashed his wife's throat. The paralyzed arm was his way of dealing with his murderous wishes, trying to keep them under control. When he lost the symptom in such a drastic fashion, he could not cope with his fury. Arthritis had been the means by which psyche and body kept him from destroying his wife (and ultimately himself, as he eventually committed suicide in prison).

Unconscious guilt over unacceptable desires can cause the psyche to be flooded with what Freud called "excitations" that must, in some way, be gotten rid of so the body can regain its physical and psychic balance. Grief, guilt, hate, unfulfilled sexual desires literally can eat away at a person, destroying tissue, muscles, blood, bone.

The only way to solve a psychic conflict that has become intolerable is to become aware of it and its causes, Painful though this may be, it prevents greater pain in the long run. But it seems far easier for most of us to bear the symptom than to bare our souls and make conscious the fantasies that cause the conflict. A man with excessive unconscious fear of castration would deem himself just this side of madness if he freely admitted he had ulcers because he was afraid, as a boy, that his father was going to cut off his penis as punishment for his desire to possess his mother sexually and his wish that his father drop dead. Instead, the man prefers to undergo an ulcer operation, which to his unconscious symbolizes the castration he fears, and which he believes he deserves as punishment for his wicked wishes. This is one reason people usually feel relieved after an operation. Their unconscious guilt has been temporarily eased through the punishment they have brought on themselves.

As the Reverend Laurence Sterne wrote in *Tristram Shandy*, in 1760, "The body and the mind are as a jerkin and its lining—rumple the one and you rumple the other."

Freud wrote of the relation between body and mind: "If anyone feels astonished at this associative connection between physical pain and psychical affect [emotion] on the ground of its being [of] such a multiple and artificial character, I should reply that this feeling is as little justified as astonishment at the fact that it is the rich people who own the most money. Where there are no such numerous connections, a hysterical symptom will not, in fact, be formed; for conversion will find no path open to it."

Freud led the way to a greater understanding by general physicians of the unity between body and mind. Today psychoanalytic theories are being accepted by more and more doctors. For instance, Dr. Henry Schneer, chairman of the Psychiatry Section of the Medical Society of the State of New York, arranged a program for the 173rd convention in September, 1979, "to alert doctors to psychosomatic medicine during different stages of life."

Dr. Schneer said, "We are all psychosomatic or somatopsychic —body and mind work together. They can affect each other either to establish health or cause disease. Heart disease, the common cold, and even cancer, may have a mental origin since it is well known that stress is linked to physical illness."

He pointed out that peptic ulcer is not only a psychosomatic illness among New Yorkers: in Uganda a study showed that more than fourteen percent of the natives suffered from it.

Unconscious fantasies may influence behavior in many ways. Accident-proneness, for instance, may be caused by the unconscious wish to keep punishing the self for "evil" thoughts. A wife who suffers beatings by an alcoholic husband, for example, may be satisfying an unconscious need for self-punishment because of unexpressed hatred for her husband probably related to a hatred she felt as a child toward a cruel father.

What Freud called "the return of the repressed" can also be seen in phobias. Fear of darkness, fear of dirt, fear of being alone, fear of falling and fear of heights are all methods of fighting threatening conflicts unresolved in childhood. Phobic persons accept a substitute, disguised and given symbolic expression, to conceal from themselves the true reason for their fear. They believe that by avoiding a certain evil, such as dirt or darkness, they can escape impending disaster, thereby achieving control over anxiety.

What is the original fear that the phobia has displaced? It is the fear, Freud said, of a repressed "dangerous" impulse threatening to break through into consciousness. An impulse that, if carried out, would violate one of society's taboos, which include: Thou must give up thy mother's breast; thou must not touch the most pleasurable part of thy body; thou must not desire a parent or brother or sister sexually; thou must not raise thy hand to strike a parent or a sibling in murderous assault. Otherwise, thou willst suffer mutilation or outright death.

The conflict between a wish and a taboo can express itself as a phobia. It may represent a frightening or painful situation in any stage or all stages of early life. For instance, the fear of being alone may be fear of separation from the mother in the first years of life, but it may also hide a later fear of masturbating—a forbidden pleasure. Fear of being confined in a small area, or claustrophobia, may be based on the fantasy of returning to the mother's womb, or fear of incestuous sexual intimacy, as may be the fears of being buried alive or the fear of suffocation. A fear of high places may relate to the fear of sexual excitement, both of erection (raising of the penis) and orgasm (falling off).

Fear of the dark is also associated with separation from mother and fear of death, as well as fear of sexual intercourse, which often takes place in the dark. Fear of ghosts and fear of strangers, originally a fear of being separated from mother, are also often related to the wish for incestuous love, displaced on the ghost or stranger and sometimes also on persons of a different color, creed or race.

No phobia exists in a vacuum. It is always associated with an actual experience around which fantasies revolve. A contemporary analyst told of a patient who could not tolerate a dog in his house; he would not even allow visitors to bring their pets. During psychoanalysis the patient remembered that at the age of seven he had watched two dogs copulate and was both horrified and fascinated. Whenever he saw a dog, displacing both his fears and sexually aroused desires on the animal, he became phobic. Another boy, less afraid of his sexual feelings, would have been able to witness the act and have a dog as a pet without feeling disturbed.

Another patient, a woman, was phobic about the color purple, which she refused to wear. In analysis she recalled that when she was about four her mother had once slapped her fiercely for leaving the house when she was told to stay in her room. At which she had felt like murdering her mother. She also recalled that on that day her mother had been wearing a pair of purple velvet slippers. She had promptly denied her wish to destroy her mother, but the purple of the slippers became a phobia hiding her matricidal impulse. A few children are driven so blind by anger that they *do* kill a parent, sometimes even waiting years for revenge, as perhaps Lizzie Borden did.

Phobias about food may be related to fear of being impregnated, connected to childhood sexual fantasies that the birth of babies takes place through the mouth or anus. A food phobia may also relate to fear of being poisoned, early fantasies of persecution by the "bad" mother.

Speech phobias may go back to erotic oral fantasies, with anal fantasies added later. Not to talk, or not to talk properly—for example, stammering—may show a repressed anal anger, a refusal to let the words out or an erotic attachment to the mouth. The words are overly caressed, the stammerer reluctant to let them go.

There are such obsessive acts as the endless washing of hands, or observing a ritual in getting dressed each morning, or incessant, uncontrollable talking, or the compulsive repetition in speech of certain words such as "you know" or "uh." These all may hide unconscious desires considered dangerous, erotic or aggressive from the oral, anal or phallic stages, perhaps all three.

The person who returns several times to make sure he has locked the door may fear that someone will break in and take what belongs to him, even though he carries his most precious bodily possession with him. Many psychoanalysts believe that indecision may mask an unconscious conflict over whether or not to masturbate.

The compulsive person tends to be obsessed by the idea that his sexual impulses are destructive. He tries to handle this in one of two ways. By exaggerating the destructive part he may conceal from himself the sexual part as he thinks, "If I keep my hands clean, I will be less likely to kill," hiding the wish to masturbate. Or, by exaggerating the sexual part, he may conceal the destructive wish, such as the woman who compulsively masturbates, hiding her desire to murder a man who is impotent with her.

In any case every obsession is an unsuccessful attempt to solve an ambivalence that is felt to be dangerous. The ambivalence stems from intense shifts between love and hate that the obsessed person felt as a child, Freud said. In obsessions, these violent swings from love to hate become centered on objects, such as doors, cracks in the walls, dirty hands. This is an attempt to ease a painful psychic state, but the attempt always fails because the love and hate are too strong and too evenly balanced. The obsessed one, Freud said, hangs, as it were, in a state of suspense midway between his sexual or aggressive desire and the taboos against his fantasies, fantasies that have been contained since childhood and are still active in the unconscious.

It took years before there was scientific proof that there does exist a part of the brain that stores our fantasies and memories. That the unconscious was not just a fantasy of Freud's, but actually existed, was finally proved in the late 1940s by Dr. Wilder Penfield, in experiments at the Montreal Neurological Institute.

Penfield "stumbled" upon his discovery by accident, as he reported in the book *Speech and Brain-Mechanisms,* written with Dr. Lamar Roberts. Penfield was trying to throw new light on the speech mechanisms of the brain as, in his words, he "listened to the humming of the mind's machinery, and where words come from." He performed 190 craniotomies under local anesthesia, which prevented pain yet left the brain normally active, so the patient was fully conscious and could talk while the brain was exposed.

As Penfield used electrodes to mildly stimulate parts of the brain, unexpectedly a patient would start to talk freely about something in his past. Penfield discovered this happened only when the electrodes were applied to spots on the cortex just above the two temporal lobes. These are the sections of the brain that lie under the temple on each side of the head, the location of our thought processes and memory.

The electrical stimulation caused a "stream of consciousness" to flow, in which patients described and emotionally relived past experiences. Penfield compared that part of the brain where memory is stored to a continuous film strip with a sound track. He described how a man first heard a piano playing, then remembered the song *Oh Marie, Oh Marie!* A woman relived a scene from early childhood, recalled the fear she felt at the time. Some called the experiential memory a dream, others referred to it as a "flashback." All agreed it was more vivid than anything they could recall voluntarily. Penfield noted that the patients did not look on their recollections as "remembering" but as a "hearing-again and seeing-again—a living-through moments of past time."

As Penfield put it, "He [the patient] enters the stream of the past and it is the same as it was in the past, but when he looks at the banks of the stream, he is aware of the present as well."

Our entire "past" appears in a steady flow from the unconscious in one of our most normal mental functions—dreaming. This was shown in Freud's monumental book, *The Interpretation of Dreams,* which appeared in 1900 and is regarded by many as his most original and creative work.

Writing a preface to the Third Revised English Edition in 1931, Freud said, "It contains, even according to my present-day judgment, the most valuable of all the discoveries it has been my good fortune to make. Insight such as this falls to one's lot but once in a lifetime."

For his foreword, he chose a line from Virgil: "If I cannot influence the celestial gods I will set in motion the infernal regions."

The scientific approach to dreams was one of Freud's most significant contributions. For centuries their meaning had been attributed to evil spirits, demons within, ancestors sending messages from the nether world or the mind trying to predict the future. Freud showed that dreams could be interpreted according to the laws of the unconscious. They were messages from the unconscious self to the conscious self—messages that could be decoded if one knew the clues.

The structure of symptoms and the structure of dreams were the same. They were both "compromise formations," the result of the interplay between conflicting forces of the mind. A dream gives discharge in a symbolic way to the secret wishes that clamor for expression. A repressed wish from childhood, related to a current wish, seeks release even as it is opposed by censors of the mind that consider it dangerous. These contesting forces bring about the disguises and distortions that made dreams—and physical and mental disorders—seem unintelligible until Freud discovered the various psychic processes that operate to disguise buried emotions in dreams, and developed an interpretation of the language of dreams. The processes of disguise include: the use of symbols, the part for the whole, displacement, identification, denial, the use of opposites, the combining of past and present. The dreamer plays all the roles in the dream, unconsciously manipulating the action to give expression to the hidden wish.

Freud described a "determining condition" that distinguishes dreams from physical symptoms that force their way into waking life, such as headaches or a paralyzed arm. The dream, though in disguised form, expresses the repressed wish as *fulfilled,* whereas the symptom expresses it as *repressed.* A symptom arises whenever an impulse from the id and the repressing thought from the ego come together and the conflict is only partially resolved. In a dream, where the ego is less strong, the wish, though in disguised form, is portrayed as fulfilled.

With Freud's discovery that dreams reveal unconscious desires —childhood wishes that had to be suppressed because they dealt with such taboos as incestuous love, the wish to express erotic feelings with someone of the same sex, the urge to kill, the desire to masturbate—Freud brought home the importance of hidden wishes not only in the lives of the deeply disturbed but in normal people as well. Everyone dreams. Dreams are the binoculars through which the dreamer takes a closer look at the specters that haunt his life. They are the safety valves for repressed emotions.

"The interpretation of dreams is the royal road to a knowledge of the unconscious activities of the mind," Freud said. Dreams prove that *"what is suppressed continued to exist in normal people as well as abnormal, and remains capable of psychical functioning"* (italics Freud's).

He explained that in waking life the suppressed material of the mind is prevented from finding expression and is cut off from internal perception, but during the night, "under the sway of an impetus toward the construction of compromises, this suppressed material finds methods and means of forcing its way into consciousness . . . By analyzing dreams we can take a step forward in our understanding of the composition of that most marvelous and most mysterious of all instruments."

Dreams are never what they seem on the surface. The heart of a dream lies not in its story but in what comes to the dreamer's mind about each detail of the dream upon waking. In addition to revealing a repressed childhood wish as fulfilled, the dreamer also incorporates with it an impression or wish of the previous day that stirred memories of the childhood wish and thereby offered the unconscious "the point of attachment necessary for its emergence into the conscious."

Why does a dream reflect a wish? Because the wish sets in motion the psychic apparatus, Freud said. One has to wish before one can act. One wishes to get up in the morning: then the limbs move. One wishes to get dressed: then one puts on clothes. But when one wishes to do something that is opposed by the conscience, a conflict ensues.

Childhood is a time of great conflict, especially when it comes to erotic and hostile desires. These infantile conflicts live on in dreams, Freud said. One of his patients, a physician in his thirties, told Freud he often dreamed of a "yellow lion," but could not account for it. One day, in the closet of his room, he came across a china "yellow lion" he had put away years before. His mother told him it had been his favorite toy during childhood, though he had long forgotten it. The "yellow lion" no doubt symbolized some early experience involving his erotic or aggressive feelings, which he preferred to forget.

Freud described the dream of an intelligent, reserved, undemonstrative woman, who told him at her analytic session, "I dreamt that I arrived too late at the market and could get nothing either from the butcher or from the woman who sells vegetables." Freud remarked that this seemed to be "an innocent dream no doubt; but dreams are not as simple as that, so I asked to be told it in greater detail." The woman then said that she had dreamed she was going to the market with her cook, who was carrying a basket. When the woman asked the butcher for some specific cut of meat, he had said, "That's not obtainable any longer." He offered her something else, saying, "This is good too." But she had rejected it. She went instead to a woman who sold vegetables. This woman tried to persuade her to buy a peculiar vegetable, tied in bundles and black in color, but she said, "I don't recognize that; I won't take it."

As she told Freud her thoughts about details of the dream, she recalled that the day before she had gone to the market but so late that she found "the meat shop was closed." When she requested meat, the butcher had said, "That's not obtainable any longer"— the very words appearing in her dream.

Freud thought to himself, he said, that the phrase, "The meat shop was closed," was the reverse of a vulgar phrase used to describe a man who had neglected to close the fly of his trousers (your meat shop is open). But Freud also realized that these were *his* thoughts, not his patient's. The question became whether anything in the dream or the thoughts it produced in the patient supported this sexual interpretation.

Freud bided his time, focusing on the spoken words of the dream, which he expected might lead to some experiences in the patient's life that had caused her to feel pain, even if the words were quoted out of context. The phrase, "That is not obtainable any longer," he recognized as a comment he had made the day before about her childhood memories. The use of his words showed that her dream involved him in a so-called "transference dream."

In talking about the phrase, "I don't recognize that," referring to the strange vegetable offered by the woman in the market, the patient recalled an actual scene between the cook and herself. She had scolded the cook for some wrongdoing, saying, "I don't recognize [accept] that." Then she had said, "Behave yourself properly." But only the phrase, "I don't recognize that" appeared in the dream. The words, "Behave yourself properly," however, represented an important, even though omitted, clue to the meaning of the dream, Freud said. It was a strong warning she was issuing to someone else, or herself, or both, connected to a taboo desire.

This hidden phrase confirmed Freud's suspicion that the dream dealt with a sexual experience in which a man had exposed himself

and his patient had replied, "Behave yourself properly." Her associations to the vegetables "tied up in bundles and of a black
color" were sexual, Freud concluded. He surmised that in her past
some man had behaved in "an improper and sexually provocative
manner," forgetting to "close his meat shop," as it were. She had
then said, "Behave yourself properly," as a reprimand but also to
protect herself from her sexual desires. Freud did not mention this,
but the fact that the woman used his words in the dream—"that's
not obtainable any longer"—might be related to a sexual wish on
her part to be involved with Freud, which she knew was forbidden, so his "meat shop" would always be closed to her and she
would have to "behave properly." This wish was related to her
childhood wish—a natural one—to possess her father.

The dream appeared at the beginning of the woman's treatment.
Later in the analysis, confirming his interpretation, she told Freud
that when she was a girl, a man had exposed himself sexually and
she had ordered him to behave himself. The experience had so
frightened her that she had promptly put it out of mind . . . The
dream was probably evoked by her erotic feelings for Freud, her
visit to the butcher shop and her fight with the cook. These experiences had revived memories of the early trauma. The dream gave
release to the premature sexual feelings aroused in her as a girl and
repressed, as well as to her anger—"behave yourself properly"—
at the man who had exposed himself to her, at the butcher for
rejecting her request for meat and at Freud for what she knew
would be rejection of any sexual advance on her part.

Freud discovered the role of symbols in dreams. He said they
referred mainly to sexual objects or attributes since this was the
area of greatest repression. He gave as an example: "All elongated
objects, such as sticks, tree-trunks and umbrellas (the opening of
these last being comparable to an erection) may stand for the male
organ—as well as all long, sharp weapons, such as knives, daggers
and pikes." And: "Nor is there any doubt that all weapons and
tools are used as symbols for the male organ: e.g., ploughs, hammers, rifles, revolvers, daggers, sabers, etc." Fruits, particularly
apples and peaches, are often symbols of the breasts. Wood, paper
and articles made from them, such as chairs and books, stand for

the woman's body, as do purses, bags, tables, closets, chests.

But Freud warned that the understanding of the primordial language of symbols is of limited use in the interpretation of a dream. There must be an understanding of what is personal and unique to the dreamer, which relates to his particular childhood experiences and conflicts and the wishes they reveal.

Freud analyzed himself chiefly through his own dreams. He wrote of this self-analysis in his letters to Fliess, who encouraged him in his psychic explorations and contributed his own—usually wrong—interpretations.

As with all else in his life Freud undertook his self-analysis thoughtfully and thoroughly. He never stopped analyzing himself, devoting the last half-hour of each day to the task. This self-analysis was his search for the causes of conflict in his own life. He began it at a time of great trauma—after the death of his father aroused ambivalent feelings as well as the grief and anger he was later to write about in connection with the death of a parent. No doubt his intense emotional distress caused Freud to examine his inner feelings at this particular moment in his life, just as many people only enter analysis when they feel desperate.

A letter to Fliess dated May 31, 1897 contains the first hint of Freud's discovery of what he later named the Oedipus complex: "Hostile impulses against parents (a wish that they should die) are also an integral part of neuroses . . . It seems as though in sons this death-wish is directed against their father and in daughters against their mother."

He recalled that when he was four years old he felt an erotic yearning for his mother when he saw her naked on a train trip the family took as they moved from Leipzig to Vienna, during which they shared the coach's small sleeping quarters. He also remembered jealousy and hatred of a baby brother who died when Freud was nineteen months old.

In a letter to Fliess written on October 15, 1897, Freud describes how he arrived at his conviction about the Oedipus complex. He named it after the hero in Sophocles' play *Oedipus Rex*, the mythical story of a man who unwittingly kills his father and marries his mother. When Oedipus learns what he has done, he tears out his eyes to atone for breaking the incest taboo and flees the land. His mother, Queen Jocasta, kills herself. In the letter Freud says:

"I have found love of the mother and jealousy of the father in my own case too, and now believe it to be a general phenomenon of early childhood . . . the Greek myth seizes on a compulsion which everyone recognizes because he has felt traces of it in himself. Every member of the audience was once a budding Oedipus in fantasy, and this dream-fulfillment played out in reality causes everyone to recoil in horror, with the full measure of repression which separates his infantile from his present state."

Freud never theorized in a vacuum. He arrived at the importance of the sexual drive only when patient after patient recalled memories related either to childhood sexual experiences or fantasies. He was struck by the persistence with which such traumatic events of early life were mentioned, especially in view of the puritanical attitude toward sex then prevalent.

One of his early patients was an eighteen-year-old girl, Katharina. Freud met her on a vacation while walking along a mountain trail in the Alps. Katharina, a waitress at the inn where he was staying, followed him and begged him for help. She complained of headaches "like a hammering in my head," shortness of breath, dizziness and a weight pressing against her chest that made it difficult for her to breathe. She also felt at times as if she were going to die. She said she was haunted by the vision of a man's angry face staring at her.

Freud did not relish the thought of working on vacation but was moved by the girl's plight. He encouraged her to talk freely. After an initial reluctance she told him that her symptoms had started two years before, on a day when her mother had gone shopping. Katharina and her younger brother went to their father's room and found it locked. It seemed strange to her that her father would bolt the door during the day. She decided to go outside and look in the window. Peering into the room, she saw her father in bed with her cousin, a girl about Katharina's age who lived with them and did the cooking.

Freud asked what she felt as she stared at the scene. She said, "I came away from the window at once, and leaned up against the wall and couldn't get my breath—just what happens to me since.

Everything went blank; my eyelids were forced together, and there was a hammering and buzzing in my head."

"Did you tell your mother that very day?" Freud asked.

"Oh, no, I said nothing," Katharina replied.

But her behavior in the next few days was so strange that her mother suspected she was concealing some terrifying secret. She demanded to know what it was. The frightened daughter confessed what she had seen. The mother then confronted the father. He admitted that the daughter's story was true and the mother promptly packed and left him, taking along her two children.

Katharina further disclosed that when she was younger, one winter she had accompanied her father on a trip into the valley, where they spent the night at an inn. He stayed in the bar drinking and playing cards and she went to bed in the room they were to share. Sometime during the night she woke suddenly to feel his body pressing against her. She jumped out of bed and asked, "What are you up to? Why don't you stay in your own bed?"

"Come on, you silly," he said. "You don't know how nice it is."

"I don't like your 'nice' things; you don't even let one sleep in peace," she rebuked him. She stood by the door, ready to run into the hall should he persist, but he fell asleep.

When Freud asked if she knew what her father was trying to do, she replied, "Not at the time."

She recalled that another night she had been forced to run out of the house because her father became drunk and made advances, and remembered still other scenes of intimacy between her father and her cousin.

In Katharina's case, as in Anna O's, when she could speak of the traumatic events and her emotions at the time, her physical symptoms disappeared. She became cheerful and healthy, no longer troubled by headaches, dizziness, pressure on her chest, shortness of breath. She said she realized that the angry face she sometimes imagined staring at her was her father's face, glowering at her as he had done when her mother accused him of seducing his niece.

Listening to other patients Freud concluded that, like Katharina, if a child were subjected to sexual assault, or undue sexual stimulation that aroused feelings the child could not handle, even if no apparent effect was produced at the time, as a result of repression physical symptoms might appear later in life.

Freud realized how much of ancient primitive life revolved around sex and violence and the resulting taboos imposed by civilized man. Classical mythology, the Greek plays based on those myths, fairy tales and folklore shared a similar content, sometimes symbolic, sometimes direct: the murder of the father, the murder of the mother, the murder of the brother, the eating of human flesh (the god Kronus devoured his own children), incest, dismemberment, castration and worship of the phallus. Freud realized that in the course of becoming civilized man had to repress many of his aggressive and sexual impulses, which nevertheless continued to demand satisfaction in disguised ways.

Freud's encouragement of his patients' recognition of repressed sexual fantasies and feelings was in no way an encouragement of promiscuous behavior.

Freud was far from an advocate of sexual license as a means of curing neurosis. Sex "is not the antidote to every ill," he once said. Living in an era of high hypocrisy and prudery about sex, he saw around him frigid wives and spinsters, husbands impotent with wives but not other women, promiscuous young men who could not marry but slept with prostitutes, and homosexuals. He sought the causes of sexual aberrations; by no means did he promote them.

Freud made sex respectable instead of obscene. Only by understanding what could happen to the development of the sexual drive, he said, could people hope to arrive at better control of feelings and achieve more harmonious adjustment between unconscious demands for sexual gratification and judicious indulgence of passions.

A revolutionary finding. One of many made by this extraordinary man. The question arises: why was Freud the one to have discovered such truths about the human mind?

3

Why was Freud the One?

What gave Freud the special courage, the special knowledge, the special sensitivity to venture into the complexity of his own mind and the minds of others—forbidden territory up to that point in history? To become a man so far ahead of his time that it might take centuries to catch up with his revelations?

"Freud's journey within—the *Interpretation of Dreams* (1900)— parallels and goes beyond that of Marcus Aurelius, St. Augustine, Dante, Pascal, Kierkegaard, Rimbaud and other more recent explorers of the soul," says Benjamin Nelson, historian and author. "None took soundings so deep as he, none focused so unrelentingly and evolved such powerful resources for mapping the innermost labyrinths as he; none described the mind's itinerary with less resort to fable, fancy or despairing leaps into faith."

Freud said of himself in a letter to his physician Dr. Max Schur, ". . . I am really not a man of science, not an observer, not an experimenter and not a thinker. I am nothing but by temperament a *conquistador*—an adventurer, if you want to translate that word

—with the curiosity, the boldness and the tenacity that belongs to that type of being."

His sense of adventure permitted him to tackle the unknown, to travel dangerous paths. But instead of electing to climb Mount Everest, he chose to plumb the unexplored depths of psychic functioning. And once he started his journey into the inner life, he never let go if there was yet one more insight to be achieved as he listened carefully to what he called "the vast world-melody of instincts."

A significant story about Freud is told by Robert Waelder in his book, *Freud.* Waelder recalled the day, "many years ago," when he and another man whom Waelder describes as a "renowned writer from Germany" (probably either Thomas Mann or Stefan Zweig), visited Freud in a little Alpine village where he was vacationing. In their conversation they talked about the German-Jewish philosopher and writer Franz Rosenzweig, who had died at an early age. During the last years of his life Rosenzweig translated the Bible into German verse. Because of an injury received in the war he had developed what Waelder calls "one of the most horrible sufferings which can be found in the arsenal of human diseases: an amyothropic lateral sclerosis, in the course of which all his muscles successively became paralyzed."

Rosenzweig was forced to recline most of his waking hours in a large armchair, his head supported by a large strap. The only muscle he could move was an eye muscle, which "had to perform the entire service of contact with the outside world." A typewriter with a large keyboard had been specially built for him and his way of "talking" was to fix his eyes on one letter, then another, as his wife would press the key he indicated. In this way he wrote the biblical translation, conducted correspondence with distinguished contemporaries and "conversed" with visitors.

In his discussion of Rosenzweig with Freud and the German author, Waelder made an admiring remark about what to him appeared great heroism. Whereupon Freud gave him a look of surprise and said, "Was there any other alternative?"

Commented Waelder in his book, "The courage of life and the will to work were a foregone conclusion to Freud. If all roads were closed except one narrow, hardly passable path—what else remains to do than walk this narrow path as well as one can?"

The "courage of life" Freud certainly had. Not the kind of courage that wins medals of honor for slaughtering enemies on battlefields. But the kind needed to face the dreaded enemies within—greed, hatred, jealousy, terror, the wish for revenge, cannibalistic impulses, incestuous desires. And the courage to apply the revolutionary insights gained from facing inner enemies to the construction of a healing process that could set men free from being their own executioners.

It was no accident that Freud was the one. It was the result of many factors, including some of the circumstances of his life.

Sigmund Freud was born at 6:30 P.M. on May 6, 1856, at 117 Schlossergasse in Freiberg, Moravia. Now called Príbor, Freiberg was then a town of about 5,000 Germans and Czechoslovakians and belonged to the Austro-Hungarian Empire. Freud's birthplace was an old two-story house built of plastered bricks and topped with a slate roof.

His mother, Amalia Nathanson Freud, was twenty-one years old at his birth. She was the descendant of a famous Talmudic scholar, the eighteenth-century Nathan Halevy Charmatz, of Brody, Poland. As a young woman Amalia was slender and pretty and kept, to the end of her ninety-five years, her gaiety, alertness and sharp wit. At an age when most of her contemporaries, if still alive, were confined to their beds, she enjoyed card parties.

Freud's mother was the second wife of his father, Jakob, who was forty-one years old when Sigmund, his first child in the second marriage, was born. Jakob was the owner of a small textile mill in Freiberg, a merchant engaged principally in the sale of wool all his life. Jakob's father, Ephraim Freud, was called "rabbi," though this was used as a title of respect, rather than implying clerical status.

Jakob was a gentleman, well-loved by his family and friends. He was also above average in intelligence, according to Freud's biographer Dr. Ernest Jones. Freud described himself as a duplicate of his father physically, and to some extent mentally as well. He depicts his father as a Jewish Micawber, "always hopefully expecting something to turn up." At the time of Jakob's second marriage, he was a grandfather by his first marriage. His elder son, who lived nearby, was the father of a one-year-old boy, so Sigmund was born an uncle, one of the many puzzles his young mind had to try to solve.

The first three years of Freud's life were spent in Freiberg— Free Mountain—a peaceful little town about 150 miles northeast of Vienna, on the Libina River. The steeple of Saint Mary's Birth Church, which rose more than 200 feet in the air, dominated the town. Most of the Moravian population were Roman Catholic, with two percent Protestant and two percent Jewish. The Jews, in language and education, were German. They were the target of Czech anti-Semitism when the revolution of 1848 erupted in nearby Bohemia, directed against Jewish textile manufacturers.

As his mother's first child, Sigmund was also her favorite. She called him *"mein goldener Sigi,"* and they remained close until the day she died. Freud wrote, "A man who has been the indisputable favorite of his mother keeps for life the feeling of a conqueror, that confidence of success that often induces real success."

At birth he had such an abundance of black curly hair that his young mother nicknamed him her "little blackamoor." He was born in a caul, an event she believed ensured him fame and happiness. An old woman she encountered by chance in a pastry shop confirmed Frau Freud's superstition, telling her that she had brought into the world a child who would become a great man. Amalia undoubtedly transmitted her feelings to her young son. As Jones says in the Freud biography, "Thus the hero's garb was in the weaving at the cradle itself."

In contrast to this feeling of being "special," Freud also suffered a great trauma early in life. When he was nineteen months old his little brother Julius, eight months old, died. Five months later Freud slipped from a stool and hit the left side of his lower jaw on the edge of a table he was exploring. The blow was so violent that his jaw bled profusely and required stitches. He had the scar all through life and later developed cancer on the right side of his upper jaw.

This accident may have been related to both the death of his little brother and the pregnancy of his mother, who gave birth to her first daughter, Anna, six months after Freud's accident. Freud was the one who later pointed out the intense jealousy of siblings and that guilt caused by repressed hostile wishes may result in drastic self-punishment.

During Freud's infancy economic depression, combined with rising nationalism on the part of the Czechs, touched off hostility against the usual European scapegoat, the Jews. Even in tiny Freiberg, the Catholic clothmakers started to blame the Jewish minority of textile merchants for their plight. Though the lives and property of Jewish families were not actually endangered, Jakob decided, since his source of income had dwindled, to leave for Leipzig, where he hoped to set up a new business.

Sigmund, then three years old, remembered the long ride in the horse-drawn carriage and his first sight of a railway. After a year in Leipzig, Jakob decided to move to Vienna, where Amalia had spent much of her childhood.

Freud's early years in Vienna were evidently not happy ones; he later said he remembered little of what happened to him between the ages of three and seven, "They were hard times and not worth remembering," and that he missed the freedom and pleasantness of country life.

Like Freiberg, Vienna was very anti-Semitic, though in 1867, when Sigmund was eleven, a new municipal constitution granted Jews equal status with other citizens, putting an end at least to the legal aspect of racial discrimination. But in attitude the *echt Wienerisher* remained anti-Semitic all of Freud's life. Freud, who had been circumcised as a baby, was later to say that he thought the unconscious reason for the world's hatred of Jews was that they introduced circumcision, which brought pain so early in life and symbolically represented castration and death, although its avowed purpose was that of cleanliness.

At first the Freuds lived in a small, crowded apartment in the Pfeffergasse, a tiny street in a largely Jewish section. They soon moved to a six-room apartment in the Kaiser Josefstrasse, to accommodate the rapidly growing number of children—after fourteen years of marriage Amalia had given birth to four more daughters and another son. Jakob never did well financially, but his wife's family gave assistance.

The "cabinet," a long, narrow room separated from the rest of the apartment, was given to young Sigmund. It held a bed, chairs, bookshelf and desk. There he slept and worked until he became an intern at the Viennese General Hospital. The only thing that changed in the room all through Sigmund's high school years and university life was the continual addition of bookcases. The future founder of psychoanalysis spent a good deal of time in his "cabinet." In his teens he ate his evening meal there, so he would lose no time at study. He even had the only oil lamp in the apartment; the other rooms used candles.

When Sigmund objected to his sister's piano practicing, claiming that it interfered with his studying, his mother had the piano taken out of the apartment. Freud's lifelong aversion to music is well known. Jones reports that there was a pained expression on Freud's face whenever he entered a restaurant or beer garden and heard a band . . . his hands would fly to his ears to drown out the "blare." A curious aversion in the compatriot of Mozart, Mahler and the Johann Strausses!

Like his mother, his father also treated young Sigmund as "special." Jakob taught his son to read and write before sending him to a private school—not many nineteenth-century Austrian boys received this much attention from their fathers. Jakob also looked on Sigmund as a companion, taking him on long walks all over Vienna, an activity Freud was to continue in later life in the company of colleagues.

Jakob Freud was not the strict *pater familias* then so common, according to Jones. He consulted his wife and children over important decisions but at the same time demanded that they show him respect. One day young Moritz Rosenthal, who later became a famous pianist, was arguing with his father in the street when they met Jakob Freud. He reproved the boy, saying, "What, are you contradicting your father? My Sigmund's little toe is cleverer than my head, but he would never dare to contradict me!" Which testified to Jakob's deep admiration for, and pride in, his older son.

Freud described a unique occurrence of his father's rejection that haunted him all his life, he said. This traumatic experience took place, as Freud recalled in *The Interpretation of Dreams*, "when I was seven or eight years of age." He said that one evening before going to bed, "I had disregarded the dictates of discretion and had satisfied my needs in my parents' bedroom, and in their presence," meaning that he had urinated in front of them. His father scolded him and remarked, "That boy will never amount to anything."

Freud commented, "This must have been a terrible affront to

my ambitions, for allusions to this scene recur again and again in my dreams, and are constantly coupled with enumerations of my accomplishments and successes, as though I wanted to say: 'You see, I have amounted to something after all.' " His single-minded pursuit of greatness and achievement, "one of the immortal infantile wishes—the wish to become great," was an effort to vindicate himself in the eyes of his father, he suggested.

He also revealed that at the age of two he had been impelled by sexual curiosity to peer into his parents' bedroom. One can theorize that the later act of urination may have been motivated by the desire to show his father that he too had a penis he could use and as a reminder to his mother, as well.

When, at seventeen, Sigmund was graduated *summa cum laude* from high school, he faced the problem of choosing his life's work, which his father left up to him. For a Viennese Jew the choice of a career was limited to industry or business, the law or medicine. As Sigmund did not want to go into business, he thought of law. He had learned many languages, including Greek, Latin, French, English, Hebrew, Italian and Spanish. He had started reading Shakespeare at eight and read his works again and again, always ready with an apt quotation. He was later to cite Hamlet as an example of the Oedipus complex, and Lady Macbeth's handwashing scene was to provide him with a classic study of unconscious guilt.

He then considered medicine, though he did not feel particularly inspired by it, later saying he was "moved, rather, by a sort of curiosity, which was, however, directed more toward human concerns than toward natural objects . . ." At this time "the theories of Darwin, which were then of topical interest, strongly attracted me, for they held out hopes of an extraordinary advance in our understanding of the world."

Just before he graduated from high school he attended a lecture given by Professor Carl Brühl, who read "Goethe's beautiful essay on nature." Freud claimed that it was this lecture that "decided me to become a medical student." The essay was titled "Fragment upon Nature" and contained a spirited challenge to man to conquer nature which, in a sense, Freud did—but his conquest was of *human* nature.

He entered the medical school of the University of Vienna in 1873 and received his medical degree in 1881, not intending to practice but to carry on scientific research. He had taken courses in zoology, biology and physics at the Institute of Physics, where he had met the director, Brücke, whose influence "affected me more than any other in my whole life."

It was Brücke who persuaded him to give up research and practice medicine to earn a decent living. There followed Freud's growing interest in neurology as he studied under Meynart and Charcot and, as a result of his work with Breuer, began his rise to glory in the world of the science of the mind.

Why was glory—not easily but finally—achieved? In a sense, "the right man" did appear "at the right time." The same year that three-year-old Sigmund Freud was taken by his parents to live in Leipzig, Darwin's *Origin of the Species* was published. This one book proved that man could be the object of scientific study, no different, except in complexity of mind, from other forms of life.

The following year when Freud was four Gustav Fechner founded the science of psychology. This great German scientist and philosopher showed, in 1860, that the mind of man could be studied scientifically and measured quantitatively, and psychology took its place among the other natural sciences. Both Darwin and Fechner, according to Freud himself, were to have great impact on his intellectual development.

Interest in the biological sciences and psychology flourished during the second half of the nineteenth century. Pasteur and Koch, in their fundamental work on the germ theory of disease, established the science of bacteriology. Mendel, through his investigation of the garden pea, founded the science of genetics. Life sciences showed a creative surge, emerging from the dark ages of ignorance and superstition.

Other scientific discoveries were coming in physics. In the middle of the century the German physicist Hermann von Helmholtz formulated the principle of the conservation of energy. This led to one discovery after another in the field of dynamics, providing man with electrical appliances, television, automobiles, airplanes —and atomic bombs. Freud used "energy" as one of the main principles in describing the functioning of the mind. The new physics made possible an even more radical view of man than that of Darwin, who conceived of man as an animal, evolving from the ape—just another "species"—and Fechner, who proved that the mind of man could be brought into the laboratory and measured. Physics now said man was an "energy system," obeying the same physical laws that regulated the movement of the planets or the steam engine.

In medical school Freud could not help being influenced by the new physics—"energy" and "dynamics" were seeping into every laboratory, flooding the minds of scientists of all nationalities. Brücke's book, *Lectures on Physiology,* published in 1874 (the year after Freud entered medical school), set forth the radical view that the living organism is a dynamic system to which the laws of chemistry and physics apply.

Twenty years later Freud's singular genius applied the law of dynamics to the mind of man. Freud created a "dynamic" psychology that studied the transformations and exchanges of energy within the psyche—which proved one of the most stupendous achievements in modern science.

In 1883, two years after Freud graduated from medical school, Theodor Lipps, a professor of psychology in Munich, wrote that he believed "in the existence of unconscious mental processes side-by-side with the conscious ones . . . We further believe that unconscious processes lie at the bottom of all conscious ones and accompany them . . . the conscious, when fortune favors, arises from the unconscious and then sinks back into it again." Freud listened to what Lipps had to say. Also about this time the Viennese professor Krafft-Ebing, with his book *Psychopathia Sexualist* broke the ban of silence on perversions, giving them names and describing them in detail.

Freud combined what he learned in physics and psychology and to this knowledge added his own philosophy. He said in 1896, when he was forty, "As a young man I longed for nothing else than philosophical knowledge, and I am now on the way to satisfy that longing by passing over from medicine to psychology." He had just written *Studies on Hysteria,* his first book and the turning point of his life.

Freud's philosophical interests were not those of the abstract professional or academic professor—his philosophy was social and humanitarian. "It took the form of building a philosophy of life," as Calvin S. Hall put it in his article, "Sigmund Freud, Founder of Psychoanalysis," published in the special edition of *Wisdom* magazine, May, 1957, on "Psychology and the Human Mind." Hall wrote, "Freud stood for a philosophy of life that is based on science rather than metaphysics or religion. He felt that a philosophy of life worth having is one based upon a true knowledge of man's nature, knowledge that could be gained only by scientific inquiry and research." Freud did not believe psychoanalysis was called upon to develop a new world-view, said Hall, but to extend "the scientific world-view to the study of man." Freud's philosophy of life could be summed up in the phrase, "Knowledge through science," according to the author of *A Primer of Freudian Psychology*.

Freud's intimate knowledge of human nature made him both pessimistic and critical, Hall believed. Freud did not have a high opinion of most men; he felt the irrational forces in man's nature were so strong that the rational forces had little chance of dominating them. A small minority might be able to live a life based on reason, but most men were more comfortable living with their fantasies and superstitions. Freud saw too many patients fighting too passionately to preserve their illusions and delusions for him to place much faith in the power of logic and reason. He demonstrated that most people resist discovering the truth about themselves. So Freud was not only a physician, neurologist, scientist, psychologist and philosopher, but also a social critic. He believed that society, fashioned by man, reflects to a large extent human irrationality, and that each generation is corrupted by being born into an irrational society, not far removed from the tribes of the jungle, with their rituals, superstitions, worship of the phallus and intense jealousies and hatreds. Freud hoped that psychoanalytic principles might be applied in rearing and educating children, but did not minimize the enormity of this task.

Freud has been hailed as a genius, even by those who do not agree with all his theories. Though Breuer's resistance to exploring his inner feelings prevented him from joining Freud in his monumental search for the causes of mental pain, he admired Freud's courage, brilliance, imagination and tenacity. On February 8, 1886, seven months before they were married, Freud wrote to his then fiancée, Martha: "Do you know what Breuer said to me one evening? That he had discovered what an infinitely bold and fearless person I concealed behind my mask of shyness. I have always believed that of myself, but never dared to say it to anyone. I have often felt as if I had inherited all the passion of our ancestors when they defended their Temple, as if I could joyfully cast away my life in a great cause. And with all that I was always so powerless and could not express the flowing passions even by a word or a poem. So I have always suppressed myself . . ."

Breuer said, in 1895, "Freud's intellect is soaring at its highest. I gaze after him as a hen at a hawk." In assessing himself Freud wrote to Lou Andreas-Salomé on July 28, 1929, that his discoveries seemed to spring "from some inner necessity." He added, "My worst qualities, including a certain indifference toward the world, have no doubt had the same share in the end result as my good ones, e.g., a defiant courage in the search for truth."

In this search Freud was able to help his children live more happily. Martin Freud, his eldest son, in his book *Glory Reflected*, said, "We Freud children had inherited a precious gift from both our parents: we enjoyed freedom from fear." Martin wrote that on summer vacations his father threw aside his professional worries and was "all laughter and contentment," showing "a merry heart."

A number of psychoanalysts and psychiatrists have written their impressions of Freud, either after treatment with him or as a colleague or friend.

First and foremost is Ernest Jones, both in his biography and his "Four Centenary Addresses" on Freud, delivered in 1956 in the United States and England. Referring to the belief that a genius "succeeds in demonstrating to the contrary" some prior conclusion that has seemed irrefutable, Jones gave as an example the fact that "many philosophers and psychologists have shown conclusively that in theory there can be no such thing as unconscious mental processes." And yet, as Charcot said (a phrase Freud was fond of quoting), "that doesn't prevent it from existing." Freud went ahead and proved that unconscious mental processes did exist.

Jones described, as among the qualities of a genius, "intuitive inspiration" and "spontaneity," as well as "the power of concentration." He also listed "absolute honesty, originality, a mysterious feeling for what is true, and a sense of sureness." The latter arises, Jones says, from the completeness with which the ego is receiving, "in an unquestioning fashion," the message from the preconscious. At that moment "there is a complete coincidence between the striving of the id, the permission of the superego, the acceptance by the ego and the external perception of the problem being studied."

Jones quoted Emerson as saying, "To believe your own thought, to believe that what is true for you in your private heart is true for all men—that is genius." Schopenhauer made a similar point, Jones added, when he wrote, "Always to see the general in the particular is the very foundation of genius."

Jones believed that if Freud had not been a Jew he would never have discovered psychoanalysis . . . "It is doubtful if without certain traits inherited from his Jewish ancestry Freud would have been able to accomplish the work he did. I think here of a peculiar native shrewdness, a skeptical attitude toward illusion and deception, and a determined courage that made him impervious to hostile public opinion and the contumely of his professional colleagues."

Freud's parents, according to Jones, were "very free-thinking people," who after arriving in Vienna dispensed with the Jewish dietary observances and most of the customary rituals except for the festival Seder meal on the eve of Passover. Jakob was fond of reading the *Torah,* a book of Jewish philosophy as well as religion. Freud attended occasional *Cheder* lessons in the synagogue during the school days. He knew the Bible and was always ready to quote from either Testament—he began to read the Old Testament at seven.

But, says Jones, Freud "grew up devoid of any belief in a God or Immortality, and does not appear ever to have felt the need of it." Nevertheless, Freud had a strong sense of Judaism as his ethnic identity; Jones described Freud as feeling himself "Jewish to the core" and said Freud made very few friends who were not Jews.

As a boy, Freud's idol was a Jew—Hannibal, the great Carthaginian general who had a Semitic background, swore undying hatred of Rome and almost succeeded in destroying it. Many years later Freud explained his boyhood hero-worship of Hannibal: ". . . when I finally came to realize the consequences of belonging to an alien race, and was forced by the anti-Semitic feeling among my classmates to take a definite stand, the figure of the Semitic commander assumed still greater proportions in my imagination. Hannibal and Rome symbolized, in my youthful eyes, the struggle between the tenacity of the Jews and the organization of the Catholic Church."

Though Freud did not believe in God, he was proud of being a Jew and a staunch supporter of the Jews. Jones said, "One cannot describe the man Freud without laying stress on the fact that he was a Jew. Though never orthodox or in any way religious he held together with his people, was a governor of the Hebrew University in Jerusalem and took an interest in the fate of Jewry." He joined the B'nai B'rith society of Vienna in 1900, explaining to the members many years later that he did so because "the longing arose in me for a circle of chosen, high-minded men who, regardless of the audacity of what I had done, would receive me with friendliness. Your society was pointed out to me as the place where such men were to be found. That you were Jews only suited me the more, for I myself was a Jew, and it always seemed to me not only shameful but downright senseless to deny it."

He said he had been raised without particular regard for the strictures of orthodox Judaism, but not without regard for its ethical demands. He said he had always tried to suppress in himself "nationalistic ardor," which he thought not only pernicious and unjust but also too similar to the spirit that moved "the people among whom we Jews live." On the occasion of a celebration of his seventieth birthday he told the B'nai B'rith that he found the attraction of Judaism and the Jews "irresistible." He described Judaism for him as made up of "many dark emotional forces, all the more potent for being so hard to grasp in words, as well as the clear consciousness of an inner identity, the intimacy that comes from the same psychic structure."

Freud lived to see honor paid to a Jew in Freiberg—himself. On his seventy-fifth birthday a memorial tablet was affixed to the house where he was born, with ceremonies—which he did not attend—honoring him and his work. The street Schlossergasse was renamed Freudova Ulice. On that day congratulatory messages poured in from all over the world to his home in Vienna, and orchids, a flower of which he was particularly fond, filled his house. The Vienna Medical Society, a group that had scorned his first lectures on psychoanalytic theory, made him an honorary member. Dr. Julius Wagner-Jauregg, the Viennese psychiatrist who had epitomized the opposition of the medical world to Freud, declared, "Recognition by enemies is worth more than any amount of praise from supporters."

Freud remained in Vienna until after the Nazis marched into the city. It was as if he tempted Hitler's myrmidons to destroy him, willing to fight until his last breath—unlike his father. When Freud was a little boy his father had told him that one Saturday when he was walking along the street in Freiberg, all dressed up, wearing a new fur cap, a Christian came up to him, knocked his cap into the mud and shouted, "Jew, get off the pavement!" When the boy Freud asked his father, "And what did you do?" his father said, calmly, "I went into the street and picked up my cap." Freud's later comment was: "That did not seem heroic on the part of the big, strong man who was leading me, a little fellow, by the hand. I contrasted this situation, which did not please me, with another, more in harmony with my sentiments—the scene in which Hannibal's father, Hamilcar Barca, made his son swear before the household altar to take vengeance on the Romans."

Freud defied the Nazis until the last possible moment, when Princess Marie Bonaparte, who had been analyzed by Freud and was his close friend as well as colleague, offered the Nazis the quarter of a million Austrian shillings she had on deposit in a Vienna bank to spare Freud the horrors of the Holocaust. Freud showed *he* would not get off the pavement on the order of any Christian.

He may not have been a religious man, as far as orthodox or ritualized religion goes, but as Helen Puner said in her biography, *Freud: His Life and His Mind,* he was obsessed by faith—"a faith somewhat different from that which permeated religion . . . He rejected the faith of his fathers and clung instead to a faith in the power of reason."

Reason led him to suggest Jung, a Swiss Protestant, as the first president of the International Psychoanalytical Association when it met, in 1910, in Nuremberg—Jews were not granted academic recognition in the University of Vienna, there was widespread anti-Semitism throughout Europe and Freud realized psychoanalysis would benefit if a non-Jew were president of the new international organization. A few analysts, led by Dr. Alfred Adler and Dr. Wilhelm Stekel, were determined to oppose this idea, which had been proposed by Dr. Sandor Ferenczi in Freud's behalf.

On the afternoon of the day on which the proposal was to be brought to the floor, some of the Viennese analysts met secretly beforehand in the Grand Hotel. Adler and Stekel stated their objections, calling Freud ruthless and simple-minded, according to Jones' report.

Suddenly Freud, uninvited, walked into the room. He said, "Most of you are *Jews* and therefore you are incompetent to win friends for the new teaching. Jews must be content with the modest role of preparing the ground. It is absolutely essential that I should form ties in the world of general science. I am getting on in years and am weary of being perpetually attacked. We are all in danger." He won his point, Jung was elected.

This did not mean, though, that Freud was denying his Jewishness. As he said at another time, "My parents were Jews and I have remained a Jew myself." His selection of Jung meant only that he was trying to be realistic, reasonable, about the best possible way to spread acceptance of his new science of the mind.

Freud had no illusions about the harshness of reality. As Jones, who knew Freud intimately for thirty years, said, Freud had endured "a very hard life and in consequence thought it a mistake to pretend that life is easy." Freud's youth was spent in near poverty. Even in his late twenties he reproached himself for the extravagance of buying a piece of chocolate to assuage his hunger, or for enjoying a rich meal to which he had been invited when his sisters and brother at home ate plain fare. Further, the picture of Freud as "dry, disagreeable and intolerant," is incorrect, says Jones, who always found Freud "a warm-hearted friend, a delightful companion with a rich sense of humor covering his underlying seriousness." Freud had great personal charm, Jones writes, "though without any trace of that facile charmingness that so often passes for the real thing. A smile, the more attractive for its sincerity, was never far from his lips . . . though not demonstrative by nature he had, it was not hard to perceive, a deep fund of tenderness as well as kindliness. It is not surprising that he inspired devotion." The values Freud esteemed most, according to Jones, were kindliness and probity, and the ones he disliked most, brutality and hypocrisy. There were no limits to Freud's tolerance of deficiencies in people he loved.

In Jones' opinion Freud's two outstanding characteristics were "an amazing intellectual courage that could face the most unwelcome facts" and "an absolute integrity of mind and love of truth that brooked no compromise in his devotion to it." He was a man of wide interests and culture, deeply versed in classical as well as modern literature. Among his personal friends were Thomas Mann, Romain Rolland and Stefan Zweig. His chief hobby was the collecting of antiquities from ancient Greece, Egypt and Babylonia, which filled his office.

By nature Freud was endowed with unusually strong emotions: he could love and hate passionately. But he also had equally strong self-control, so that he hardly ever showed his emotions to outsiders. His powerful emotions were devoted to intense concentration in his search for knowledge. He had, Jones says, a "tenacious reserve."

He was a "natural psychologist," possessing the rare faculty of recognizing a psychological fact and respecting instead of discounting it. Jones said he learned much from observing Freud's "delightful tolerance," and praised Freud's sense of humor. He recalled one time Freud said the best sign of the acceptance of psychoanalysis would be when the Viennese shops advertised "gifts for all stages of the transference." Jones commented, "That has not happened in Vienna, but I am told it has in New York."

In his eulogy Jones spoke of Freud as possessing the "simplicity that seems always to accompany true greatness in men," along with a "true nobility of mind." Freud would have been "prepared to die rather than to yield in a conviction over anything he was persuaded was right. The courage, the skepticism, the honesty, the search for truth and knowledge and his other characteristics . . . were fused together into a remarkably harmonious whole," Jones told the mourners at Freud's funeral in London. "They became all of a piece . . . In any discussion of psychical integrity one must always think of Freud as a supreme example of it."

Freud's utter devotion to one single aim in life—a passion for finding out the truth about the human mind—was stressed by Hanns Sachs, who as a young lawyer became interested in psychology, attended Freud's first lectures and gave up law for psychoanalysis. In his book *Freud, Master and Friend,* Sachs gives a warm, loving portrait of Freud, whom he knew thirty-five years, almost all of Freud's career.

"Psychoanalysis was the main interest of Freud's life," he said. "The magnetic needle of his nature pointed toward this pole and never wavered from it . . . Freud admired and often quoted Cromwell's words, 'A man never mounts so high, as when he does not know where he is going'." Freud's wife and children, like his mother before him, honored his absorption, never interfered with it.

In the thirty-five years of their friendship and work together, Sachs says he never heard Freud raise his voice "in anger or excitement." Freud's dislike of ostentatiousness showed itself in his manner of speech: "He never used a hollow phrase. What he said sounded so simple and unimpressive that its full meaning would escape an inattentive listener." In discussing his theories, Freud "did not assume the role of the prophet who tells of the mysteries that were revealed to him. The prevailing tone was a simple, conversational one, often interspersed with witty or ironical remarks; his conviction of the far reaching consequences of the new truth was too deep to stand in need of emphatic asseveration."

While listening to Freud's lectures and studying his technique of explanation, Sachs wondered how Freud succeeded "in producing something unexpected and stupendous while his talk moved in simple terms, dispensing with the fireworks of baffling profundity or of glittering paradoxes." Sachs asserts Freud made use of Schopenhauer's recipé for a good style: "Say extraordinary things by using ordinary words." Freud followed this advice intuitively: according to Sachs, Freud borrowed his "handy pocket-edition" of Schopenhauer for the summer, years later, to read him for the first time.

Sachs praised Freud's ability to sum up in a short sentence a striking thumbnail sketch of a person. Freud described an old friend, who had once been a powerful figure in politics, as: "Aged lion, well on his way to becoming a couch-cover."

Sachs also talked about Freud's predilection for telling a joke or anecdote to illustrate a point. When he wanted to explain the cause of a neurosis he showed a picture postcard of a country yokel in a hotel bedroom, trying to blow out the electric light as though it were a candle. Freud said, "If you attack the symptom directly, you act in the same way as this man. You must look for the switch."

And when Freud wanted to explain how many people can accept their moral deficiencies and misdeeds with an unruffled conscience, whereas something comparatively minor that "hits the spot" may upset them completely, he told of a member of the most exclusive club in Budapest who made a bet with another member that he would eat a large portion of fecal matter. It was served on a golden plate and the good burgher began to eat without any noticeable disgust. But suddenly he stopped, spluttered and could eat no more. He had a found a hair in it. In presenting his students with the concept of "reaction-formation" Freud explained that when a German professor pleaded urgently for the suppression of unnecessary noises, advocating rigorous police enforcement and the forming of an anti-noise league, "He wants to make all the noise himself."

His pessimism occasionally came through in conversation, Sachs reported. When a prominent Bolshevik told Freud that Lenin, who had been the Bolshevik's personal friend, predicted Europe would have to go through a period of desolation much worse than that caused by the Revolution, the civil war and famine in Russia, but that afterward a period of unbroken happiness and stability would follow, Freud said, "Let's make it fifty-fifty. I will accept the first half."

Sachs says when he asked himself for his own dominating and lasting impression of Freud, "the answer is always the same: he was different. This feeling was present from the beginning and during the many years of our acquaintance; our comparative intimacy certainly did nothing to diminish it. I always knew that he was different—it is true that his psychological insight was a gift of the gods—as much as music or poetry. But I felt that Freud would have become as different from the average variety of humanity even if he had not turned his back on the physiological laboratory and had never meddled with psychology or psychopathology. I simply could not believe that he was made of the same clay as others. Some special substance had been infused into him and gave the finished product a higher grade of perfection."

Freud persistently "refused to pose for others as the great man, the teacher of wisdom, the mind-reading genius, or the enigmatic personality . . . His indifference to popular acclaim and admiration was as complete as it had been in former days to detraction and slander."

In speaking to Sachs about the sudden popularity of his name, Freud mused that Cromwell, when asked, "Are you not proud that so many came to see the chosen of the Lord enter in triumph?" had answered, "Three times as many would have come to see me hanged."

Sachs also praised Freud's "intellectual independence," which "has to do with obstinacy and is not far removed from a certain form of severity. Perhaps it is best expressed in the simplest words: the determination not to be fooled at any price, neither by others nor by oneself." What mattered to Freud "was to come as near to the truth as possible, to make no concession to prejudice, tradition, authority or to one's own wishes and weaknesses." A favorite saying of Freud's was, "One must learn to bear some portion of uncertainty."

Independence, courage and pride were the hallmarks of Freud's character and out of these three characteristics he formed his answer to the "Why?" which has stood, in Sachs' words, "as a challenge and often as a tormentor before the human mind since the first dawn of reason. Why are we here? . . . What is the purpose of life? If happiness is the purpose, why can't we find it? Why not give in and disappear when we are convinced that happiness does not exist, either on earth or beyond the grave?"

Freud's answer was not that happiness "can be caught by any of the techniques used by mankind"—he examined them and found them all wanting—nor was his answer "rosy optimism." Freud recognized, Sachs says, that the impulse of destruction was inherent in every form of civilization, that no effort of love could eliminate the death instinct. "He took life as a task that had been set, as a duty, imposed on every one of us by the past of which we are the product. This inheritance is always with us in the form of our superego, invisible, intangible, and yet the most indubitable reality that shapes our life. We have no choice. We cannot reject our inheritance and return to animalism. Bargaining, trying to beat down the demands of the superego would be a sign of meanness, which his pride condemned."

Apropos of this philosophy Sachs tells a joke he believes Freud would have appreciated: A Jewish coachman whips his horse mercilessly. The Jews who see him beg him to spare the poor beast. He says coolly, "Since he has undertaken to be a horse, he must run." And Sachs comments, "Since we have taken it upon ourselves to be men . . ."

Sachs recalled Freud himself, "with mischievous glee," telling the story of a critic—a professor—who told his students there was not a grain of truth in the Freudian theory. He then proceeded to describe a patient who complained of an obsession causing him great suffering—the urge to turn up the petticoats of every woman he met. When the professor saw the smile on the faces of his students, he said, "Just wait a bit. You will see the superficial aspect of this system is quite misleading."

He then asked the patient, "Do you have this obsessional impulse also in relation to your mother?"

The patient said, "Yes, Herr Professor, very strongly, that is the worst of it!"

The professor said to his students, "So you see, gentlemen, that there can be nothing sexual in this symptom." . . .

In describing Freud outside of his work, Sachs mentions his love of flowers, reports that during summer vacations Freud rented houses with gardens and observed every particle in the garden with the same "zest" he gave to an analytic theory: "He contemplated the life-cycle of a flower, its growth and decay and rebirth as he had looked at the struggle between Eros and death-instinct in the history of the human development."

Freud had endless patience with those suffering mental pain, but he was impatient when kept waiting. Sachs recalls Freud once said "good-humoredly" to him, "The most unnecessary expenditure I know of is for all the coal that's needed for hell-fire. It would be much better to go through the usual procedure, have the sinner condemned to so many hundred thousand years of roasting, then lead him into the next room and just let him sit there. To have to wait would soon become a worse punishment than being actually burned." Sachs adds the only occasion Freud "squandered away his time" was when he had to make a train. He was always at the station far ahead of the scheduled departure and had to wait sometimes for an hour or more.

He was known for one indulgence. From breakfast until he went to sleep after midnight, following hours of studying and writing, Freud smoked practically without pause. According to Sachs, "He was a chain-smoker in the fullest sense of the word. His usual quantum was twenty cigars a day, usually *Trabuccos . . .*" He was irritated when men around him did not smoke, so nearly all the "inner circle" became "passionate smokers," Sachs says. Even in the weeks preceding Freud's death he did not give up smoking. Once Sachs refused the cigar Freud always offered him, saying he had just finished one. "He laughed at this—and that was the last time I heard him laugh."

In recalling Freud's love of truth, Sachs states that Freud "did not flinch when he had to look, standing at the brink of the precipice. Most others who followed in his tracks got at first a fit of giddiness [when they discovered what 'unholy stuff' lay in the unconscious] and had to hold on to him to steady themselves when the mountains seemed to reel." Sachs adds, "What could those do who were too proud to be supported by him and yet too weak to stand alone? They covered their eyes with their hands and slunk away."

Sachs concludes his biography with an account of a visit to Freud in London just before Freud's death. He was in great pain, spoke every word with great effort. Sachs was then living in Boston and Freud "discussed problems and personalities of the psychoanalytic movement in America with full knowledge of the details, without a single slip."

When the hour of parting arrived, knowing he was seeing Freud for the last time, Sachs said he spoke only a few indifferent words about his trip home. Freud pressed his hand and said, "I know that

I have at least *one* friend in America." These were the last words Sachs heard from Freud's lips.

Freud has many friends in America today, some of whom have written about their analysis with him. After Dr. Joseph Wortis was analyzed under a fellowship in 1933, seeing Freud daily for four months, he wrote *Fragment of an Analysis with Freud.* Freud was then in his eighties and quite ill, but still saw a few selected patients. Wortis recalled: "Freud was an eminently human person. This was one of his striking characteristics. You don't often meet someone so down to earth in his dealings, so direct. . . . His maid spoke of him with warmth . . . she said she never saw the Professor angry. . . . He loved to tell parables to make his points. One day he was critical of something I said. I remarked, 'Herr Professor, since you understand me so well, you should excuse anything I say. To understand is to excuse'.

" 'I'm not so sure', he said. 'I'll tell you a story. My son, who is an architect, has been living in Berlin. Not long ago he took a lady friend of his to a gathering. One of the guests acted in a rude manner to his lady friend. When my son remonstrated, the man said, 'You know who I am? I am the Count von Bismarck.' My son replied, 'That's an explanation. That's no excuse'."

Freud was "brilliant at dream interpretation and was very intuitive in interpreting free associations," Dr. Abraham Kardiner says in his book *My Analysis With Freud: Reminiscences.* (Freud once said he could judge the ability and psychological insight of an analyst best by seeing how he handled the interpretation of a dream.)

Kardiner described what he called "an amusing thing" that happened during the course of analysis, when he mentioned William James and asked Freud whether he had ever met James. Freud said he had on several occasions, including his visit, in 1909, to Clark University in Worcester, Massachusetts. James also went to Vienna to see Freud shortly before James died in 1917. Freud called James "the only American genius" he had known, adding, "This was a great man. Furthermore, he had one attribute for which I have unstinted admiration. He spoke German better than I did. That's quite an achievement."

"Well, Professor, what did he think of you?" Kardiner asked.

"Oh," said Freud, "he thought I was crazy."

"It is this laconic wit and ease with himself," Kardiner comments, "that I most remember with feelings of great warmth, even to this day."

Gordon Allport, professor of psychology at Harvard University, attending a meeting of the American Psychiatric Association in Swampscott, Massachusetts, told an anecdote to illustrate the special ability of Freud to understand the language of the unconscious. One day, finding himself in Vienna, Allport telephoned Freud and made an appointment to see him. This was at the time Freud's theories, with their emphasis on sexuality, first shocked a prudish world. Allport took a streetcar to Freud's home, arrived late. After greeting Freud, he explained apologetically, "I was delayed by the streetcar. It was so crowded I was forced to sit next to a filthy old man. I was afraid I'd be contaminated."

Freud said quietly, "And are you now afraid you will get contaminated by *this* filthy old man?"

The late Dr. Ludwig Eidelberg once told this writer his impressions of Freud. He had attended lectures given by Freud and meetings in Freud's home. "Freud had a certain warmth and kindness that some of his biographers missed," Eidelberg recalled. "It was reflected in his whole body. In his gestures. In the tone of his voice. Listening to him, you were aware this was a man who spoke with conviction. He was one of the few men I have met whom I feel had complete integrity, one for whom the search for truth was the major aim. This was why he repeatedly changed his ideas or modified them when he realized that what he believed was not as near the truth as could be achieved."

"What was he like as a speaker?"

"Pity we didn't have a tape recorder at that time. There was magic in his voice—it was a voice that went through you. I usually have trouble not to talk. But whenever I was with Freud, it wouldn't occur to me to open my mouth. Listening to him I felt overwhelmed by the mastery with which he expressed his ideas. I felt that what he said represented truth. He had trouble speaking because of the prothesis. But even so, listening to him, one felt overwhelmed."

"Did he often speak with humor?"

"With a fantastic sense of humor. I remember one meeting where Dr. Herman Nunberg [who later practiced in New York] gave a paper on 'The Synthetic Function of the Ego'. There was always one paper presented at a meeting, then Freud led the discussion. This night Dr. Nunberg explained how the patient's ego assimilates the unconscious material brought up in an analysis. After he finished, Freud started the discussion by saying that, while listening to the paper, he thought of a painting he had just seen, well-known in Austria, by Moritz von Schwind, representing an episode from the legend of Saint Wolfgang. It shows a devil who has made a contract with a saint, pushing a load of stones uphill on a wheelbarrow. At the top of the hill stands the saint blessing the stones, to be transformed into a beautiful church. Freud said, 'I am the devil who brings up all the material from the unconscious and you, Dr. Nunberg, are the bishop who, by blessing the ugly stones, changes them into a church'.

"At which Dr. Paul Schilder whispered in my ear, 'He means rabbi, not bishop'.

"Freud's remark was ironic, and to soften the irony the next day Dr. Nunberg received a gift from Freud, who had bought a copy of the painting and sent it to him."

Eidelberg described Freud's home at 19 Berggasse, to which the family moved in the summer of 1891: Freud's office on the mezzanine consisted of a room where patients waited, the room with the couch where he treated patients and his private study. Each room had a window opening on a courtyard, in the middle of which stood a tall, spreading tree. The rooms were comfortably furnished in the style of the day. Only Freud's study differed—bookshelves covered the walls almost to the ceiling and glass cases contained Freud's collection of antiques.

"Did Freud serve coffee?" I asked.

"He served dessert. Petits fours from Dehmel's—the most important place in Vienna. I don't recall if there was coffee but I shall never forget the petits fours."

I chuckled at the scene of those erudite pioneers of the charting of the mind discussing the royal road to the unconscious as they munched petits fours. Eidelberg recalled particularly one meeting, in 1930 or 1931, where Freud described how he first discovered the concept of psychic reality and "a great feeling of excitement swept the room. He told us that at first, after many years of analyzing patients, he arrived at the conclusion there had always been seduction in childhood by parents or nurses or others taking care of the child and he considered this seduction of the child responsible for the later neurosis. But one day, in talking to a patient, he realized there was not the slightest doubt that no seduction could have taken place. Yet the patient insisted she had been seduced. This was a great shock to Freud, Obviously he had been fooled by former patients as well. What they had told him was not true. He said that as he meditated about this problem he came to the conclusion that at an early age, whether seduction actually took place or was merely desired and imagined, made no difference. It was as though it *had* occurred, in the mind of the child. It was *psychic reality.*

"This discovery not only solved the problem of whether the actual seduction was important but illuminated another concept that became very important—that the infantile wish becomes repressed, stays in the unconscious, and the person does not differentiate between the wish and the act."

He explained, "For instance, whenever a patient has a hostile wish and wants someone to die, he behaves as if he had killed him. Instead of patting himself on the back for rejecting an immoral wish, he develops a feeling of remorse, considers himself a criminal and seeks punishment to atone for the crime. Patients are not aware of this when they start analysis. We show them there is a basic error in confusing a desire with an action."

"Isn't it incredible how Freud made one great psychological discovery after another?"

"He was a genius, though he always denied it. He thought he was no genius because, if he were, he would have arrived at his discoveries with less effort. He always worked very hard. He repeatedly expressed the belief artists arrive at similar truths without such hard work."

"It's not quite the same."

"Of course not. The artist arrives at a philosophical truth. Freud gave us a scientific method for reaching the unconscious and helping men live more happily."

"His generosity seems to be well-known," I said. "Can you give an example?"

"In his biography of Freud, Jones describes the time I wrote a paper pointing out something contrary to one of Freud's theories. The paper was written partly on my experiences in analyzing perverts. I discovered perversion was not a simple break-through from the unconscious but represented a complicated defense mechanism. As my book *The Dark Urge* showed, a man will commit rape as a defense against what he considers a greater crime— homosexuality or murder or incest. The perversion represents his way of trying to escape putting into action the deeper wish. It was not easy to demonstrate such a theory, because not many analysts were interested in analyzing perverts. So I looked for an example in which I could express a similar idea applicable to everyday life. I thought of one of Freud's concepts which was widely accepted —the slip of the tongue. This, Freud said, represented a break-through from the unconscious. With each slip of the tongue, we separate the word which is omitted, which Freud referred to as representing a 'harmless' idea, from the word which appears as the slip of the tongue, which Freud described as representing a 'harmful' tendency which, for some reason, succeeded, against the will of the person on coming into the open. I asked myself, 'What makes this break-through possible?'[7] I wondered whether Freud's idea that the omitted word had no significance was really correct. In working with my patients I discovered the omitted word was *not* a harmless word but represented some dangerous, unconscious wish. The word that appeared instead, while coming from the unconscious, represented a defense against this wish from the id. The slip of the tongue, thus, becomes similar to other defense mechanisms."

Then he asked, "Would you like an example?"

"Certainly. Theories are much easier to understand when personalized."

"A patient of mine, whom I had analyzed for many months, told me that one evening when he entered a restaurant with a girl, he intended to ask the head waiter, 'Do you have a table?' What came out was, 'Do you have a room?'

"He became very embarrassed because it was obvious to him, the waiter and his girl friend—who, in his mind, he had nicknamed 'Miss Forepleasure'—that he was so anxious to go to bed with her that he had asked for a room instead of a table. In analyzing this slip of the tongue, I tried at first to get additional material connected with the word 'room' which, according to Freud, represented the 'harmful' unconscious tendency with the power to break through and appear in the conscious. Often a slip of the tongue does not make sense unless we analyze it with the help of the patient's associations. But sometimes, as in this case, the hidden meaning of the so-called 'harmful' tendency is obvious without further associations, though I later asked for them. This man's associations showed he was so preoccupied with the idea of going to bed with 'Miss Forepleasure' that he considered it a waste of time to eat first. Further associations revealed the slip represented a punishment. In admitting in public what he wanted, he had to accept a certain amount of embarrassment.

"But I thought we ought to find out why the word 'table' had been omitted, although Freud originally said the omitted word represented a 'harmless' conscious tendency and did not require further analysis. The associations of the patient to the word 'table' showed that *eating* had a very important meaning to him in terms of his infantile wishes. Rather than representing a 'harmless' tendency, it became more and more evident that the word 'table' was omitted because it would have been used for the infantile gratification of a repressed oral, aggressive wish connected with his mother when he was a baby. In other words, 'room', which represented a normal adult sexual wish was less dangerous than the word 'table'. The use of the word 'room' was an unconscious defense against his oral, aggressive wish. It was easier to say, 'I wish to sleep with a woman' than 'I wish I were back on my mother's breast, wishing to bite it when I felt angry'. I sent my paper, titled 'A Contribution to the Study of Slips of the Tongue' to *Imago* [an international psychoanalytic journal]. The paper was rejected. Convinced my explanation was correct and important, I then sent it to Anna Freud. After a week," Eidelberg said, "I received a letter from her telling me she showed the paper to her father and he told her to write me that he agreed with my criticism of his theory."

Eidelberg's face lit up. "This was one of the most beautiful days of my life. Not only because I was pleased Freud accepted my theory but because I was overwhelmed by the generosity of this man. His willingness to accept criticism by a younger man. A quality very rare among scientists."

"What happened to the paper?"

"It was published in *Imago* and in the *International Journal of Psychoanalysis*. In Jones' book he refers to the letter Anna Freud sent me which said: 'Your criticism of the word 'harmless' for the trend that is disturbed is thoroughly justified, and further investigation of the apparently 'harmless' is undoubtedly important. He [Freud] suggested that the relation of the two tendencies is probably a variable one. Further investigation along these lines would probably be very rewarding.'

"I saw Freud briefly in London when I visited Anna. He looked much older. I knew there was not much hope. He died just before midnight on September 23, 1939, a few weeks after the war started. I went to the funeral."

"Were there many there?"

"Perhaps about a hundred of us, gathered at a cemetery called Golder's Green. We were all holding our gas masks. The war had started, there was a restriction on traveling and not many people knew about the funeral. This was as Freud would have wished. He always avoided any public appearance."

Freud's body was cremated at his own request. His ashes now repose in one of the two Grecian urns given to him by Princess Marie Bonaparte.

"Stefan Zweig made a speech in German and then Jones delivered the funeral oration. He gave us each a copy."

The last lines of the oration, reprinted in full in Volume III of Jones' *The Life and Work of Sigmund Freud* sum up eloquently:

"A great spirit has passed from the world. How can life keep its meaning for those to whom he was the center of life? Yet we do not feel it as a real parting in the full sense, for Freud has so inspired us with his personality, his character and his ideas that we can never truly part from him until we finally part from ourselves in whom he still lives. His creative spirit was so strong that he infused himself into others. If ever man can be said to have conquered death itself, to live on in spite of the King of Terrors, who held no terror for him, that man was Freud. And so we take leave from a man whose like we shall not know again. From our hearts we thank him for having lived; for having done; and for having loved."

Eidelberg recalled, "The orations were like background music to me because I was so moved by many of my own thoughts. . . . Fortunately Freud died at a time when most of his work was finished, although I'm sure if he had lived longer he would have modified and added many ideas. Psychoanalysis is one of the few sciences where the contributions of one man still dominate whatever we know. I was thinking, too, that his death was delivery from pain. Freud had suffered very much."

The late Theodor Reik also granted this writer a special interview, in his home-office on West End Avenue, New York, where photographs of Freud lined the walls. Freud had approved Reik's decision to start the National Psychological Association for Psychoanalysis, one of the first non-medical institutes for psychoanalysts in the United States.

"You have written a book about your thirty years with Freud," I said. "But perhaps there were things you didn't put in the book."

"There are many details," he said. "I'll start at the beginning."

Speaking with a Viennese accent, looking directly at me with keen, blue eyes that often twinkled, he said, "The first time I heard of Freud I was nineteen years old and a student of psychology at the University of Vienna. Our psychology professor, Friedrich Jodl, discussed the association theories of Wundt and Ziehen, psychologists of that day, and said, 'There is a lecturer in our city who asserts that forgetting is not only determined by associations but by a psychic process he calls repression'. Jodl said this with a fine, ironic smile. A few months later I read *Psychopathology of Everyday Life*. It made a deep impression on me. I then read everything Freud had written.

"When I wrote my Ph.D. thesis on Gustave Flaubert's *La tentation de Saint Antoine,* I sent the manuscript to Freud. He called me up and asked to see me. I went to his home at Number 19 Berggasse. As I walked up the steps I felt like a young girl going on a date, my heart was beating so fast. I stood for the first time in the room where Freud worked, looked at his desk, at the Egyptian and

Etruscan figurines, the phantoms of the past he loved so dearly. He knew Flaubert's book very well, much better than I, and we discussed it at length. That year I was introduced as a guest at a meeting of the Vienna Psychoanalytic Society by Dr. Wilhelm Stekel. I did not only listen but, having read the psychoanalytic literature, felt I could take part in the discussion . . . After I had my Ph.D., I went to Freud and asked if I should now study medicine. He said no. He said he had other plans for me. He urged me to give my life to psychoanalytic research.

"For two years then, he gave me—I was very poor—from his private pocket a certain amount monthly to study psychoanalysis. This was at a time Freud was supporting his own children and other relatives. He got me also a job in a book store in Vienna so I could earn a little money. In one of our brochures, we asked prominent people their favorite books and I remember that Freud said one of his favorites was Anatole France's *Sur la Pierre Blanche.*

"Until after I married, Freud gave me a certain amount monthly. He evidently believed in my talent for psychoanalytic research. Especially after I wrote an article on 'The Puberty Rites of Savages'. One day he appeared in our shabby Berlin apartment. I had moved from Vienna to Berlin because, although I had wanted to go into a training analysis with Freud, at this time he wasn't taking any student of his for training and instead, wrote Dr. Karl Abraham in Berlin, who offered to give me a training analysis for nothing. I went to Dr. Abraham until I was called into the Austrian Army in 1915. After the great war I returned to Vienna to practice psychoanalysis.

"On this day Freud came to see me in Berlin, in January, 1915, he walked up four flights of stairs to bring the news that the Psychoanalytic Society had decided to award me the prize for the best scientific work in the field of applied psychoanalysis for my article on the puberty rites of savages. I can still see the smile on his face as he told me this. I was the pupil who had justified his belief in me.

"There was no such thing as supervision then. Today a young analyst learns not only through his personal psychoanalysis but through supervision by an older psychoanalyst who discusses with him the patients he treats. When I wanted to know something about one of my patients, I would catch Freud as he took a walk.

I knew he always walked down certain streets in Vienna, Ring-strasse and Kärtnerstrasse, and I knew what time he went. So I accidentally on purpose met him and would ask him about certain cases of mine.

"Freud was really a writer and did not like much to speak. He seemed uneasy giving a formal lecture. He gave a chat, *'une causerie'.* He spoke extemporaneously. When I presented my first lecture in Vienna I read from a manuscript. He praised what I said but reproached me for reading. He said that when he had to speak he chose one person in the audience and pretended he talked only to this person.

"I remember once he gave a lecture in the psychiatric institute where the audience was mixed—physicians and laymen. He spoke about repression. He used the following comparison: 'In this audience, which follows me with such rapt attention, there is a man who makes noises that disturb us. We try to calm him down. He refuses to listen. Finally several of you throw him out of the door'. Freud used this to clarify the nature of repression as he went on to describe the return of the repressed.

" 'But this man who is outside the door doesn't keep quiet, shouts that he wants to come back and make trouble. Someone goes to the door and says, "Look here, my dear fellow. When you promise to keep quiet, we'll let you in." That is what we do in analysis. We let the repressed return so it will not disturb us any longer'."

"Can you give any examples of how Freud helped you with your cases?"

"I had a patient at the time who did not talk about his childhood. It seems he didn't want to remember it. I told Freud this. He said, 'A man who does not like to think of his past is a ne'er-do-well'. I wanted to object to that. Then I realized Freud was right. There must be certain pathological disturbances in a man who breaks off all bridges to the past.

"Then there was an allied case. I treated once a member of one of America's leading families, then living in the Hague. After he started his analysis, I expressed my astonishment that he never mentioned his mother. He informed me, 'A gentleman never discusses his mother nor his religion'.

"I also had as a patient a young girl in Vienna who never, over many months, showed the slightest sign of transference, of personal interest in me. I complained about this to Freud. He said, 'Make her once jealous'. The next time another patient, a young girl, sat in my waiting room, as the first patient came out of her session, I greeted the second amiably, saying, 'How are you?' At her next analytic session—analysis was then six days a week—the first patient, about whose remoteness I had complained to Freud, started off with a flood of abuse at the other girl, saying, 'That hussy, how dare she—' and then abused me. Freud had been right."

Reik was silent for a moment, then went on, "Another advice that Freud gave: There was a British diplomat who came to Vienna for analysis with Freud. Freud had no time and sent the diplomat to me. This was the time of the Peace Conference of the League of Nations and this man had to live for a while each year in London, then a few months in Geneva, and only came to Vienna for a few weeks from time to time. I was doubtful whether an analysis could be done in this way. But Freud advised me to do it. He called it 'fractured analysis'."

"How did it work out?"

"Quite well. I saw the man at intervals for three years."

"What did you think of Ernest Jones' biography of Freud?" After all, Reik had known Freud thirty years, usually saw him once a week either at meetings at the psychiatry clinic in the Lazarettgasse or held by the Vienna Psychoanalytic Society, as well as the Wednesday evening gatherings at Freud's home. Reik was also secretary of the Vienna Psychoanalytic Society in 1923 and again in 1925.

"Two things Jones didn't understand in his book. One was Freud's Jewishness. Jones connected Jewishness with a Talmudic type, which Freud wasn't. Freud loved Jewish jokes but otherwise he was not what we think of as typically Jewish. Jones, who knew only the London Jews, did not understand you could be Jewish deep in the pit of your personality without representing the so-called Jewish stereotype. The other thing Jones did not understand was the relationship of Freud to Vienna. All the time I knew Freud, he abused and cursed Vienna, made fun of the Viennese *'gemütlichkeit'*. Yet he never left Vienna although he had many offers to go to London, Paris, America. He was bound to Vienna by a kind of hate-love."

"Was this perhaps because he did not want to leave his mother?" I asked. "He did leave after she died."

"Then he felt free to do it. He said, 'Now I can die'. He wanted to live only as long as she did."

"It's interesting he said 'Now I can die' rather than 'Now I can live.' "

"I knew the old lady," Reik said. "She regularly went to Ischl, near Salzburg, for the summers and I would see her there. She was made an honorary citizen because she went so many years."

"Was the play, 'The Far Country' true to Freud?" (This hit Broadway drama by Henry Denker was performed in 1961, with Steven Hill playing Freud and Sam Wanamaker, Breuer.)

"Yes, there were some very realistic things in the play. The scene where Freud falls asleep at his desk late at night, exhausted, wakes in the morning and the first thing he does is to grasp a cigar. He always had a cigar."

"Did you like the way Freud was characterized?"

"It was too vivid a portraiture. Freud had more self-control. He was a more reserved man."

"Was Freud's mother as tyrannical as she appeared in the play?"

"No, she was not a tyrant. But you can't expect a playwright to be accurate in all respects. For instance, in the play she calls Freud 'My dear Sigmund' which she would never have done. She always called him, 'Siggy, *mein Gold*'. My golden one. She did not speak in high German but Galician Yiddish."

"What did you think of the portrayal of Martha, Freud's wife?"

"Quite good but not quite accurate. She really never understood why her husband became famous. Nor did she understand his work. She was not particularly interested in his research. She had little awareness of the important role of the unconscious. Once she said to me about a hysterical woman, 'She'll get over it if she'll use her will.'

"But she was a wonderful housewife, doing all her own shopping, rather than trusting it to a maid. She was also a wonderful wife. I remember once when we went out together, Freud and I, it was raining and she ran down the stairs saying, 'Your galoshes'.

She loved the opera but always was late because she wanted to be at home when he ate dinner, and he ate late.

"She also had humor. She told me once, 'I get along famously with my daughters-in-law. I never see them'."

"Was Freud attracted to the ladies, as we have sometimes heard?"

"He liked them. He was always very gallant to women. I was attending the International Psychoanalytic Congress in March, 1914, with my bride. She didn't know much about psychoanalysis. I introduced her to Freud. She said to him, 'There's really no place for me here'. He said to her, 'You are the pearl of this congress'. In conversation with me, he compared her to one of the madonnas of Botticelli. Only later in life did Freud talk more freely about his relationship with women. He might have felt very much attracted to certain women but it was never more than that. He was a highly moral man. He was very stimulated by women, especially by Princess Marie Bonaparte, a very beautiful woman. But it never went far."

Reik seemed to be searching for other stories about Freud. He recalled, "There were two times Freud tested me. Once when I was invited for dinner—dinner in Vienna would correspond with lunch here, a light meal. There was salami, butter, bread, prunes and cheese which was strong-smelling. Anna did not eat it. Freud looked at me. I ate the cheese. I understood his glance. If I refused, it meant too strong reaction to the anal.

"The other time is the following. On his watch-chain there hung a little machine to cut off the tip of the cigar. Once he offered me a cigar, cut the tip, handed the cigar to me and looked at me. I knew he was watching to see my reaction to this symbolic castration. I kept a calm expression."

There came another recollection. "A young psychoanalyst gave a lecture in which he outlined other fields in which psychoanalysis could be used, drawing a blueprint for psychoanalysis. Freud asked him, at the end of the lecture, 'Do you feel less hungry after you read the menu?' "

"Meaning?"

"That the blueprint had no content."

And another remembrance. "Freud had a Russian patient who

was educated in Paris. She wanted to learn a little German so she could at least talk with people in the streets of Vienna, with the taxicab drivers, the waiters in the restaurants. I had studied French and Freud recommended I give her lessons in German, since I also spoke French. As she learned German, every day she told me what had happened in her analysis with Freud. One day Freud called me. He said, 'This has to stop. There are a thousand things you can discuss, this patient and you. But not analysis'.

"Freud explained further to me, 'There is a waterfall. You want this waterfall to drive a mill, with its mighty energy. You will not therefore dig channels to take away some of the water'."

Reik also recalled a summer Freud spent in a villa he had rented at the Kurhaus Semmering, high in the mountains, about three hours from Vienna. "I lived near him in the Südbahnhotel. Almost every day I went over and we took a walk. Once I met Sinclair Lewis, who had come to visit Freud with Dorothy Thompson. We spent the evening together during which Lewis proved very witty and amusing. He was making fun of being a writer." Dorothy Thompson saw Freud rather frequently, according to Dr. Reik, who mentioned other writers Freud knew—Thornton Wilder, Romain Rolland, Arthur Schnitzler and Thomas Mann. . . . "I lived in the Hague from 1934 to 1938 and had a good practice there. I spoke then better Dutch than I speak now English. I had several young analysts in training and several laymen in therapy. Among the training analysts was a Dutch lady psychiatrist—no names— a woman near middle age, mother of two children. During her analysis, I made a very grave mistake. I stupidly uttered a few derogatory remarks about the Dutch, especially about the residents of the Hague, calling them very *burgerlich*, which means pedestrian. This aroused in her a terrible resistance. I was immediately sorry after I had said it. She could not forgive me. Our analysis became blocked. She decided Freud should be arbiter in this argument. As the summer approached, she suggested we both go to see Freud, otherwise the matter would never be settled. So we went to Vienna, she in one car, I in another. She had written Freud there was a conflict between her analyst and herself and we were both coming to hear his opinion.

"We sat in the waiting room together, exchanging only amenities. When Freud came out of his consultation room, he turned to me, signaling me to enter alone. After he closed the door, he said, 'Did anything traumatic happen?'

"I looked at him without understanding, at first, what he meant. Then it dawned on me he meant an affair with the patient. 'No', thinking she was not quite my type. Not to mention all the other reasons for not having an affair with a patient. Then I told him of my mistake—criticizing the Dutch. He called in the lady psychiatrist and in her presence reproached me. He said I had no right to say what I did. It was wrong not only from a technical point of view but also from a social one. He told me I could not afford to express displeasure or criticism of a country in which I was living as a guest. I apologized to the woman and Freud dismissed us. She and I returned to the Hague, this time on good terms. I took the analysis to a successful conclusion."

In his book *From Thirty Years With Freud*, Reik says: "Let us have no legends woven around Freud. He was human, with human weaknesses, and we loved him even for these. His character was rooted in that black earth out of which all of us grow. But most trees remain small or of middling height, and only the rare ones grow from their underground roots to such astonishing heights . . . He was capable of much love, but he was also a good hater. He tried to suppress his desires to avenge injustices he had received; but often they broke forth in a word, a gesture or an intonation. In old age, despite his self-control, more than one bitter word broke through the bars . . . But at such times he always spoke without strong emotion; these remarks sounded quite matter-of-course, like a final, calm judgment. Once—and only once—I saw him terribly angry. But the only sign of this anger was a sudden pallor and the way his teeth bit into his cigar."

I asked Reik to describe this time in more detail.

"Actually, I did not see it. This was told to me. Freud referred a patient to me. A perverted masochist who let himself be beaten by women. This man, an aristocrat, said Freud had treated him several years with some success. One day however at the end of a session he told Freud, as they walked out of the consultation room, that he thought he was not making much progress with his analysis and that better he should go to Alfred Adler. Freud did not answer but the patient observed Freud's teeth were digging into his cigar. Freud had an exceptionally high self-control."

Adler was one man for whom Freud had little respect. In Freud's *Autobiographical Study* he says Adler "threw all the psychological discoveries of psychoanalysis to the winds." Freud wrote in a letter to Ferenczi, his closest friend over the years, "the tactlessness and unpleasant behavior of Adler and Stekel make it very difficult to get along together. I am chronically exasperated with both of them." And again, "I am having an atrocious time with Adler and Stekel." Freud also mentions Reik as among the ten men "who have worked with me for some fifteen years in loyal collaboration and for the most part in uninterrupted friendship."

The late Dr. Franz Alexander, founder of the Chicago Institute for Psychoanalysis, first met Freud when he was sixty-three. In an interview in 1953, Alexander told this writer some of his impressions of Freud . . . "Freud was a strong, overpowering figure but a very jovial man at the same time," he said. "In small talk he was like a typical Viennese—humorous, casual. But when it came to serious talk, to which he was very much committed, he could be very, very negative and uncompromising. But only on those matters in which he had investment. He was highly sensitive not only to criticism but also to non-understanding acceptance. He had an extremely succinct way of coming to the essence of a subject. I never will forget, after his visit to the outpatient clinic of the Berlin Psychoanalytic Institute, I asked what it was like and he compared it to a compulsive patient. Then he said, 'You know, Alexander, that what is so characteristic about these compulsive patients is that they never get to do what they want, on account of their endless preparation. It is like a man with glasses who forever keeps cleaning the glasses but never uses them for reading'.

"Once he invited me to a meeting at his home when I was still a young analyst to give a paper which everyone then discussed. I presented the story of a Berlin waiter who had a passion for riding in taxicabs, who would go into a trance as he sat in the back of the taxicab. He would ask the taxi driver to accompany him for a meal in a restaurant, spending hours over a long dinner. Then he would refuse to pay the taxi fare. It was completely senseless. After a number of times in which he tried to get away without paying, he was put in jail. There I studied him, seeing him every day in interviews. In my paper I brought out the unconscious motivations, tracing them back to his childhood and their development. Freud listened. He was the first discussant. He made a few acknowledgments, saying he thought it a very fine paper, very convincing. Then he said, 'But, I do not think all these motivations suffice to explain why this man became a criminal'. Then he turned to me and explained, 'Dr. Alexander, don't you think if he had been the son of a rich man, instead of a poor merchant, he would have become a national hero in breaking records in auto-racing?' . . . Freud never forgot the economics. He was saying that if the man had been wealthy, his unconscious might well have sublimated the same desire in more acceptable form."

Alexander first met Freud in 1921 and saw him for the last time in 1935, just before Alexander came to America. After that he visited Freud every summer and also corresponded with him . . . "He was always very encouraging toward me and expected from me a great deal, I think, even though he didn't approve of my going to America. He thought the American approach to psychoanalysis was superficial and utilitarian. That Americans were not so much interested in psychoanalysis itself but what use they could make out of it materially. He said to me as I left, 'I hope America will leave something intact of the real Alexander'. He said I was too optimistic and gullible. He was afraid his teachings would be diluted in America. That psychoanalysis might become popular but also watered-down and ineffectual. He feared psychoanalytic principles would be abandoned in order to become more acceptable both to the medical profession and the public. He worried that America would give lip service to psychoanalysis but no real understanding or conviction."

Freud's personal physician the last year of his life in London was Dr. Vladimir Gurevich, who took care of Freud when Dr. Max Schur left for America. Gurevich, now living in Manhattan, consented to be interviewed but seemed reluctant to say much, explaining, "There are others who knew Freud far better."

"How well did you know him?"

"I met him on and off during the summers ever since 1930,

before I became his personal physician. We saw each other first in Berchtesgaden and then when Freud went, in the last years, to Grundlsee in the Austrian Alps, where he took the same house for several summers. My wife and I had a house there too. We would see his patients pass our house regularly at the same time each day. At twelve o'clock, Princess Bonaparte would pass."

During one of Freud's final summers in Austria, Freud and Gurevich would meet outdoors and sit together without talking, sometimes for as long as an hour, because it was painful for Freud to speak with his much-operated-upon jaw. "Although he didn't talk much, you felt here was a special person of great caliber," said Gurevich. "At this time he was shrunk by age, withered. But he was always very gentle, very polite. And, as a patient, he was always very intelligent and cooperative. He never complained. He always submitted to all medical measures as a matter of fact."

Gurevich, who also was personal physician to Freud's sister-in-law Minna, attending her after the heart attack she suffered when she went to England with the Freuds, said that in thinking of Freud he was reminded of a description given by one of Freud's pupils: "If you had a room full of one hundred people and you were asked to pick the man who discovered psychoanalysis, you would select anyone but Freud. He looked like an average Victorian gentleman, in the way he dressed and in his manner."

Gurevich also recalled, "At one of his summer houses there was a piano in the room and Freud asked that it be removed. He couldn't stand the sight of the piano. I think music to him may have been too irrational. He dealt with the irrational in his work and that was enough."

The late Dr. Ives Hendrick, author of *Facts and Theories of Psychoanalysis,* once said, "I was devoted to Freud as a scientist but I did not have awe of him. I never felt that personal response one feels to an idol."

Whereas Rudolph Eckstein remarked that one day in Vienna when he caught a glimpse of Freud at the window, as he entered the house to visit Anna Freud, "I felt like a religious person deeply attached to a symbol of faith."

Dr. Lawrence J. Friedman, as a student at the Medical School of the University of Vienna, at a lecture one evening found himself sitting next to Freud. He was studying to be an obstetrician, not yet committed to psychoanalysis, so he was not interested in Freud . . . "I didn't say a word to him all night. What a chance I missed!"

Freud followed the advice of Charcot, who told him to keep looking and looking at something until finally it "spoke" to him. Freud said he wanted to understand "some of the riddles of nature." What is the greatest riddle of nature to a child? How babies are born, said Freud. And finally, in all its awesome ramifications, he understood the powerful nature of the sexual impulse, understood, too, how repression of or fixation on sexual fantasies might lead to neurosis, perversions, psychosis. And how a heightened aggressive impulse, clouded with hate, could distort the sexual impulse in its development.

Of the science he discovered, he observed, "It is certainly not the whole of psychology but its substructure and perhaps even its entire foundation."

Psychology benefited from the knowledge Freud gained as a physician. If he had not studied medicine, he might not have created psychoanalysis. He knew enough to rule out organic illness as a cause when men and women suffered from paralyzed limbs or facial tics or migraine headaches. He then started the search for a cause that lay elsewhere and it led to the fantasies of the mind.

But it was Freud's respect for the power of the psyche that won him his glory. He not only honored man's every spoken thought but his every unspoken thought. In trying to reach the unspoken —"the unspeakable"—the couch was Freud's only piece of physical equipment. He used his mental equipment to reach out and explore "the far country" both in his patients and himself as he persisted in the one "goal" of his life: "to infer or to guess how the mental apparatus is constructed and what forces interplay and counteract in it."

He trusted his own unconscious. He wrote Fliess that in periods of doubt he "adopted the expedient of renouncing work by conscious thought, so as to grope my way forward into the riddles by blind touch." To be able to do this he needed great inner strength, a strength which stemmed in part from his early years with a mother who obviously loved him, made him feel emotionally secure, thought him "special" and encouraged him to become famous. His father also treated him as "special," saying, "My Sigmund's little toe is cleverer than my head." Both parents were highly intelligent, wanted their son to learn to think for himself, taught him the value of inner discipline. His father had humor and skepticism as well as a free-thinking attitude towards the world. From his mother, according to Freud, he inherited his temperament, the passionate emotions he learned to control and sublimate so effectively.

But the more intense the early love of the mother, the greater the loss when she bestows it on others, and Freud saw a stream of "others," seven in all, follow him at his mother's breast before he was ten years old, when his last sibling, his brother Alexander, was born. The first loss came when Freud was weaned, suffered as a loss of the mother's breast. At the age of nineteen months he suffered a traumatic loss, the death of his eight-month-old brother. This was followed five months later by the blow to his jaw which required stitches and would have been a painful experience. Then, when he was four, the Oedipal stage meant the loss of his beloved mother forever, in a sexual sense. All these losses would make his need and wish for restitution a strong one, along with his desire to regain the feeling of being "special." As he said, "The wish to be famous is an infantile wish."

Freud was no doubt sexually precocious. He said he wet his bed until the age of two, later related bed-wetting to masturbation. He told of the time when he was seven and urinated in his parents' bedroom, symbolically a defiant sexual act as well as a regressive one. The feeling of being "special" to his mother would evoke early erotic desires, as he pointed out in his famous study of Leonardo da Vinci.

A boy's heroes tell us of his wishes. Freud's heroes were conquerors—Alexander the Great and Hannibal. Freud referred to himself as a *"conquistador*—an adventurer." He waged battles on many fronts—against his own strong passions of love and hate, against the prejudice inflicted on Jews, against man's ignorance of and blindness to the power of sexual and aggressive feelings. Freud's "Rome" was the human mind, for which he created a "scaffolding," and the land he conquered was the illicit desires he felt within. He conquered not by giving in to them but by *understanding* them.

"He had a veritable passion to *understand,*" says Jones. To understand why he had lost his mother's love, why she had so many other babies if she loved him, why he could never possess her sexually, why he was born with a father old enough to be his grandfather, why he was born already an uncle, why he was born Jewish so that irrational hatred would be directed against him all his life.

Freud fought in his own way, with a brilliant mind and unfettered imagination. He dared what no man had dared before because of his ability to allow himself to *know* the intensity of his love and of his hate, realizing there was no other way except through the knowing to understand it.

He both won his battles and got his revenge, as we all do in one way or another, on those he believed hurt him. He awakened mankind to the naked truth—not a pretty truth, but a truth that would help man survive if he understood it. It was the finding of truth that was his personal way of survival. There was for him, as he said of the crippled Rosenzweig, "no other alternative."

Freud's way led to revolutionary theories about the sexual instinct in the life of man. He discovered the sexual drive existed in its primitive form at birth and developed in stages until it reached maturity. Such unpalatable theories cost him Breuer's friendship, brought the scorn of the medical profession down on his head and aroused fear and anger toward him throughout the world.

A world not yet ready to face the facts of man's sexuality.

Freud at the age of eight with his father, Jakob, who predicted of the future founder of psychoanalysis, "that boy will never amount to anything." *(Courtesy of Austrian Press and Information Service)*

The discoverer of the Oedipus complex, at the age of sixteen, with his mother, Amalia Freud. *(Courtesy of Austrian Press and Information Service, New York, N.Y.)*

19 Berggasse, Freud's residence in Vienna, where he lived and worked for forty-five years. *(Wide World Photos)*

Freud and his fiancée, Martha Bernays, a year before they were married in 1886 following a four-year courtship. *(Pictorial Parade)*

Freud at fifty-one, on his way to fame as the first traveler along the "royal road to the unconscious." *(Austrian Institute Library)*

Freud with his sons, Ernst and Martin, as they go off with the Austrian Army to fight "the war to end all wars." *(Pictorial Parade)*

Freud in 1912, strolling in the Dolomites with his daughter Anna, whom he once called "my favorite son." *(Pictorial Parade)*

Freud at age 73, with his grandson Stephan, whose father Ernst was Freud's oldest son. *(Keystone Press Agency)*

In 1938, a year before his death, Freud at 82, flanked by his daughter, Mrs. Mathilde Hollistschek, and his eminent biographer, Dr. Ernest Jones *(Keystone Press Agency)*

4

The Sexual Revolution

Freud made his most stunning discovery in 1905. Aptly called by Freud himself "the 'red rag' of the sexual factor," it shocked and antagonized not only Breuer but most of the world. Even today the antagonism has not yet disappeared though it has abated as more people have come to accept Freud's belief that ". . . from the beginning everything sexual should be treated like everything else worth knowing."

To his Victorian contemporaries Freud's sexual hypotheses marked him as a dangerous iconoclast. He blasted the age-old myth that childhood was a time of "innocence," insisting that sexuality started in the infant, developed in the child and matured in the adult. He warned that if for any reason sexual development was impeded in its natural growth, the person would suffer either from a failure to express mature sexual desire freely or from a need to express one of its early stages, which society called "perversion."

Though he occasionally changed his mind about other things, Freud never deviated from his theory of infant sexuality. In 1920, in a preface written for the fourth edition of his revolutionary book *Three Essays on the Theory of Sexuality* (which appeared originally in 1905), Freud said this theory was based on "careful and impartial observation," and that "the beginnings of human sexual life which are here described can only be confirmed by investigators who have enough patience and technical skill to trace back an analysis to the first years of a patient's childhood."

Then he added, with customary ironic humor, "If mankind had been able to learn from a direct observation of children, these three essays could have remained unwritten."

He recalled that the book's "insistence upon the importance of sexuality in all human achievements and the attempt that it makes at enlarging the concept of sexuality" had from the first provided "the strongest motives for the resistance against psychoanalysis." He added that some people "have gone so far in their search for high-sounding catchwords as to talk of the 'pan-sexualism' of psychoanalysis and to raise the senseless charge against it of explaining 'everything' by sex."

Freud theorized that psychosexual development takes place in four main stages—oral, anal, phallic and genital. The earlier stages overlap and pervade the others. The degree of pathological pervasion depends on what Freud called the "vicissitudes" the sexual drive encounters along the way.

The first stage, the oral stage, starts at birth and is followed by the anal stage, which, Freud said, begins whenever a parent decides to toilet train a child and focuses the child's attention and concern on controlling his urine and feces. This usually occurs between one and a half and two years of age. After the anal stage comes the phallic stage, which starts at three or four, when children notice differences in the genitals of boys and girls, and become very aware of the penis. The final or genital stage occurs in the mid-teens, at the end of puberty, which starts at eleven. Young men and women are then ready for genital sex, to mate and to procreate.

The infant's first sexual feelings are stirred at his mother's breast. According to Freud, ". . . the sucking of the child at the mother's breast is the model for every love relation."

In other words, in the beginning is not the Word but, closely allied to it, the Mouth. During their first months of life babies find out about the world by the sensations of sucking, swallowing, spitting out. The baby's world is primarily an oral one. Its first pleasure in life is to suck at the breast or bottle, reveling in the warm flow of milk as it eases hunger and provides sensual stimulation. Freud painted the following picture: "He who sees a satiated child sink back from the mother's breast and fall asleep with reddened cheeks and blissful smile, will have to admit that this picture remains as typical of the expression of sexual gratification in later life."

Sucking for nourishment is the starting point of our whole sexual life. As Freud put it: "The desire to suck includes within it the desire for the mother's breast, which is therefore the first *object* of sexual desire; I cannot convey to you any adequate idea of the importance of this first object in determining every later object adopted, of the profound influence it exerts, through transformation and substitution, upon the most distant fields of mental life."

He described the desire to suck as "the unattainable prototype" of every later sexual satisfaction. Our fantasy reverts to it in later life when we become anxious or tense, he added. In support of this theory Freud cited an authority, a Hungarian pediatrician named Lindner, who, twenty years earlier (in 1885) had noticed an erotic element in sucking. After carefully observing the sucking habits of children Lindner concluded that a child often sucks even when he is not hungry, to get erotic gratification. The sucking is carried out with intensity and excitement and after gratifying his erotic hunger the child relaxes enough to fall asleep. Lindner also called attention to the grasping motion associated with sucking, usually of a blanket, and theorized that this represented the transition from sucking to masturbating, the next step in sexual development.

While Freud spoke of the sucking process solely as the start of sexual development, psychoanalysts who following him expanded this to include the security and love the baby gets at its mother's breast, which also sets the stage for his future ability to love. Although the feelings of a nursing baby cannot be called adult love, they can affect his later attitudes and sexual feelings, and so his adult love life.

The mother who gives a baby at her breast the feeling that she loves him is the mother who will also give him this feeling as he grows up, who will guide and help him over the difficult tasks he faces. The anxious, worried mother, full of self-hatred, cannot make her baby feel loved at the breast or at any other time during his life. She will resent feeding him, calming his screams, changing his diapers, bathing him. All these activities become part of the infant's erotic life and if they are performed coldly, or hastily, or angrily, or worriedly, or disgustedly, he will know it and know too that he lacks love.

The mouth is the first erotogenic zone, an area of the body with the capacity for erotic emotion. In infants the gratifying of the need for nourishment and of the mouth as an erotic zone cannot be separated from each other. The failure to separate them successfully occurs in those who, as adults, must eat or drink beyond what they need to satisfy hunger or quench thirst—eating and drinking serve an erotic rather than a nutritional purpose; food is consumed and liquor imbibed not because one is hungry or thirsty but rather possessed by an inner oral-erotic urgency.

Any bodily organ from which one demands too much as a way of meeting sexual needs may as a consequence refuse to function properly. Those who are still too deeply attached to oral gratification may show it directly through a kind of misbehavior of the mouth, such as stammering, or finding it hard to speak in times of tension, or experiencing eating difficulties or trouble with the teeth.

The partial failure to separate the function of taking nourishment from that of the sexual urge may also be seen in those who suck candy all day or chew gum incessantly or have a cigarette continually in their mouths, feeling they are combating a gnawing hunger. Those who take pills may need to swallow something that stirs sensations of their earliest pleasurable memories, obliterating the painful realities of the present. Some people are even soothed by medicines that are worthless, placebos that have no effect whatsoever on the body. And those who must bite their fingernails or chew a pencil in order to concentrate also need oral gratification to be able to function.

If life after infancy becomes too difficult, it is understandable that one would want to return to a time when he felt more loved.

A parent, no matter how lacking in affection for, or angry at, a growing child, will seldom let a baby starve. And even an unloved baby will register the experience of being fed (assuming there is no cruelty or force-feeding involved) as pleasurable. Moreover, a solicitous parent, unable to communicate with a child through speech, may focus on breast- or bottle-feeding to show love. As the child grows up, feeding him may continue to serve as an emotional outlet for the mother, as shown in the stereotypes of the Italian mama urging her brood, *"Mangia, mangia!"* (Eat, eat!) or the Jewish mother soothing all hurts with homemade chicken soup.

The intensity of infantile oral eroticism and its carry-over into adult life is reflected in the various oral images used in speech. Love is sometimes spoken of in terms of eating: "I love you enough to eat you." "Eating" is also a term applied to the licking or sucking of the clitoris or penis. In a more general sense one talks about being "hungry for love," "sex-starved" or "thirsting" after someone's body.

On the negative side the word "sucker" is used in a derogatory sense and adolescents will often disparage something they don't like with the phrase, "It sucks." One warns, "Be careful not to get sucked in," or refers to someone who "sucks around" as if this were the crime of crimes. Dr. Leo Stone, in his article "On the Principal Obscene Word in the English Language," tracing the history of the word "fuck" and its appearance in literature and lexicons, concluded that the word "suck" was actually more obscene. He pointed out the similarity in "unconscious rhyme relation" of the heretofore taboo word "fuck" and the word "suck." He suggested that "the pleasure and often guilty excitement" which accompanies the use of the word "fuck" is displaced on it from the earlier, more taboo process of "sucking," associated unconsciously with the mother who was once "sucked."

It is essential that the mouth play a vital part in early life. It is the only way a baby has of getting acquainted with the world, including mother. He wants to swallow her, believing this the way to know her. He wants to take her inside himself, as only weeks before he was inside her. Indeed, learning begins with this "taking in" or incorporating into the self, called *"introjection,* the psychic equivalent of physical swallowing. Actually one can never really separate psyche and body—physical being cannot operate independently of the ability to wish, an important psychic function. Before one can move, one has the wish to walk, before one eats, the wish to eat. Learning develops from one of the first wishes, to keep within the self all pleasurable experiences over which one has no control. It begins with the mother's breast or bottle, which the baby would like inside himself so he might have it whenever he wished and thus escape rage at the inevitable delay which he feels is aimed solely at making him uncomfortable.

A baby must take in more than food. He needs the psychic equivalent of food, the warmth of a maternal body and the reassurance he is loved—the meaning of "man cannot live by bread alone." Babies abandoned by their mothers or whose mothers have died and who spend their first few months in a hospital with no love bestowed on them, who have no one to give emotional warmth, often die. Dr. René Spitz's studies of babies, conducted from 1928 to 1938 in Vienna, demonstrated this.

A baby is extremely sensitive to how mother feels about him, whether she holds him in love or hate, whether the flow of milk is easy or difficult, the expression on her face as she diapers him, the many moods that indicate either her pleasure or her anger. When an experience with the mother brings pleasure, the baby feels what he takes in from her is "good" and it becomes a good part of his own self. If his experience with her is frightening or painful, he feels what he takes in is "bad" and this becomes a bad part of his own self. His feelings are either totally good or totally bad. There is no in-between for a baby.

Only when there is enough "good" taking-in during infancy will psychic development proceed naturally. When the early ingestion creates psychic pain for the baby, he protects himself from this pain, which he can escape no other way, by propelling it out psychically, just as physically he vomits bad food. He cannot get up and do anything to combat a painful thought, nor can he talk it away. He can only imagine it away—which is called *projection,* the expulsion of what is distasteful to the psyche.

One engages in projection whenever a painful wish or feeling occurs, denying that the emotion belongs to the self and instead blaming someone else for having that wish or feeling. The practicer of projection reacts as though he had to defend himself against the other person, who is out, he feels, to injure him. He can then feel righteous anger instead of the guilt that would normally follow the forbidden wish. Carried to an extreme, projection becomes paranoia.

What Freud called the "colossal capacity for displacement"—indulged in by both individuals and nations—is a hangover from the age of childhood when, having no other way to deal with psychic pain and unable to use reason, the infant blames everyone else for his discomfort. A baby cannot accept responsibility for the strong impulses that overwhelm him, such as his wish to destroy his mother when he is hungry and she fails to bring food.

Everyone makes use of these two processes, introjection and projection, throughout life, seeking pleasure, trying to avoid pain. The right balance of both leads to the ability to love. An imbalance can be seen in those who are very moody, who swing from the extreme of taking in something extraordinarily wonderful to the despair of expelling something agonizing.

Psychic "taking in" also leads to the development of the conscience. A child takes in from his parents what they want him to know, as well as what they do not want him to know—their unconscious wishes—which come through to the child no matter how the parents try to hide them. Children also absorb the ways their parents handle the world outside. By two years of age a child seems to possess a conscience. This moral sense is originally based on fear of punishment. A child knows not to harm a new baby even though he may wish the baby dead. One occasionally reads of an older child killing a younger brother or sister, a child who has not received the proper help from parents in controlling his primitive impulses.

At first a baby recognizes only "parts" of his mother—her breast, her hand, her hair. He thinks his mother and he are one and the same. As Freud wrote, "Against all the evidence of his senses the man in love declares that he and his beloved are one, and is prepared to behave as if it were a fact." Such a feeling of total love is connected to a baby's very early feeling toward its mother—of being merged with her.

As reason develops and the child sees the mother as a human

being in her own right, he starts to use the process called *identification*. Children imitate, copy the mother, believing if they are like her, they will never lose her. Also, that she will love them more. One psychoanalyst explained, "A baby thinks, 'If I can't have her inside me, the next best thing is to be her'."

As the child matures he starts to use what Freud called *perception*, to learn about the world by giving things attention, becoming conscious of them. Perception includes not only receiving impressions but rejecting those that cause pain. Whether one acts one way or another depends on one's use of judgment. Freud described judgment: "Originally the property to be decided about might be either good or bad, useful or harmful. Expressed in the language of the oldest, that is of the oral instinctual impulses, the alternative runs thus: 'I should like to eat that, or I should like to spit it out;' or, carried a stage further: 'I should like to take this into me and keep that out of me'."

A horrifying illustration of the fantasy behind the process of identification occurred several years ago when a farmer in Wisconsin was discovered to have skinned women's bodies (it was not proved whether he killed them or merely stole corpses) and then draped the skin over himself. He would stand in front of a mirror staring at himself covered by a woman's outer form. He was literally trying to get inside the skin of his mother. One can only surmise that he was among the most angered and frustrated, or else overindulged, of babies. As an adult he was living out the fantasy that if he were somehow able to get inside his mother or take her inside him, he would possess all her attributes, gain her strength and thereby keep alive. The threat to his psychic life as a baby must have been almost intolerable, and one can imagine how deeply his mother was disturbed. This man had never married, nor had he ever been seen with a woman and his unnatural acts took place right after the death of his mother. In fantasy, he may have been trying to make up for her loss by assuming her identity, one way Freud found people tried to ease their grief when they lost someone they loved.

The loss of a mother, even temporarily, when a baby wants her, seems catastrophic. Severe depression may ensue and become a lasting part of life if she leaves him in someone else's care for months or years at a time. His anger will eventually explode against the "bad" mother he now wants to destroy, specifically her breast, that part of her with which he has been in closest contact and which he knows best.

When forced to give up the breast or bottle, to ease his anger a baby will use his thumb as a substitute for the denied pleasure. In symbolic form he now possesses the "good" breast inside. He can have it whenever he wants it. The pleasure of sucking his thumb replaces the missing pleasure of feeding at the breast or bottle. While it is not quite the same, the baby is at least saved from being overwhelmed by his rage.

If a baby's rage becomes too intense, if the "bad" mother is in fact a bad mother, he will hate her excessively and grow into an angry, hostile adult, incapable of love. His mother, his first love, who satisfies his hunger, is also his protection against a terrifying world. He is completely helpless and must look to her for all solace. If she does not provide protection, his psychic life will be endangered. If a mother is in reality cruel, either consciously or unconsciously has not wanted the baby, he will take in more of the "bad" mother than the baby whose mother loves and wants him, and whom he takes in primarily as "good."

Babies are pint-sized cannibals who cheerfully wish to devour their mother without a second of sympathy if she frustrates them. The emotions of pity and compassion develop much later in life than the primitive urge to bite. Adults find it difficult to accept the thought they might have once wanted to devour human flesh, one of the most repugnant and most repressed of infantile wishes. Yet it is not unusual for a child, in a moment of excitement or anger, to sink his teeth into someone's arm or leg. When a murderer has bitten his victim, as some do, often on the breast, it is a sign of acute rage from the oral stage, which Freud called "the cannibalistic-oral stage."

Primitive man sometimes ate his captured enemies, not because he needed food, but because he magically believed that by "taking in" the strong opponent (sometimes only the penis, which he believed contained the real power), he would assume the characteristics of the one devoured. Which is how an infant unconsciously thinks, according to Freud, before developing the capacity to reason.

When a child is angry he may have fantasies of devouring (from the oral stage), or drowning (urinating upon) or burning alive (the sensation of anger from the anal stage), or cutting off the penis (from the phallic stage). The fantasy is followed by the fear his intended victim will retaliate by doing the same to him (an eye for an eye—more of the thinking of the unconscious). The adult knows it is not a crime merely to wish someone dead. But a child cannot yet tell the difference between a wish and a deed, will feel guilty and believe he deserves punishment.

Freud thought that elements of the infantile sexual impulses that do not become an actual part of sexuality may instead show themselves as character traits—traits that may be either unchanged perpetuations of the original impulses or an expression of the exact opposite impulse as a defense. The latter Freud called *reaction formation.* Someone who possesses a great need to be cared for as in childhood may deny what he believes a dangerous feeling by acting in a dominating, controlling manner, showing the opposite characteristic, hiding his passive wish by acting aggressively. And so some of the early erotic feelings enter into the final stage of sexual life, some become sublimated, and some form part of character.

The discovery of the various sexual stages was Freud's, and he also discussed character traits as related to sublimation of erotic wishes. His close colleague and friend, Dr. Karl Abraham, elaborated on these findings. Abraham divided the oral stage into two parts—the sucking phase, followed by the biting phase. He said there were numerous ways this important process of development could be impeded. Because the pleasure of the sucking period is largely the pleasure of taking in, of being given something, if a child receives either too much or too little nourishment, his later character will be disturbed. Those infants who have had a reasonably pleasurable sucking period will find later life enjoyable, Abraham said. They will be optimistic, tranquil, generous and self-assured. Those who have been overindulged are apt to be exceedingly carefree and will grow up believing someone will always be around to take care of them. Their attitude is one of expecting "the mother's breast to flow for them eternally, as it were." At the other extreme, those whose sucking period has been ungratified and meager, as adults seem to beg all the time, asking either aggrievedly, demandingly or shyly, expressing their wishes in a manner that has "something of the nature of persistent sucking about it," Abraham said. They are "leechlike," afraid to be alone, and impatient, sometimes cruel with themselves and others.

The excessively "oral" person, Abraham said, may show an insatiable urge to talk, believes his fund of thoughts inexhaustible, and ascribes a special power to what he says. He relates to others primarily through speech, or "oral discharge," which has an erotic quality. Such persons are good talkers but poor lovers, as their passion goes into their words. Their talking may also possess a quality from the second oral phase when sadism first appears, in that they use words to kill, or biting remarks to obliterate.

Following the oral stage in Freud's hierarchy of psychosexual development comes the anal stage, which Abraham also divided into two phases: the retentive, when the feces are held back, and the expulsive, when they are discharged from the body. Many of the character traits that belong to the anal stage are, he said, "built upon the ruins" of an oral eroticism whose development has miscarried. Impulses belonging to any of the later stages of sexual development either support or conflict with those of the previous stages, depending on how fully the child's emotional needs at the previous stages have been met.

Abraham pointed out that some who show a great mental capacity for absorbing (overindulged in their oral stage) become inhibited in producing (harsh training in the anal stage). Others produce too rapidly, hardly taking in an idea before it comes out of the mouth. Abraham suggested there should be a satisfactory combination of forward-moving oral impulses with retarding anal ones. The "normal character," he said, contains derivatives from all the original instincts "happily combined with each other." Every variety of character trait is present in each one of us to some degree.

The anal stage holds many hazards, according to Freud, as the child is taught to control the pleasurable sensations of urinating and excreting. He learns that he must not dirty himself or his surroundings with urine and feces but perform the excretory functions at regular times and in specific places.

Children agree to learn this control because they do not want to lose the love of the mother, which suddenly, to the child's amazement, seems to hinge on this one, all-important task. It is as though he crucifies her if he does not regulate his bladder and anus according to the clock. He is grateful for her love in return for this mammoth achievement though part of him will hate her for interfering with what, at this time in his life, is a great pleasure.

A child is not disgusted by his excretions; he thinks of feces as a cherished possession. What else has he got to give his mother and father in return for their feeding and caring for him? He does not know that feces are waste but only that they come out of his body and belong to him. Babies urinate and defecate only on those they love. They take pleasure in the smell, sight, touch of feces. The most valuable possession in later life, money, is symbolic of what was once the most precious possession of childhood. The excessive value collectors place on the objects they gather together so avidly corresponds, Freud said, to the value children place on their feces, and also to the lover's over-estimation of the object of his sexual desire, which he tends to lose somewhat when he starts to see his beloved as a human being.

Before a child is taught to control his bodily functions, he has no shame about them. It is only when he sees a look of disgust or anger on his mother's face if he balks at control that he begins to feel that what he produces is dirty, disagreeable, despicable. He may, when he is angry, use retention (constipation) or expulsion (diarrhea) as an expression of hostility. The reason man chose as an abusive epithet the name of his best friend in the animal kingdom is that dogs have no horror of their excrement as well as being creatures of smell, Freud said.

The child who becomes over-obedient and a little paragon of politeness has probably learned control too soon and too severely, and may possess an unconscious desire for revenge that may explode in other ways as he fights the battle of the bathroom. One cannot push nature, which has its own quiet pace, without some ill effect on the psyche and body. Freud's discoveries have made both parents and doctors aware of the damage that may be done by too-early toilet training. Freud also warned against the giving of laxatives, saying a child could go for several days, if not weeks, without moving his bowels and not harm himself.

When one unconsciously or consciously hates a parent for making one control a pleasurable sensation too early in life, one may become inhibited in the ability to defecate comfortably while living with others. One may also transfer the hate to those who are close, refusing to give of the self in other ways as well as this elemental one on which all other ways of giving are patterned, according to Freud. One may become "constipated" in the ability to produce, or unable to give the self sexually.

Or the opposite may occur—one may suffer from psychic diarrhea, over-giving emotionally or sexually in an attempt to mask anger, then feel weak and exhausted afterward. If either extreme occurs, one is not accepting defecation as a natural function but endowing it with the anger felt in childhood when one was harshly forced to exercise this first control over pleasure.

Many adults show mixed feelings about the anal function. They may speak of the toilet as the "throne," attributing to it a sense of power. Expressions referring to toilet functions or the part of the body involved are often used to indicate utmost contempt. Freud pointed out that many jokes focus on toilet functions, as through laughter one releases repressed feelings connected to this very anxious period of life when, if a child mastered control, his mother called him "good" and he felt he had earned her love—though always there was the wistful wish that she might have loved him as he was: uncontrolled and dirty.

The area between the anus and the genital organs is full of sensuous nerves in which pleasurable sensations are aroused by the passage of feces through the anus, Freud said. Adults, except those who use the anus as a substitute for the vagina in sexual intercourse, do not remember these feelings as pleasurable both because of the repression that took place when they were made to feel their feces dirty and disgusting, and because the genitals have taken over as the primary area of pleasure.

One forgets most of the first six years of life in what Freud called "infantile amnesia," because so many repressions took place then in connection with the sexual impulses. During a child's first years, he has to learn what it took mankind hundreds of thousands of years to learn as civilization developed.

When a child is taught to postpone expulsion of feces until certain hours, he realizes he can heighten pleasure by holding back. The retention of stools gives a sensuous feeling that may lead in later life to constipation, Freud said.

The child also learns he possesses a strong weapon with which to threaten his mother, either in withholding feces or in giving way too completely. Through constipation or diarrhea he can assert a power that will bring a look of consternation, concern, anger, or pleasure and approval to her face. He recognizes, for the first time, that he is master over at least a small part of his fate.

Constipation is more customary than diarrhea as a weapon of revenge, Freud said, because it is less painful. He warned against giving enemas to children because of the sexual fantasies aroused —the insertion of any object between the buttocks may be interpreted by a child as either a sexual or a hostile attack.

Some mothers find it difficult to accept the genital organs of the child but give the anus their undivided attention. These mothers warn against masturbation and are careful to avoid touching the child's genital regions. But they frequently caress the child's buttocks, refer to his "cute little bottom," show intense interest in his defecations and want to know each time he performs and the quantity and quality of what he produces.

The child of such a mother is apt to grow up fearing his genitals, Freud said, and will instead focus his sexual feelings on the anus, since it appears to have his mother's approval as an erotic channel. Some psychoanalysts believe a mother's undue interest in the anal function is one of the earliest and most dangerous enemies of the sexual development of a child.

The child's anger against the threatening or frustrating mother, an anger that may have started in the oral stage, becomes reinforced during this second stage, which is strongly charged with what Freud called "anal-sadism." The desire to be cruel and sadistic, to take revenge, overlays and intensifies the anger of the oral period when the baby wanted to sink his teeth into his mother out of fury. According to Freud, if a baby is very angry during the oral stage, he will certainly be angry during the anal stage when called upon to give up the pleasure of urinating and defecating at will.

During the anal stage certain traits may dominate the personality and produce what Freud called "the anal character." He came to this conclusion after noticing among his patients a type of personality in which certain traits were strongly marked. At the same time, he observed the behavior of these persons "in regard to a certain bodily function and of the organ connected with it during their childhood." They showed a regular combination of three definite peculiarities: exceptional orderliness, parsimony and obstinacy.

Each of these characteristics covered several traits, all related to one another, Freud discovered. "Orderly" included bodily cleanliness, reliability and conscientousness in the performance of petty duties, often exaggerated to the point of absurdity. "Parsimony" could reach the point of greed, miserliness and meanness. "Obstinacy" could become defiance, irascibility and vindictiveness.

Freud found that many of these patients had taken a long time to learn to control their urinary and anal functions, and when they did, found pleasure in holding back. They had learned control but unconsciously had not given up the forbidden pleasure. Their later character exaggerated the qualities of cleanliness, miserliness and defiance, as though caricaturing the whole unhappy procedure.

He suggested these traits of orderliness, avarice and stubborness, so prominent in those who as children attached great pleasure to the anal function, were the first and most constant results of the sublimation of this erotic feeling. The sublimation developed between the ages of four and eleven when reactions of shame, disgust and morality become strongly entrenched.

He pointed out the direct relation of each trait to the anal period. Cleanliness and orderliness were a reaction against what was felt as unclean and dirty. Concerning the third trait, obstinacy, Freud said it appeared no easy task to relate that to defecation until one remembered that infants very early showed great self-will about parting with feces and often parents spanked or struck them as a way of breaking this self-will. The obstinacy was a reaction against being forced to be submissive. . . .

A child's esteem is greatly affected by the way in which parents accept his pace in learning control. Recently a mother cracked her three-year-old daughter so severely across the mouth when she did not have a bowel movement that the child had to be rushed to the hospital. Psychic readiness begins when the child starts to transfer to his mother and father some of the feelings of narcissism that, at the start, he holds only toward himself. Once the child acquires this capacity to give love, he will become clean for the sake of the one he loves. But if cleanliness is demanded too soon, the child may acquire the habit through fear, not love. The inner defiance will remain, the child will continue to hate, rather than love, his narcissism will remain fixed on himself and his capacity to love will be impaired.

Love is a developmental process, according to Freud. Feelings of love and hate that develop in connection with the oral and anal stages and later the phallic are transformed into the ability to give or take love as an adult. If toilet training has been easy, if the parents were understanding and caring, the adult will tend to be amenable, generous, punctual, understanding of the needs of others and able to lead a reasonably serene, orderly life.

Abraham elaborated on the three characteristics of the anal period described by Freud. Those whose adult lives possess an anal quality are apt to believe they can do things better than anyone else, he said. They do not like to share and resent encroachment on anything that belongs to them. They expect everyone to accommodate to them but are not flexible with others. They live by strict rules and regulations and are upset when they must deviate. Unconsciously they are afraid that without such compulsions they will defecate over everything and everybody. They are also, in their inflexibility, caricaturing the power they felt their parents possessed. They enjoy making needless lists, take pleasure in indexing, cataloging, collecting, playing with statistics (as though unconsciously reliving the pleasure of reporting and describing bowel movements to their parents.) They show ardent interest in possessing things, hardly ever throwing anything away. They save in large amounts (displacing the holding back of feces to money). They will often limit their saving to small things, then embark on a spree and spend lavishly (as they once stubbornly held back feces then expelled them in one sudden burst of power). They will refuse someone's demand or request, then give when *they* choose. The important thing for the anal character is that he be the one to make the decision, to control things. These people like to arouse desire and expectation in others and then give gratification only in small amounts. (Abraham cited as an extreme example a stingy old man who fed his goat one blade of grass at a time.) Anal characters also worry about wasting time, the real worry being the "waste" in their own body as they equate work with feces. Anything that interrupts their work irritates them. They think only the hours spent at work are well spent. They hate inactivity and resent leisure activities, which they tear through in desperate, furious fashion. They tend to read in the bathroom, needing to "take in" something before they will give out. They rationalize that they are saving time by doing two things at once, not realizing the normal amount of time for defecation, when it is not erotically tinged, is only a minute or two.

One of Freud's most important discoveries was that the same fantasies occur in all children as they apply what they know about their own bodies ("the first ego is a body ego," he said) to explain whatever puzzles them sexually. In the oral stage they imagine that babies are born through the mouth. In the anal stage, they believe that babies, like feces, come out of the anus. The child's ignorance of the vagina's role makes it possible for him to imagine that if a baby grows in the body of the mother and is then detached from it, this can only happen by way of the anal aperture, as the child thinks the baby "must be expelled like excrement, like a motion." Babies are equated in the unconscious with feces, Freud said. If babies are born through the anus, then a man can give birth as well as a woman, a child is able to believe. A boy imagines he can have a baby without anyone accusing him of being a girl.

In the oral stage, when the mouth is the chief erotic zone, begins the fantasy that one may get pregnant from a kiss, Freud theorized. In his experience, this applied exclusively to women, usually "girls whose sexual curiosity had undergone very strong inhibition in childhood."

The third stage of sexual development, the phallic stage, occurs as the child, usually at the age of three or four, becomes aware of sexual differences. It is a stage when the penis is the focal attraction for both sexes. The little boy fears he will lose his penis if he is "bad" and the little girl, envious, wishes she had a penis, according to Freud.

The phallic stage is related to what Freud named the Oedipus complex, which he described in his early theories as "the core of neurosis." As a result of his self-analysis and the analysis of patients Freud concluded that "every psychoanalytic treatment is an attempt to free repressed love." The loved one was the person who during the early years of life was the true love—the parent of the opposite sex. It was an all-consuming love, as Freud described it: "Childish love knows no bounds, it demands exclusive possession, is satisfied with nothing less than all."

Everyone's first love is "regularly an incestuous one," and the most stringent prohibitions are required to prevent "this sustained infantile tendency" from being carried into effect. This early love has a power beyond belief. Were it not such a compelling force, so demanding of fulfillment, there would be no need to forbid it. Mankind's taboo against incest arises out of the strength of this sexual desire.

It took hundreds of thousands of years in man's development before the nearest blood relatives were excluded as objects of sexual love. In mythological tales incest was indulged in by the gods —myths are age-old wish fulfillments. Incestuous marriage with a sister was encouraged among the Pharaohs of Egypt and the Incas of Peru, to provide royal mates for their rulers. Some primitive tribes still allow incest between father and daughter, but not between mother and son.

In the early days of primitive man fathers murdered sons to keep them from possessing the mother, Freud noted, quoting Sir James Frazer's *The Golden Bough*. Whereupon sons banded together and turned on the fathers. As Freud's memorable words near the end of *Totem and Taboo* remind us, "In the beginning was the deed."

The desire for the parent of the opposite sex is, Freud said, universal, whether one lives in the darkest jungle or the most sophisticated city. There exists an embryonic Oedipus in every man and an Electra in every woman. While growing up, each person, in Freud's words, "must devote himself to the great task of *freeing himself from the parents;* and only after this detachment is accomplished can he cease to be a child and so become a member of the social community" (italics Freud's).

The son must give up his wish to possess his mother and seek a woman who can become his wife. If he has remained hostile toward his father as a rival, either openly or hiding his childhood rebellion by being outwardly submissive, he must free himself of this hatred. The daughter must give up her desire for her father and her rage at her mother for being the one to possess him.

The attachment to the parent of the opposite sex is part of our natural growth, Freud pointed out. It is a step toward eventually loving someone outside the family. If this detachment is not accomplished, he warned, neurosis will result.

Freud had the chance to study why so many men and women became disillusioned after falling in love—why the passionate feelings did not last, as the poets of the ages sadly agreed. He came to the conclusion: "It has an ugly sound and paradoxical as well, but nevertheless it must be said that whoever is to be really free and happy in love must have overcome his deference for women and come to terms with the idea of incest with mother or sister." He was speaking of men but applied this also to women in their relation to father and brother.

He pointed out that one reason Hamlet vacillated so long about killing his uncle and avenging his father's murder (the core of his famous soliloquy beginning "O what a rogue and peasant slave am I") was because he unconsciously knew he would be killing his uncle for doing the same thing he, Hamlet, wished to do—murder his father and possess his mother. The fantasy held by some, that if they had only been seduced by a parent they would not live in such torment of desire, is, though, a false one. After Oedipus murdered his father and slept with his mother he called this "the woe surpassing all woes."

Freud's courage in facing his own wish to possess his mother and get rid of his father was undoubtedly one of the most daring confrontations with the self ever made. He had no psychoanalyst —since he was the first—to reassure him or guide him along the perilous psychic path he charted.

Freud was also the first to recognize the urgency of a child's need for complete closeness with a parent. He understood that the warm, friendly contact the child seeks may include sensations that are sexual in nature, though not expressions of adult sexuality. As Freud worked on he uncovered many evidences of childhood yearning for the parent of the opposite sex, which in later years became masked by "romantic love."

To ensure "a fully normal attitude in love," two currents of feeling have to unite, Freud said: tender, affectionate ones and sensual ones.

Tender feelings are learned by a child as he feels them in his parents, expressed toward him and toward each other. Sometimes feelings of tenderness and sensuality, instead of fusing as love, split into opposing camps, become deadly enemies. This is apt to happen if a child possesses too great an erotic attachment to the parent of the opposite sex. He lives in the illusion he cannot be unfaithful sexually to the parent whom, in fantasy, he cannot give up as his secret lifelong mate.

A child's fantasies revolve chiefly around his erotic and aggressive feelings because these are the strongest and the most forbidden. Sexual urges may flood his body before he is mature enough to handle them and he may try to ease their pressure through excessive use of fantasy.

All experiences connected to birth hold danger and fascination to a child, Freud said, the chief stimulus to sexual curiousity being fear of displacement by new rivals and the wish to find out how babies are born. A child lives in a state of suspense from the time he watches his mother's stomach grow until he hears the wails of the new baby. During the birth, even though his mother may be in a hospital, the child at home has fantasies about what is happening to his mother at the hands of doctors, even fearing (wishing) her death, angry at her for leaving him and for giving birth to a rival. A little boy recently asked his mother, after the birth of a younger brother, "I know you know how to have babies, but do you know how *not* to have them?

Freud said that when the child first becomes aware of his father's penis he may think of it as a third breast, an appendage like the two he remembers so fondly that his mother possessed. Often when the adult penis is sucked or stroked, in fantasy it has remained the breast, Freud added. The child will also have the fantasy that "baby" and "penis" are connected—in some languages they are both called "the little one."

As a new baby arrives, an older child may regress to wetting his bed to attract attention and get the love he once knew, now given to the unwelcome stranger. It is impossible for a child to realize a new baby needs constant care. He knows only that he wants his mother's and father's full love. One of the first mental activities, according to Freud, is regression. The baby, after being put to bed, will naturally fall asleep. But adults who must sleep unusually long hours are regressing to the state of sleep and its fantasies in dreams. Regression represents an attempt by the psyche, when in pain, to return to former states of pleasure. When one finds no other pleasure in life, one returns to the pleasures of infancy.

One very important fantasy of childhood, Freud said, was "the sadistic conception of coitus." When children witness their parents in sexual intercourse or hear noises from the bedroom, they imagine "something that the stronger person inflicts on the weaker by force, and compar[e] it, especially the boy, to a fight as they know from their childish play, in which, by the way, an admixture of sexual excitation is not wanting."

So children tend to interpret the act of love as an act of violence. A child believes that what goes on in the bedroom between his mother and father is rape, or at least a mutually destructive act. An infant may, if he sleeps in his parents' room, see them writhing together, not knowing where one ends and the other begins. Freud said the monsters of mythology, partly male, partly female, were examples of horror aroused by fantasies about parental intimacy. Or, he said, the child may think of women and men in sexual intercourse as vampires sucking each other's life blood. If a child sees menstrual blood on the sheets, this confirms his fantasy that the sexual act is one of brutality inflicted on his mother.

Freud also pointed out, "At other times the whole marriage presents to the observant child the spectacle of an unceasing quarrel, expressed by loud words and unfriendly gestures, so that the child need not wonder that this quarrel goes on in the night, too, and is finally decided by the very same means which the child himself is accustomed to make use of in its intercourse with its brothers, sisters and companions, that is, by a fight."

The infantile ideas about the nature of marriage, seldom retained by the conscious memory, nevertheless have "great significance for the symptoms of later neurotic illness," he warned.

When we are adults these fantasies usually become unconscious. We are reminded of them by the words and acts of children, or by the mentally ill who are unable to maintain the defense of repression. The fantasies also appear nightly in our dreams, though in such disguised fashion that they usually do not alarm us, except for nightmares.

One of the most destructive things a mother or father can do to the psychosexual development of a child is to be excessively seductive or engage in incest, Freud declared. That parents do seduce children is attested to by court records. A fifteen-year-old boy told a psychiatrist that his mother lured him into sexual intimacy with the explanation she was "keeping him from bad women." A ten-year-old girl was called by her father into his bedroom so he could show her "what an erection was" because, he said, he wanted her "to learn the facts of life early."

Some parents walk naked in front of a child. Others allow a child to touch and explore their genitals, or to wash their bodies under the guise of "educating" the child or satisfying the child's curiosity. Freud called this the unconscious attempt by a parent to seduce through exhibitionism, and warned that such activities stimulated the child beyond what he was able to handle psychically and physically.

Some mothers use sexuality as a defensive process, unconsciously encouraging a child in an early, pre-genital seductive relationship, which is gratifying to the mother in that it keeps her from facing underlying feelings of "intense depression, deadness, unresponsiveness, loneliness, rage and humiliation," according to Dr. Stanley J. Coen in his article "Sexualization and the Choice of a Sexual Mode of Defense."

Sexualization can occur in a number of ways, Coen points out. He cites Freud as saying that in obsessional neurosis even the thought process becomes sexualized, as the sexual pleasure normally attached to the content of thought "becomes shifted onto the act of thinking itself, and the satisfaction derived from reaching the conclusion of a line of thought is experienced as a sexual satisfaction."

Seductiveness may be only one aspect of a mother's disturbance. Both mother and child may focus on sexual feelings and hypochondriacal anxieties instead of knowing what each really feels or thinks. Such a mother emphasizes the seductive relationship "to obscure her deficiency as a mother." Because of the "unpredictable quality" of the mother's responsiveness to the child and the child's ensuing feelings of helplessness, rage and depression, his role as enjoying a special relationship, forbidden to most children, is used defensively, according to Coen. The child fantasies himself as an omnipotent, irresistible seducer to counter his rage at feeling exploited and manipulated by his mother as she keeps him from moving toward independence and self-esteem.

The highly seductive parent is also a highly rejecting parent. The parent who loves his child in a mature way will be neither over-seductive nor withhold affection, but will provide an atmosphere of love and tenderness as well as protection. Wherever there exist intense incestuous feelings, there also lurks intense hidden hatred. A mother or father who unconsciously or consciously provokes deep feelings of sexual yearning in a child, who steps beyond the bounds of tender parental love into seduction, is apt to be the kind of parent who fails to protect the child in other areas, who has little understanding of a child's emotional needs. Parents no longer in love with each other will sometimes use the children—who are younger, more beautiful or more handsome versions of the mate—as substitute loves reminding them of the one with whom they were once in love.

The childhood desire for the parent is mirrored in many a fairytale. The story of the beautiful princess awakened to love by the monster who is really the handsome young Prince in disguise hides the fantasy of the little girl who desires her "monster" father, a noble man underneath. The wolf who obligingly eats up the grandmother for Little Red Riding Hood is, in fantasy, getting the mother out of the way so the little girl is free to have her father, though conscience (the woodman who kills the big bad wolf) triumphs in the end, as it does in all fairytales and is supposed to do in life.

It may seem strange that Freud coupled "deference" with "the idea of incest," as he wrote that one must overcome "deference" and "come to terms with the idea of incest" to be "really free and happy in love." He admitted this had a paradoxical sound. Yet the deference, the wish to please, to be loved completely and forever by the parent, is very much a part of the idea of incest, he said. Coming to terms with the idea of incest means accepting the impulse to love the parent of the opposite sex as natural, even though taboo. If one can consciously accept the *idea* of incest, one can handle the guilt about taboo feelings, knowing they spring from the natural need to be loved and to give love. It is a need which may, if excessive, give rise to the delusion of incest and, in lesser degree, to the illusion of finding the perfect parent in one's love partner. This wish—that the one who is loved be the perfect parent—deals the death blow to adult love. A mate cannot be a parent, perfect or imperfect, and to ask consciously or unconsciously that he or she serve as one is to demand the impossible. The one time in literature when a man married his mother, even though unknowingly, the inevitable outcome of flouting this strongest taboo was tragedy. Oedipus fled the land, symbolically castrating himself as he put out his eyes, while his mother Jocasta committed suicide.

It must be remembered too that children do not see their parents as they really are. To a little girl her father is a combination of Sir Galahad, God and Prince Charming, while a little boy thinks of his mother as Cleopatra, the Madonna and Miss America all in one. This is fantasy spun on fantasy. It becomes self-destructive in later life if one demands of his mate not only that he be a parent but a parent originally idealized beyond all reality.

One needs to learn to steer the course between what Freud called "the Scylla of giving the instincts free play and the Charybdis of frustrating them." One learns from parents and society how to chart the course, avoid the currents and hidden rocks.

Humans differ from animals, whose young grow up quickly without much concern on the part of their parents. Freud called "the human condition" the many years a child has to depend on his parents. Children come into the world helpless and weak. They cannot survive without several years of intense care for their most elementary needs. The fact that a child has to depend on his mother to fulfill his needs for such a long time means that he will have to repress many of his hostile and erotic feelings. He cannot give way to his desire to destroy or to possess erotically everyone he wants. The long firm arms of parents and society interfere and make him feel frustrated, a feeling described by Freud as "the lack of fulfillment of one of those eternal uncontrollable childhood wishes rooted in our composition."

A parent may be jealous of a child, and if this feeling is too intense it will produce harmful fantasies in the child, quick to sense the jealousy and protect himself against it. A father may feel that his child, especially a little boy, is a rival and "this gives origin to an antagonism against the favorite son which is deeply rooted in the unconscious," Freud said.

He felt very strongly that sexual enlightenment should begin from the moment a child starts to ask questions and that it should keep pace with the child's continued curiosity and intelligence. He said all children have a "strong, unquenchable" curiosity about sex, that no child, "none at least who is mentally sound, still less one who is mentally gifted," can avoid being preoccupied with the mysteries of sex. The child is well aware his parents indulge in sex and may be confused as to why they may say one thing, do another.

When children do not receive the explanations they seek from adults, they go on "tormenting themselves in secret," Freud said. They produce solutions in which the truth they have guessed "is mixed up in the most extraordinary way with grotesque inventions" or else whisper secrets to each other that, because of their feelings of guilt, "stamp everything sexual as horrible and disgusting."

Children refuse to believe the "stork" story and from the time they are told "this fairytale" mistrust adults, feel something forbidden is being withheld from them, Freud pointed out. The observation of animals, who "hide so little of their sexual life and to whom children feel so closely related," strengthens their disbelief.

He suggested that schools give classes in the facts of reproduction, in gradual and progressive courses of instruction. In this way, he added, the curiosity of a child will never become very intense, because at each stage in his inquiries he will find the answers he needs. Explanations about the specific circumstances of human sexuality and some indication of its social significance should be provided the child before he is eleven, Freud said.

Following the phallic stage comes the genital, or final stage. According to Freud, the primacy of the genital zone as giving ultimate sexual satisfaction should be established by the age of eleven or twelve and all other erotic parts of the body should become subordinated to the genital zone.

During the eighth to the eleventh year, Freud said, the genital zone behaves "almost as if it had reached the age of maturity" as it becomes the site of exciting sensations and gets ready for adult sex as pleasure is experienced through the gratification of other erotic zones, in touching, embracing and kissing.

In primitive societies young boys and girls in their early teens, sometimes even younger, prepare to marry and have children. But in the western world, though the genital stage occurs naturally at adolescence, until recently sexual activity was postponed and adolescents were required to plunge into intellectual activities, work or sports, delaying sexual activity—affairs or marriage—until after college or working a number of years. But the birth control revolution and relaxed sexual mores have caused a massive upsurge in sex during high school and college years.

One achieves the full capacity to love in this final genital stage, according to Freud. Adult erotic feelings, unlike those of the oral and anal stages, hold the tenderness, affection and friendliness essential to mature love. The goal is not to rule, not to possess, not to subjugate, but to share, to give and accept love. As Freud said: "A man who doubts his own love may, or rather *must*, doubt every lesser thing" (italics Freud's).

The original love for a mother starts off as a *need* rather than a mature give and take. The adult who still thinks of love as hungry, possessive and demanding may fail each time in his attempt to find a love that lasts.

The normal development of psychosexual life ends by our being capable of loving one person of the opposite sex with whom one spends the rest of life bringing up children, Freud said. This is not, as millions have discovered, easy. We have a long and fairly difficult way to go from the complete self-centeredness of our first months on earth to the point where we can freely bestow what was originally self-love on someone for whom we care. To be able to love means to become civilized and to become civilized means frustration of many of our primitive desires. This alone causes a certain amount of anger and natural suffering. When suffering inflicted on us as children by a mother and father who themselves were once troubled children is added to this, we may find ourselves severely restricted in our capacity to love.

So "mature love" is fully realized genital love—sex freed in large part from the hunger and anger of the earlier sexual stages of life. If this is achieved sex becomes part of love, and love part of sex. If it is not, if we remain trapped in the earlier stages and their fantasies, then our capacity for love is what Freud called "impeded."

Every stage of our sexual development contributes either to the eventual success or failure of our ability to enjoy genital sex and to love. It depends on whether we have been able to give up a sufficient amount of dependency on our mother and give up, also, the erotic attachment to the parent of the opposite sex.

Freud started what he believed was his second most important work, *Three Essays on the Theory of Sexuality,* published in 1905, with the chapter, "Sexual Aberrations." He announced, ". . . in short, *perverted sexuality* is nothing else but infantile sexuality, magnified and separated into its component parts" (italics Freud's).

He said that at every stage in the course of development through which all human beings "ought by rights to pass," a certain number "are held back." They have never "got over their parents' authority and have withdrawn their affection from them either very incompletely or not at all." He added that sexual love and what appears to be nonsexual love for parents are "fed from the same courses." Nonsexual love merely corresponds to "an infantile fixation of the libido."

The closer one comes to the deeper disturbances of the psychosexual development, "the more unmistakably the importance of incestuous object-choice emerges," Freud said. He found that in neurotics a large portion, or the whole of their psychosexual activity in finding someone with whom to enjoy sex, remains in the unconscious as a result of their "repudiation" of mature sexuality.

One of the psychic tasks of the genital stage is that the libido find its way to the opposite sex, Freud said. This is not accomplished without a certain amount of "fumbling."

Referring to what he called "aberrations in sexual behavior," Freud said, "it is perhaps in connection precisely with the most repulsive perversions that the mental factor must be regarded as playing its largest part in the transformation of the sexual instinct." It is impossible to deny, he went on, that in perversions "a piece of mental work has been performed which, in spite of its horrifying results, is the equivalent of an idealization of the instinct." He added "The omnipotence of love is perhaps never more strongly proved than in such of its aberrations as these. The highest and the lowest are always closest to each other in the sphere of sexuality."

He described perversion in an adult as an aberration of the sexual instinct "in regard to object and aim." Study of the perversions shows that the sexual instinct has had to struggle against certain mental forces that act as resistances, of which "shame and disgust" are the most prominent. These forces play a part in restraining the sexual instinct within the limits regarded as "normal," but if they develop in the child before the sexual instinct has reached its full strength, "it is no doubt that they will determine the course of its development."

The perversions are only made intelligible, he said, "if we assume the convergence of several motive forces" that represent "amalgamations which have disappeared from view in the uniform behavior of normal people." There is reason to suppose that abortive beginnings of normal sexual development have occurred before the perversions become "fixated." He cited the case of fetishism, which substitutes for the body of another person some part, such as the foot or hair, or some inanimate object such as a lace undergarment or fur piece, which bears a connection to the person it replaces "and that person's sexuality."

Freud anticipated what later psychoanalysts were to substantiate when he wrote: "Analytic investigation has already been able to show in a few cases that perversions are a residue of development toward the Oedipus complex, and that after the repression of that complex the components of the sexual instinct which are strongest in the disposition of the individual concerned emerge once more."

He said it was "inappropriate to use the word perversion as a term of reproach," even in certain cases that were far removed from the normal, such as "licking excrement or intercourse with dead bodies, where the sexual instinct goes to astonishing lengths" in successfully overriding the resistances of shame, disgust, horror or pain. He added that even the most pathological sexual behavior indicated the person has not been able to develop normally in a sexual fashion because of fear stemming from childhood experiences.

Society has classed as perverts: sadists, who inflict beatings as part of the sexual act; masochists, who must have pain inflicted on them before they can become sexually aroused; exhibitionists, who display their genitals in public; voyeurs, who must watch others in sexual intimacy to become sexually stimulated; transvestites, who wear the clothes of women to become sexually aroused; fetishists, whose sexual desire is an object rather than a person; rapists, who assault women and children in order to be aroused sexually; and satyrs and nymphomaniacs, men and women who are sexually insatiable. Until recently, homosexuality was considered a perversion by most people. By some, it is still held to be deviational behavior.

Society has been all too swift to condemn these groups without understanding the ways in which such people have been sexually terrified as children, unable to emerge from the kindergarten of sex. Freud said, "Perverts are more likely to be poor devils who have to pay most bitterly for the satisfactions they manage to procure with such difficulty."

He specifically related perversions to the earlier stages of sexual development. He showed how the so-called pervert is afraid to face genital sex and remains instead in the safety of earlier stages, seeking childhood sexual pleasures that are less dangerous. Freud also showed how each perversion, at an earlier time of life, formed part of the natural sexual development in all of us. The pervert has remained enmeshed in the fantasies appropriate to earlier stages of psychosexual growth.

According to Freud, perversion includes any expression of sexual desire which does not have procreation as its aim. It is sex that he called "polymorphous perverse"—sexual satisfaction achieved in partial, incomplete, childlike gratifications such as touching, looking, smelling, kissing, exhibiting, masturbating or being masturbated.

Adults cannot find gratification in an infantile sexual pleasure without feeling debased. This was eloquently portrayed in the play *The Boys in the Band,* when in the moment of crisis, the homosexual hero cries out poignantly, "Why do I hate myself so?"

Freud said there was no doubt that a large part of the opposition to his views on sexuality "is due to the fact that sexuality, to which I trace back psychoneurotic symptoms, is regarded as though it coincided with the normal sexual instinct. "But, he added, "it is by no means only at the cost of the so-called 'normal' sexual instinct that the symptoms of neurosis originate." He added that the symptoms give expression, through conversion, to instincts that "would be described as *perverse* in the widest sense of the word if they could be expressed directly in fantasy and action without being diverted from consciousness." Then he added his famous statement: "Thus symptoms are formed in part at the cost of *abnormal* sexuality; *neuroses are, so to say, the negative of perversions*" (italics Freud's).

The unconscious mental life of all neurotics, without exception, according to Freud, shows "inverted impulses, fixation of their libido upon persons of their own sex." He added, "I can only insist that an unconscious tendency to inversion is never absent and is of particular value in throwing light upon hysteria . . ."

For instance, a man who unconsciously wishes to be a voyeur and steal up fire escapes, peeping in windows to watch women undress or couples having sex, denies this impulse and becomes very near-sighted, as though to prove he would never want to see anything so shameful. He sublimates his sexual wish in the symptom. To possess this excessive need indicates that at some time in childhood this man may have been exposed to the sight of his parents having sex and was overstimulated at an age he could not handle his sexual feelings.

Freud also said that whenever there is found in the unconscious an instinct, such as love, that is capable of being paired off with an opposite, such as hate, the latter will be regularly found in opposition as well: "Every active perversion is thus accompanied by its counterpart: anyone who is an exhibitionist in his unconscious is at the same time a *voyeur,* anyone who suffers from the consequences of repressed sadistic impulses has masochistic inclinations, even though in the actual symptoms one or other of the opposing tendencies plays the predominating part."

He also pointed out that adult sexual foreplay includes acts that, if performed only as an end in themselves, are considered perversions. Freud defined such acts as perversions only when they served as a substitute for sexual intercourse rather than as a prelude to it. Even kissing may be a perversion if kissing is all two adults do, if out of sexual fear they cannot go beyond the kiss.

Cunnilingis and fellatio, the kissing of the female and male genitals, are widely accepted today as part of normal sex. Freud would have called them perversions, however, if used as alternatives to intercourse. He believed that perversions represented either "anatomical transgressions" of the bodily regions destined for sexual union, such as the use of the mouth or anus as a substitute for the vagina, or else "a lingering at the preliminaries," which should normally end after a certain time on the way to the final act of sex —the insertion of the penis into the vagina.

Thus Freud drew a distinct comparison between forepleasure as part of the mature sexual act and forepleasure as an end in itself. Where there occurs a perversion, he said, such as the use of the anus, either in homosexuality or heterosexuality, the area or the impulses that led to the finding of pleasure in that area were used in infancy to gain an unusual amount of pleasure.

A compulsion then resulted which made it impossible for the person to merge forepleasure into genital sexuality. The perversion represented a "lingering" at what normally would be a preparatory act of sex. The threat of genital sex becomes so dangerous the person dares not think of it except with hatred, scorn and disgust. Somehow parents made the child feel that sex in its adult form was dirty and shameful, thereby dooming him to settle for sexual gratification at one of the earlier stages. The gratification homosexuals give each other is actually a form of masturbation, not of genital sex, Freud said.

So perversions represent: 1) The inability to pass through the Oedipal stage successfully, to give up the parent of the opposite sex. 2) The fear on the man's part that he will be castrated if he enters a woman's vagina and the fear on the woman's part of penetration (being wounded) by a penis. 3) The inability to give up the mother as visualized in the early days of life when she was nurse, nurturer and feared as well.

The pervert both longs for and hates the mother of infancy. His hatred comes from the traumas she has inflicted on him that have interfered with his sexual development. The disturbances start in the oral stage. The homosexual's obsessive interest in the penis is preceded by the earlier object of love and hate—the mother's breast—the penis is equated with the breast in the pervert's fantasy. Perverts who have gone into analysis often speak of the penis as though it were the breast, telling of the wish to suck or bite it or get nourishment from it.

One of the fantasies of the pervert is that he is getting revenge on a mother who took away her breast too soon, thereby not giving him enough love. He is telling the world what a failure she was as a mother as he tries to be a better mother or seeks a better mother in his male partner.

Freud uncovered another universal fantasy among men, which he thought explained the pervert's fear of the vagina. Freud called it "the dream of the dentate vagina." A small boy will imagine his mother's vagina as lined with teeth, like her mouth, and if he is a very frightened little boy will believe that if he ever puts his penis in a woman's vagina, she will bite it off.

Freud also discovered what Kinsey later substantiated in his surveys—that our natural sexual instinct, if thwarted, may become diverted to a great variety of sexual objects, including corpses and animals. The latter, Kinsey found, especially occurred in rural areas. During World War II soldiers sent overseas later reported that some men from the remote parts of our country would seek out goats and other animals at night for sex, as they had done when boys. A man of fifty, a doctor, during his psychoanalysis confessed that when he was growing up on a lonely farm in Wisconsin he had sex with animals rather than seduce a younger sister for whom he felt intense passion.

In discussing the fetishist Freud said this was a man who chose a substitute for not just "any chance penis but for a particular quite special penis that had been extremely important in early childhood but was afterwards lost."

The purpose of the fetish, according to Freud, is to preserve the fantasy that the mother of childhood had a penis (which all children believe, he said). The fetishist has refused, unlike most children, to accept the fact that women do not have a penis because, in his mind, if a woman does not have a penis then his own body is in danger, he too could be mutilated. Because of this fear and his strong aversion to the female genitals, he cannot bear to look at them, much less enter them. In his fantasy the fetish represents an acceptable alternative for the vagina. Often the object that is the fetish is put on the body with foot, finger, penis or nose thrust into it, Freud said, and has an anal quality in that it is a used object with a distinct odor.

The fetishist tends to use the psychic process of denial, retaining his unconscious belief in the phallic mother, thereby lessening his fear of castration. The fetish represents a psychic compromise—it is the penis with which the fetishist endows his mother to reduce his own sexual anxiety. Freud suggested that possibly the fetish selected was the last object perceived before a boy's discovery that a woman lacked a penis, such as an undergarment pulled off by his mother before she revealed herself naked—the last moment in which he could regard her as possessing a penis. Fur pieces, a popular fetish, may symbolize pubic hair.

The transvestite indulges in a form of fetishism when he dresses like a woman to achieve sexual release. To the transvestite women's clothes unconsciously symbolize the penis, by hiding it, Freud said. The transvestite has to pretend he is a woman with a penis to feel safe having intercourse, which comes out of his intense identification with a mother he believes to be phallic, together with his fear of castration.

The man who can express himself sexually only through rape and the woman who is frigid except when she has fantasies of rape both imagine sex as an act of violence, degradation and shame. Rapists are terrified of women and afraid of their own masculinity. They use the penis as a weapon to hurt, not to give pleasure. That so many inflict sodomy on their victims indicates they are still in the anal stage of psychic growth.

The exhibitionist tries to reassure himself against his castration fear by showing his penis to the world. He lives in the days when, as a little boy, he proudly displayed his penis to his mother, wanting her admiration and reassurance that he would not lose it if he were "bad" and masturbated.

How does love turn into the hate that is so obviously a part of sadomasochistic sex? The transformation of love into hate takes place through the connection between the libido and cruelty, Freud said. The sadist gets sexual pleasure out of inflicting pain because in his childhood cruelty and sex were somehow associated.

The submissiveness of the masochist masks his unconscious identification with the partner who turns on him the cruelty inflicted by his parents, which, in turn, he would like to inflict on others. As punishment for this wicked thought, the pain must first be inflicted on him—then he is free to enjoy sex.

"A sense of guilt is invariably the factor that transforms sadism into masochism," Freud said. Guilt follows repression of the instinct to hurt someone. He explained: ". . . the more anyone refrains from aggressiveness toward others the more strict and sensitive his conscience." The masochist conceals intense aggressive urges, revealed by the fact his conscience propels him to such terrible punishment. He submits to punishment by the sadist, who in fantasy represents the mother or father of infancy. In his paper, "A Child is Being Beaten," Freud describes the child's wish, at various stages in his life, to be beaten by the father, connected to the wish for a passive sexual relationship.

Freud described three kinds of masochism: 1) "Erotogenic masochism," or the need for physical pain as a condition under which sexual excitement may be aroused. 2) "Feminine" masochism, which includes chiefly the use of fantasies. 3) "Moral masochism," in which the person inflicts physic pain on himself in order to feel humiliated and degraded.

In the first two types of masochism the person suffers pain at the hands of another during actual acts in which he is either bound, pinioned, beaten painfully, whipped or in some way mishandled and defiled. The masochist, according to Freud, "wants to be treated like a little, helpless, dependent child, but especially like a naughty child."

Moral masochism is not directly sexual. The moral masochist's suffering comes from some unkindness thrust on him by someone or something. He may eternally seek criticism from someone whom he loves, or react with extreme pain to the remarks of someone to whom he is fundamentally indifferent. Or "fate" keeps dealing disasters. As Freud put it: ". . . the true masochist always holds out his cheek wherever he sees a chance of receiving a blow."

Masochism is a many-pronged punishment. The masochist hides numerous unconscious wishes for which he believes he deserves to be hurt. He wishes to be back at his mother's breast. He wishes to defecate and urinate at will as he once did. He wishes to kill his mother. He wishes to kill his father. He wishes to have sex with his mother or his father or both. He wishes to castrate his father. He wishes to kill his brothers and sisters.

The masochist provokes brutality. He places himself in the role of innocent victim, denying his own aggressiveness. He arranges his life so he always appears victimized, not admitting he seeks out only those eager to victimize him.

The male sadist overexaggerates what in normal sexual desire would be manliness because he feels so unmanly. His natural aggression turns into brutality. He believes he will give up what precarious manhood he is able to muster if he does not assert himself to the point of beating a woman. He may take up a whip, symbolic of a powerful penis, because he feels so impotent, Freud explained, believing he can function sexually only if he is armed with an additional penis. He bestows the symbolic penis on the woman through the beating, making her in his fantasy the phallic mother—like the fetishist and the transvestite he must deny his mother lacked a penis because of his own fear of castration.

The sadist also identifies with the masochist in the punishment the sadist feels he deserves, just as the masochist projects upon the sadist the cruelty he wishes to inflict. There ensues a mutual exchange of projections in the interest of maintaining childish fantasies that make adult sex too dangerous.

Freud said there were four ways of handling our instincts. He called the first "reversal into its opposite." This includes two processes—a change from active to passive and a reversal of the content. A man may wish to hurt someone but cope with this wish by becoming the one who is hurt. The reversal affects the aim of the instinct, in that a passive act is substituted for an active one. Reversal of content is involved as love changes to hate.

The second way of defending ourselves against a strong instinct is through "turning 'round upon the subject," as Freud put it. The one who is hurt believes he "enjoys" being tortured. The essence of this psychic process is the change of object; the aim remains unchanged.

The third way is repression, in which awareness of the instinctual wish is banished from consciousness, a way most of us use.

The fourth defense is sublimation. Here the instinct becomes expressed in a more socially acceptable manner—in work, recreation, philanthropic activities.

The sexual instinct survives despite attempts to subjugate it through these various defenses. As we grow up, one hopes, tender feelings conquer the hostile ones, or, as Freud said, the hate becomes "overlaid" by a tender feeling that manages to triumph in spite of hazards.

Freud went on to describe differences between the sexual development of men and women. His views about female sexuality and the role of women have been widely misinterpreted, mostly, ironically, by women, to whose liberation he contributed so much. What are these views?

5

The "Riddle" of Femininity

Freud changed the worldwide concept of woman as a passive, inhibited creature who endured sex only to please man and create babies to that of the sexually liberated woman entitled to her own strong erotic desires and their gratification.

He opened the doors to women's right to enjoy sex, to indulge in it according to her needs, to feel free and uninhibited in the act of sex, not humiliated, subordinated, and, most of all, frustrated.

He set the stage for woman's liberation in other areas as well, since his stand on emotional liberation for women had repercussions on all of the ways in which women were exploited by men and by society—socially, economically, politically.

He did not know all the answers nor did he pretend to know them. In his paper "Femininity," written in 1933, Freud wrote, "Throughout history people have knocked their heads against the riddle of the nature of femininity." He ended the paper by stating that what he said about femininity was "certainly incomplete and fragmentary and does not always sound friendly. But do not forget that I have only been describing women insofar as their nature is determined by their sexual function. It is true that that influence extends very far; but we do not overlook the fact that an individual woman may be a human being in other respects as well. If you want to know more about femininity, inquire from your own experiences of life, or turn to the poets, or wait until science can give you deeper and more coherent information."

Contemporary psychoanalysts have been contributing to that "deeper and more coherent information" by building on the theoretical foundations set by Freud. These were constructed in his three papers on female sexuality. The first, in 1925, was called "Some Psychical Consequences of the Anatomical Distinction Between the Sexes," the second, in 1931, "Female Sexuality," and the third, "Femininity."

Able as always to change theory if new facts arose in his work with patients, in the third paper Freud pointed out that originally he had equated "passivity" with "femininity" and "activity" with "masculinity." But now, he stated, he believed women could display great activity in a variety of ways, and he no longer considered "active" synonymous with "masculine" or "passive" with feminine. He added, however, that perhaps woman, on the basis of her share in the sexual function, had a preference for passive behavior, and that passive aims were carried over into her life to a greater or lesser degree in proportion to the limits, restricted or far-reaching, within which her sexual life served as model.

At this time he still considered that "masochism" was "truly feminine" and that "if, as happens so often, you meet with masochism in men, what is left to you but to say that these men exhibit very plain feminine traits." He was later to change his mind about this theory too.

Psychology was unable to "solve the riddle" of femininity, Freud admitted, adding that psychoanalysis did not try to describe what a woman is—"that would be a task it could scarcely perform —but sets about inquiring how she comes into being, how a woman develops out of a child with a bisexual disposition."

He paid tribute to "several of our excellent women colleagues" who were working, he said, on the question of femininity. He commented that "the ladies, whenever some comparison seemed to turn out unfavorable to their sex, were able to utter a suspicion that we, the male analysts, had been unable to overcome certain deeply-rooted prejudices against what was feminine, and this was being paid for in the partiality of our researchers."

He mentioned specifically Dr. Ruth Mack Brunswick who, in 1928, was the first to describe a case of female neurosis that went back to a "fixation" in the pre-Oedipal stage and took the form of "jealous paranoia." He also cited Dr. Jeanne Lampl de Groot who, in 1927, "established the incredible phallic activity of girls towards their mother," and Dr. Helene Deutsch, who, in 1932, "has shown that the erotic actions of homosexual women reproduce the relations between mother and baby." Deutsch's two-volume *The Psychology of Women* traced female sexual and emotional development from birth to old age.

Freud was also the first to study the sexual responses of women as reported by them, though he did this on an individual basis with his patients, rather than conducting wholesale surveys as is done today. He was the first scientist to care about discovering the difference between clitoral and vaginal responses and deserves recognition as a pioneer in this area of such paramount concern to women today. He described the various stages of sexual development and the trauma that could occur along the way and interfere with a woman's full sexuality.

He said the decisive "turning points" for a woman were "prepared or completed" before puberty. While a little girl might be "less aggressive, defiant and self-sufficient" than a boy, with a greater need for affection and more dependent, pliant, intelligent and lively than a boy her age, Freud declared that both sexes seemed to pass through the oral and anal phases in the same manner.

But when the phallic stage is entered, differences appear. They occur primarily in fantasies that surround the mystery of the penis and the clitoris. Freud said, "We are now obliged to recognize that the little girl is a little man," in that she thinks of her clitoris as "a little penis" when she discovers the existence of the latter organ in a boy, and imagines that someday she too will have one that size, when her clitoris grows.

He said, ". . . this little organ, the clitoris, does actually play during childhood and in the years before sexual intercourse the same part as the male organ" as the chief erotic zone. ". . . it is easy to observe that little girls are quite in agreement with their brothers' estimate [of the penis]. They develop a great interest in this part of a boy's body but this interest is at once dominated by jealousy. They feel themselves injured; they make attempts to urinate in the position that is possible to the boy by his possession of the big penis, and when they express the wish 'I should love to be a boy,' we know what lack the wish is to remedy."

For a woman to be "fully feminine," she has to give up the fantasy of possessing a penis and transfer her erotic feelings from the clitoris, where they started when she masturbated in earlier years, to the vagina.

In discussing childhood masturbation, Freud said neurotic patients seemed to think this responsible for all their troubles and "we have the greatest difficulty in persuading them that they are mistaken." He added, however, in one sense they were right: "masturbation is the executive agent of infantile sexuality, from the faulty development of which they are indeed suffering."

Neurotics blame their problems on the masturbation of puberty, which occurs at the age of eleven or twelve, having forgotten that of early infancy, "which is what is really in question," Freud said. He described three phases of infantile masturbation—early infantile masturbation, brief masturbatory activity about the age of four and masturbation during puberty. The masturbation of early childhood and "the more or less violent suppression of it" is attached to the Oedipus complex and serves as a discharge for erotic feelings aroused by the parent of the opposite sex, Freud said, or by a brother or sister.

Early masturbation may have an effect on later character or neurosis, depending on whether it was discovered, how the parents struggled against allowing it or forbidding it and whether the girl or boy succeeded in suppressing it alone. If, in a girl, envy for the penis provokes "a powerful impulse" against clitoral masturbation but this nevertheless refuses to give way, "a violent struggle for liberation ensues in which the girl, as it were, herself takes over the role of her deposed mother and gives expression to her entire dissatisfaction with her inferior clitoris in her efforts against obtaining satisfaction from it," Freud said. Many years later, when masturbatory activity has long since been suppressed, an interest still persists as a defense against "a temptation that is still dreaded." He added, "Disposing of early infantile masturbation is truly no easy or indifferent business."

Freud helped liberate men and women from the repression of Victorian sexual mores, part of which was a fanatical belief in the evils of masturbation, a subject on which much literature was written encouraging parents to forbid masturbation in their children. Parents made dire threats of mutilation to children, not only because religious leaders saw masturbation as morally wrong but also because the medical myths of the day insisted it would lead to insanity, syphilis of the brain and loss of physical energy.

Freud said he originally formed the impression that in general women tolerated masturbation "worse than men," that they more frequently fought against giving in to it and were unable "to make use of it in circumstances in which a man would seize upon it as a way of escape without any hesitation." It appeared to him, he said, as though masturbation were further removed from the nature of women than of men. This was explained, he added, by the fact that masturbation of the clitoris, a masculine activity (similar to the stroking of the penis), had to be eliminated as a necessary precondition for the development of femininity. Analyses of the remote phallic period taught him, he said, that in girls, soon after the first signs of penis envy, "an intense current of feeling against masturbation" makes its appearance, which cannot be attributed exclusively to parents forbidding it.

"This impulse is clearly a forerunner of the wave of repression which at puberty will do away with a large amount of the girl's masculine sexuality in order to make room for the development of her femininity," he explained. "It may happen that this first opposition to auto-erotic activity fails to attain its end . . . Many of the later manifestations of sexual life in women remain unintelligible unless this powerful motive is recognized."

He stated that anatomy had recognized the clitoris within the female pudenda "as an organ homologous to the penis, and the physiology of sexual processes has been able to add that this little penis which no longer grows behaves in the childhood of the woman like a genuine and real penis, that it is the site of excitations which leads to its being touched, that its excitability gives the sexual activity of little girls a male character, and that it needs an effort of repression in the years of puberty to make the woman develop through discarding this male sexuality."

Along with the abandonment of clitoral masturbation a certain amount of general activity is renounced, he said. Passivity gains the upper hand as the girl turns to her father principally with the help of the passive instinctual impulses. This wave of development clears the phallic activity out of the way and "smooths the ground for femininity." And, "if too much is not lost in the course of it through repression, this femininity may turn out to be normal."

But the "feminine situation" is only established, Freud warned, "if the wish for a penis is replaced by one for a baby, that is, a baby takes the place of a penis in accordance with an ancient symbolic equivalence." He was referring to the dolls a little girl first played with, saying this was not an expression of her femininity but identification with her mother aimed at substituting activity for passivity.

"*She* was playing the part of her mother and the doll was herself; now she could do with the baby everything that her mother used to do with her . . ." "Not until the emergence of the wish for a penis does the doll-baby become the baby she wishes from her father." And thereafter, "the aim of the most powerful feminine wish."

A woman's happiness is greater, Freud stated, if the wish for a baby finds fulfillment in reality and particularly if it is a son who brings "the longed-for penis with him." He described the mother-son relationship as "altogether the most perfect, the most free from ambivalence, of all human relationships."

When the clitoris is the little girl's chief erotic zone, one of her fantasies is that if it grows into a penis she can become the lover of her mother—her own first love—taking the place of her rival father. But when her erotic feelings center on her vagina, the feminine receptacle for a man's penis, her fantasies turn to love of her father and she proceeds on the way to sexual maturity.

"With the change to femininity the clitoris should wholly or in part hand over its sensitivity, and at the same time its importance, to the vagina," Freud said. The second "task" with which a girl's development is "burdened," he added, was to transfer her first love for her mother to someone of a different sex, her father. A boy's mother, the first object of his love, remains the same during the formation of the Oedipus complex, "and, in essence, all through his life," but a girl has to "find her way" from love of her mother to her father and then "to her final choice of an object."

The duration of a daughter's attachment to her mother has been "greatly underestimated," Freud wrote in "Female Sexuality." He speculated, ". . . many a woman may remain arrested at the original mother-attachment and never properly achieve the changeover to men." Which, he added, proved that the pre-Oedipal phase in women was more important than "hitherto supposed."

Then he made a statement that once again showed he could change his mind when the evidence suggested a different conclusion: "Since there is time during this phase for all the fixations and repressions which we regard as the source of the neuroses, it seems that we shall have to retract the universality of the dictum that the Oedipus complex is the nucleus of neurosis."

He added, "Our insight into this early pre-Oedipal phase in the little girl's development comes to us as a surprise, comparable in another field with the effect of the discovery of the Minoan-Mycenaean civilization behind that of Greece."

He suggested giving "due recognition" to the new findings by accepting that women reach the normal, positive Oedipal situation only after "surmounting" a first phase dominated by negative feelings toward the father. To a little girl her father is not much different from "a troublesome rival," even though her hostility does not reach the pitch of a boy's.

Opening the way to an area under study by today's psychoanalysts, Freud reported that he had established "some surprising facts" about women who remained "tenderly dependent" on their fathers or some other "paternal object" until a late age. In earlier papers he attributed this to a woman's strong attachment to her father. Now he said this was rooted in an original deep attachment for the mother, an attachment subsequently transferred to the father.

"In short, we get an impression that we cannot understand

women unless we appreciate this phase of their pre-Oedipus attachment to their mother," he said. This attachment included the girl's oral, sadistic-anal and phallic wishes, which represented her active as well as passive impulses, accompanied by feelings that were ambivalent—both affectionate and of a hostile, aggressive nature.

It is not always easy to point to a formulation of the little girl's early sexual wishes toward her mother, but what is most clearly expressed, Freud said, was "a wish to get the mother a child and the corresponding wish to bear her a child—both belonging to the phallic period and sufficiently surprising, but established beyond doubt by an analytic observation."

He described the mother as regularly "the seducer" in the girl's infantile life—in the course of tending to the child's bodily hygiene she "inevitably stimulated, and perhaps even roused for the first time, pleasurable sensations in the genitals." He added as answer to those who might object to this theory, "Enough can be seen in the children if one knows how to look."

This second step in a girl's sexual development does not involve only a simple change of object, Freud said. The girl's turning away from the mother is accompanied by great hostility—"the attachment for the mother ends in hate." The girl reproaches her mother for many things, some of her resentments common to children of both sexes, like not giving enough nourishment at the breast (every baby is insatiable) and having other babies (no child wants to share its mother's love). Intense jealousy is aroused each time a brother or sister is born, Freud said, "nor does it make much difference if the child happens to remain the mother's preferred favorite." He may have been speaking of his own feelings, since he was the oldest child and his mother's favorite but saw two brothers and five sisters follow him into the world and nurse at her breast.

A girl often hates her mother for forbidding pleasurable activity with the genitals. And in fantasy she holds her mother responsible for her lack of a penis and never forgives her mother for being "thus put at a disadvantage." Here a daughter's resentment is unique—a son has no such grudge. As Freud described it: " . . . daughters are apt to feel for their mothers a mixture of compassion, contempt and envy which does nothing to increase their tenderness for them."

When a girl discovers she lacks a penis, she blames her mother either for taking it from her or for creating her without that important part of bodily equipment. She hates her mother for making her a woman and also hates her mother because her mother is just like her own inferior self.

Freud's theory of penis envy came in for much criticism and skepticism from the very first. He maintained that when the phallic stage starts there is only one genital organ in the world for both boys and girls—the penis. At this age both sexes believe people are divided into two groups: those who have a penis and those who once had one but lost it. The girls, whom Freud described as "the little creature without a penis," is taken by surprise when she makes what Freud called "a momentous discovery." She notices the penis of her father or brother or a male playmate. She imagines that her clitoris was once a penis, which has been lost or taken away from her because she was "bad" (masturbated with incestuous fantasies). She then feels inferior because of the evident superiority of the penis to her own small and inconspicuous clitoris. From that time onward, said Freud she "falls a victim to envy for the penis," which "will leave eradicable traces on her development and formation of character" and which "will not be surmounted in even the most favorable cases without a severe expenditure of physical energy."

The little girl envies the facility with which her father and little boys urinate with the penis. "She has seen it and knows that she is without it and wants to have it," said Freud. He added that "shame, which is considered to be a feminine characteristic *par excellence* but is far more a matter of convention than might be supposed, has as its purpose, we believe, concealment of genital deficiency."

Many women deny this childhood wish, long repressed, conveniently forgetting dreams in which they see themselves as possessing a penis or imagining other women with a penis. It is difficult for them to remember the days when they may have been preoccupied with the penis. Studies of primitive man and woman show in what esteem they held the phallus; even today some tribes erect shrines to it, build phallic images to worship. And women have only to listen to the words of little girls who say wistfully, "I wish I were a boy," and imitate boys in their dress, games, way of walking and talking, to recognize female discontent with their physical equipment.

Recently a five-year-old girl, whose father had left home when she was two to remarry, was introduced to a man taking out her mother and said hesitantly, "I want to ask you something." And then, "No, I can't." She blushed and ran away.

Later the girl's mother, putting her to bed, asked what she had wanted to say to the man.

"I wanted to know if he had a thing—" and she touched her genitals—"like Bobby." Bobby was her eight-year-old brother.

Never having seen (or not remembering) the naked body of her father, she was trying to find out if men had penises like little boys and trying to puzzle through why she had none, only what Freud called "the stunted penis."

Another five-year-old girl, according to the report of her mother, was heard singing softly to herself, "Penis, penis, beautiful penis." And a four-year-old girl in a playground told a social worker, "I'm growing a penis under my arm so I can get everybody's attention." This desire for a penis, Freud said, survives long after all hope of getting one is extinguished. No fantasy ever disappears from the unconscious—though forgotten, it may remain operative there.

At first the little girl thinks she is the only one on earth without a penis, then she realizes that other little girls have none, and finally, blow of blows, that even her mother lacks a penis. Little girls and little boys believe originally in the phallic mother and may spend many anxious moments trying to discover if their mother has a penis.

A psychoanalyst told this writer of a little girl of six who would go into her mother's bedroom, open the drawers of her bureau and search endlessly for what she called "treasures." She was unconsciously searching her mother's other "drawers" to find out if her mother possessed the coveted penis.

A little girl's love, Freud said, is directed to her *phallic mother* and when she discovers her mother is "castrated," it becomes possible for her, though disillusioned, to drop her mother as a love object. So the motives for hostility, which have long accumulated, "gain the upper hand." Femininity becomes "debased in value" for her, just as it does for boys "and later perhaps for men," he said.

But the little girl's anger at her mother for lacking a penis enables her to turn from her mother to her father in the hope that *he* will give her the penis he obviously possesses. Freud called this the start of the Oedipus complex. When this hope is also shattered, the little girl adopts a passive, "feminine" attitude and substitutes the wish to have a baby by her father for the wish to have his penis. All this is part of natural development, leading to the eventual resolution of the Oedipal complex when the girl's wish for a baby is transferred to a man outside the family.

Freud said the discovery "that she is castrated" may lead to one of three possible lines of development in a girl's life: sexual inhibition or neurosis; change of character of a masculine nature; normal femininity.

Women who cannot give up the wish for a penis will continue in fantasy to think of the clitoris as a penis. They will not have been able to transfer the sexual zone of excitement to the vagina, thus remaining suspended in childhood sexuality.

Freud warned that the hope of someday obtaining a penis and thus becoming like a man, in spite of knowing otherwise, may persist in a woman "to an incredibly late age and may become a motive for the strangest and otherwise unaccountable actions." Without negating Freud's theories, Dr. Rebecca Z. Solomon, president of the American Psychoanalytic Association, said in her paper, "From the Viewpoint of a Woman," that the intensity of a girl's penis envy will depend on whether she feels deprived in other ways and on the value placed on the one who possesses a penis. "If she and her mother have been valued by her father, if her father does not demand deferential treatment and if the mother values herself, the lack of a penis will not be especially troublesome," Solomon stated. "If on the other hand, the possessor of a penis is accorded special power and prestige, her envy will persist."

Some degree of penis envy is inevitable in girls, Solomon said, just as boys are inevitably concerned about the size of their penises. "It is not merely the presence or absence of the penis which has an impact on psychic functioning but the fantasies associated with it—the meaning and value attributed to it," that has an influence on development. The penis can be viewed "as a magic symbol of power or it can be viewed as an organ which is a source of great pleasure and which also serves excretory and reproductive functions."

Psychoanalysts have observed that from an early age men and women "highly invest" emotionally in the penis. But the power attributed to it is gradually modified, Solomon said, though it always retains a certain magical quality. The degree of magic a woman attributes to the penis "will influence the value which a woman places on herself in relation to men and will be reflected in her thought and behavior in many ways."

In the past, she pointed out, women did not have the opportunity to demonstrate their worth and the superior status accorded to men was based on their achievements, attributed to their biology. But as opportunities have been equalized and accomplishments of women have become comparable to those of men, the importance of biology has receded.

Contemporary women can choose from a much greater variety of occupations than their predecessors and also have greater freedom in choosing whether or not to have children. With these choices come conflicts. Solomon warns, "We must eschew stereotypes. It is no more appropriate to urge a woman to pursue a career in line with so-called feminist aspirations than it is to persuade her to accept the 'traditional role.' Women cannot be characterized as passive, dependent, nurturant, intuitive and submissive, to name a few of the so-called feminine characteristics, nor men as active, independent, aggressive and logical. These characteristics are found in varying combinations in both men and women. All persons struggle with passive longings, wishes to care for others, desires for self-assertion, the need to contain aggression and the maintenance of self-esteem. We must be ever mindful of the tyranny of stereotypes and the psychic pain which has resulted from attempts of persons to fit themselves into molds of what they think they should be rather than to recognize and cultivate what they are and can be."

In accordance with Freud's theory of sexual development, the woman who is frigid—whether a career woman or a housewife—unconsciously still wants to be a man. She is taking revenge on the man she envies and to whom she transfers her original wish that her father give her a penis, by not giving herself to him sexually. Frigidity has varying degrees of intensity. Acute anesthesia, where the vaginal mucuous membrane has lost all sensitivity to touch so that penetration by the penis is actually denied, is rare. In most cases some sensation of pleasure is felt, but the woman does not proceed to orgasm.

Many prostitutes are frigid. The woman who uses sex as a business is unconsciously seeking to humiliate and castrate men, Freud said, to take revenge on her father for not giving her a penis. Each time the man ejaculates she has the fantasy she has taken his penis from him, and for the moment it becomes hers.

For the lesbian, sexual pleasure is possible only if no penis is involved. The homosexual woman fears penetration by a man, the sight of male genitals reminds her of her fantasy that she once had them but was maimed or mutilated (castrated). She also fears her desire to castrate men, to take the penis from them.

If a mother, perhaps out of jealousy, shows extreme disapproval of a girl's yearning for her father during the Oedipal stage, the girl, to keep the love of her mother, may give up the idea of sex with a man. Also, if the mother and father stress too much their feelings that a boy is preferable to a girl, the girl may never give up her wish to be a boy.

In his treatment of a young lesbian Freud said that her analysis revealed "beyond all shadow of doubt" that the older woman she had selected as her lover "was a substitute for—the mother." She had searched "for a mother-substitute to whom she could become passionately attached." Freud said that in this young woman's "actual relations with her mother," there was a practical motive which might be called an "advantage through illness." He said the mother herself still attached great value to the attentions and the admiration of men, and thus if the girl became homosexual and left men to her mother, "in other words, 'retired in favor of' the mother," she would be more likely to earn her mother's love.

Sometimes this applies to a father who is intensely jealous of a daughter who then feels that, to keep her father's love, she dare not have sex with another man. She turns to women to appease her father, saying, See, I love only you, have no fear that I will ever love another man.

A moving story of a woman's wish for a penis was presented by

Princess Marie Bonaparte in her article, "The Case of Madame Lefebvre." Bonaparte tells how she visited Madame Lafebvre, convicted of murder, in prison, persuaded her to talk about the crime and her feelings. The murder, committed in 1925, aroused international excitement. Madame Lefebvre was a wealthy, respectable, quiet woman, the mother of two grown sons, who inexplicably shot her daughter-in-law through the left temple when she became pregnant.

Why did this staid, prim woman commit murder? Bonaparte interviewed the convicted murderess in prison, then interpreted the unconscious motives for her crime. Bonaparte asked: "What did Madame Lefebvre feel her daughter-in-law stole from her that was so precious she had to kill her to avenge the thievery?" And answered: Madame Lefebvre killed her daughter-in-law when the latter became pregnant because she could not tolerate the idea that her daughter-in-law should have, from her own son, what she herself lacked, a child, which to her unconscious meant a penis. The coming birth revived in her feelings that had been present at the birth of her own son, which unconsciously meant the acquiring of a penis. Her daughter-in-law had not only taken her son (penis) from her but was also getting a second penis in the expected child, while she, the deprived mother, was left with none.

Bonaparte pointed out that a little girl must resign herself to the permanent lack of a phallus, accept that she never had one and never will get one, which Madame Lefebvre was unable to do. Her childhood anger at not having a penis finally exploded when she was driven, in a fury she never understood, to murder the daughter-in-law who had done her an imagined wrong.

Bonaparte also concluded that on a conscious level Madame Lefebvre committed the murder because of jealousy: "The Oedipal nature of Mme. Lefebvre's crime—in her case reversed, not Oedipus but Jocasta—is so obvious that the fact that the word 'incest' was never once pronounced during the trial and not even in the series of interviews with doctors, lawyers and psychologists published in *Figaro*, shows how deep is the horror incest inspires in the mind of man."

One can only speculate that Madame Lefebvre's childhood held such psychic disturbances that she was unable to cope with the wish for a penis. In families where the mother and father openly prefer a son, the little girl desires a penis for the additional reason that she thinks her mother will love her more if she has one. She may also fantasize that if she had a penis she could give her mother a baby, prove her father is not needed and have her mother all to herself. Freud pointed out, as mentioned earlier, that the little girl may also have the fantasy of stealing her father's penis not only for genital satisfaction and power but also to replace the mother's breast, now denied her. She has impulses to suck, eat and swallow the penis as an act of love, as she once had similar impulses toward the breast.

A girl may even imagine that during the sexual act her mother takes her father's penis into her body and hides it there. She may want to break into her mother's body and steal it from her. There is no limit to what a child may fantasize in the attempt to understand the mysteries of life and include most of all the answer to the question, "Where do babies come from?"

Freud said that some psychoanalysts boasted that in the years they had worked with patients they had never found a sign of the castration complex. Commented Freud, with his famed irony, "We must bow our heads in recognition of the greatness of this achievement, even though it is only a negative one, a piece of virtuosity in the art of overlooking and mistaking. The two theories form an interesting pair of opposites: in one of them not a trace of castration complex, in the other nothing at all but its effects."

The true sense of any feeling of "inferiority" is an erotic one, Freud held. If a man feels inferior, it means he fears he is inadequate sexually. If a woman feels inferior, it means she feels unworthy because she has no penis.

He said: "After a woman has become aware of the wound to her narcissism [that she does not possess a penis] she develops, like a scar, a sense of inferiority." When she has passed beyond her first attempt at explaining her lack of a penis as "punishment personal to herself" and realizes that it is a characteristic of the sex, "she begins to share the contempt felt by men for a sex which is the lesser in so important a respect, and, at least in holding that opinion, insists on being like a man."

Dr. Bernard Brodsky, president of the New York Psychoanalytic Institute, has suggested that penis envy may not be the cause of the girl's jealousy of boys, that it merely aggravates an envy already present. Intense penis envy may mirror breast envy, which is perhaps the forerunner of penis envy, he points out. The difference in degree of penis envy is very great, and may depend on the depth of early pre-Oedipal problems.

The fantasy that she has been wounded and thus deprived of a penis is newly confirmed for girls by their first and all subsequent menstrual periods and later by defloration, both connected to loss of blood, Freud said. In his essay, "The Taboo of Virginity," he cited the custom of certain primitive people who forbid a bridegroom to deflorate his bride. Defloration was accomplished by a priest as a sacramental act, or by an older woman, either through manual or instrumental means, or by an act of intercourse. This prevented the bride from hating her husband for shedding her blood and causing pain, which would keep her from having a satisfactory erotic life with him.

The menstrual period can either be interpreted by a girl as evidence of damage, in which case she will fear and hate the monthly periods, calling them "the curse," or welcomed as a sign of approaching womanhood and independence and the chance to eventually move away from her parents.

At the time a little girl becomes disillusioned with both her parents, whom she originally idolized, discovering they are not "perfect," there develops in her a fantasy Freud described as "the family romance." She believes her mother and father are not worthy of her and imagines she was stolen in infancy from her real parents—who were of noble and exalted nature—and brought up instead by these plebian people.

The early stage of this romance, Freud said, takes place before the little girl is aware of sexual intercourse. The later stage occurs after she knows about sex between her mother and father and imagines herself in erotic situations. Her fantasies are more palatable if she can imagine them as taking place not within her own family, with whom sex is taboo, but in a different family.

"Girls with an exaggerated need for affection," Freud said, "and an equally exaggerated horror of the real demands made by sexual life have an irresistible temptation on the one hand to realize the ideal of asexual love in their lives and on the other hand to conceal their libido behind an affection which they can express without self-reproaches, by holding fast throughout their lives to their infantile fondness, revived at puberty, for their parents or brothers or sisters."

At every stage in the course of development through which all human beings "ought by rights to pass," a certain number are held back, he said. They have never "got over their parents' authority and have withdrawn their affection from them either very incompletely or not at all."

These are "mostly girls, who, to the delight of their parents, have persisted in all their childish love far beyond puberty." It is "precisely these girls who in their later marriage lack the capacity to give their husbands what is due to them; they make cold wives and remain sexually anesthetic." He might also have added the large number of women who never marry, who are still looking for the elusive Prince Charming.

It is essential to a woman's happiness that she give up the overvaluation of parents, a fantasy of the early years of every child, and accept a more realistic view of her mother and father. If she does not, even if she marries, she will overvalue her husband at first and when he fails to live up to her highly distorted image of him, will turn on him in hate.

A woman's choice of husband is often made in accordance with the narcissistic ideal of the man the girl had wished to become, Freud said. He noted that the second half of a woman's life may be characterized by a struggle against her husband, just as the shorter first half was characterized by rebellion against her mother. Threatened by becoming a mother herself, she may re-experience an identification with her own mother against which she had always fought, resulting in the compulsion to repeat her parents' unhappy marriage in her own.

Freud further said that a woman's identification with her mother has two strata: the pre-Oedipal one that rests on "her affectionate attachment to her mother and takes her as a model," and the later one, from the Oedipus stage, "which seeks to get rid of her mother and take her place with her father."

Neither may be adequately "surmounted" in the course of development. Freud called the phase of the "affectionate" attachment the decisive one for a woman's future. During it preparations are made for the acquiring of the characteristics which the little girl will later fulfill in her sexual role and perform in her "invaluable social tasks." In this identification she acquires sexual appeal for a man, whose Oedipal attachment to his mother, Freud said, "kindles it into passion . . . How often it happens, however, that it is only his son who obtains what he himself aspired to! One gets an impression that a man's love and a woman's are a phase apart psychologically." As perhaps they were in Freud's relationship with his wife in connection with their three sons and three daughters.

Surgical operations of any nature, but particularly hysterectomies, removal of cysts and tumors, other vaginal operations, and mastectomies, may revive a woman's early fantasy of genital mutilation and deprivation of a penis. If a breast is lost, she may have the unconscious fantasy of mutilating not only her own body but that of her mother, destroying the "bad" mother of infancy—the operation being her punishment for early infant anger.

Psychoanalysis often reveals to women their wish for a penis, among other fantasies of early life. A successful woman artist could not control the habit, as she lay on the couch (and sometimes in her life outside), of putting her hand to her left eye every so often in a quick, anguished gesture, as though to cut off its vision. Also, when she looked at people, she usually gazed into the left eye, ignoring the right. One day she told the analyst about her grandmother, to whom she had been very close until age five, when the grandmother died. This grandmother had lost her left eye in an automobile accident when the little girl was a year old. During the analysis she came to realize that she put her hand over her left eye every time a painful feeling arose. She was unconsciously identifying with her beloved grandmother in closing off sight in that eye. In a sense she was trying to bring back her beloved grandmother whenever she suffered pain because she believed her grandmother had loved her more than her parents did, would often comfort her when she felt hurt.

But why did she choose the eye, of all bodily organs, to symbolize her wish? One morning she was talking to her analyst about a painting she had submitted to an art gallery, hoping it would be accepted and sold during an important art show. Her hand automatically went to her left eye.

"What are you thinking of?" the analyst asked.

"I'm afraid the gallery will reject my painting and I'll feel worthless instead of on the top of the world, as I do when someone likes my work," she said.

Then she said quietly, "It's as though when I'm successful in my work, I am a man, I have—a penis. If I fail in my work, I'm not a man, I'm just a deprived female, and then I'm miserable." She had discussed her envy of men in previous therapy sessions, but only now did she connect this wish with the seemingly unrelated impulse to cover her left eye.

She placed her hand over her left eye at moments she felt mental pain because she was a woman. She equated the eye being put out (as her grandmother's had been) with being feminine and castrated. Whenever her unconscious wish to be a man became endangered she signaled this fear, indicating symbolically the missing penis by putting her hand over her eye—an eye literally missing in her grandmother.

Her gesture was founded in what Freud called "a fragment" of historical fact. It was not a random gesture, it had specific meaning to her unconscious—and now her conscious—indicating not only a painful experience in her life but a childhood fantasy that was still powerful.

Freud's theory of the oral, anal, phallic and genital phases in sexual development in women and of female penis envy still holds true, but to them has been added a concept he often mentioned but did not work through in detail—a girl's identification with her mother and the extent to which unconscious and conscious fantasies about her mother affect her femininity.

Psychoanalysts are discovering, in studying the first years of life, that a girl's sexual development takes place within an emotional relationship to her mother and father, one that may either be destructive or constructive. If a little girl has a physically or psychologically (or both) cruel mother or father, this may intensify her normal wish during the phallic stage to have a penis—be a boy and powerful so she can someday take revenge on her harsh parents.

Psychoanalysts today also consider that a little girl's femininity is formed in large part—consciously and unconsciously—by her mother's attitudes about being a woman. The mother conveys to her daughter the way she feels about her body, principally the genitals, as well as all her feelings about the feminine sex.

The women's liberation movement has made an issue of the clitoral orgasm, claiming it is sufficient for a woman to achieve this: she does not need to be able to experience the vaginal orgasm in order to feel feminine. This is in direct opposition to Freud's theory that a woman cannot be "fully feminine" unless she transfers her erotic zone from the clitoris to the vagina.

Psychoanalysts say a woman should enjoy clitoral orgasms and that stimulation of the clitoris is an important part of foreplay, but if *the only way* a woman wishes orgasm is through the stimulation of her clitoris, she has not achieved femininity—she is showing that she fears penetration by the penis. She is unconsciously afraid that during sex she will be torn apart, perhaps even killed. This fear is based on her childhood fantasy that sex is a brutal act in which a man assaults a woman—the horror of rape. Men cannot be raped because they cannot be forced to have an erection. But a woman can be penetrated against her will and rape is often physically as well as emotionally painful.

Some psychoanalysts believe a woman is not fulfilling herself if she denies the urge to have a child, which Freud said was the strongest feminine instinct. The human race would soon be extinct if every woman decided the clitoral orgasm was enough. Survival of the species depends on woman's desire for vaginal penetration, which hopefully results in orgasm for the woman as well as the man. Lesbians find it easier to bring their sexual partners to climax through stimulation of the clitoris than of the vagina. The lesbians' fear of vaginal orgasms—both having them and giving them—is related to their fear of penetration by the man's penis.

The physiological responses to either the vaginal or clitoral orgasm are no indicator of what goes on at a psychological level, according to Dr. Walter A. Stewart, author of *Psychoanalysis: The First Ten Years.* Declaring that the relationship of vaginal sensitivity to emotional maturity is a complex one, he says that Freud's formulations "unfortunately equate behavior, that is, vaginal orgasm, with psychological maturity." Potency is popularly defined in terms of "performance," he says. In a woman this means the frequency of sexual activity and the number of orgasms she can have in one night, and in a man the capacity to control the tempo, such as delaying his orgasm to satisfy the woman, or to have multiple ejaculations. "But the central issue of potency is not performance, it is the pleasure derived from the sexual experience, which includes awareness of the other person as distinct from his being a sexual object," says Stewart.

He points out that there are some women for whom the need to have vaginal orgasms includes the wish to be perfect, and that to others the lack of orgasm stands for a general feeling of deprivation, a suffering they inflict on themselves for fantasized wrongs committed against others.

Two important papers devoted to the further understanding of feminine psychology were presented at the Thirty-First Biennial Congress of the International Psychoanalytical Association held in New York in August 1979. The main topic of the congress, attended by 2,500 delegates representing thirty-six countries, was "Clinical Issues in Psychoanalysis."

Defining psychoanalysis as "an effort to reach a scientific understanding of the function of the psyche," Colette Chiland, a leading French psychoanalyst, added that she did not understand what brought Freud to write "the little girl is a little man," in spite of everything his daily observation showed him. She said that Freud was hindered, on the one hand, by his conception of the relationship between biological and psychological fields and, on the other hand, by the fact that he listened with another ear to his male patients: what they said was in tune with his own experience of self-analysis. Of femininity he could scarcely imagine anything— "except how a man would feel if he were transformed into a woman—a thought that inspired some degree of horror." Freud "moved back before the identification with a woman, which for him entailed a narcissistic danger"—to identify with a woman in order to understand her "was to identify with a castrated being." Therefore, she felt, he was not able to discover the deep range of feminine feelings or to share a woman's special problems.

Each culture has defined its own concept of masculinity and femininity, Chiland pointed out: "There is practically no quality, no attitude, no behavior, no task, which has not been deemed at one time or another masculine or feminine." There are differences between the sexes, she said, giving as examples penis envy for women and envy of the female's ability to give birth and have multiple orgasms for men. Each sex is disappointed in certain respects when it comes to childhood fantasies that evolve from the special envies.

Womanhood, in the sense of what women possess as women, is not a purely "negative content," as Freud presented it, but rather an "uncertain content." According to Chiland: "The vagina is no more and no less a hole and a wound than the penis is a bone or a weapon." Freud failed to give a "positive content" to femininity; he did not recognize that "to be a girl is to be a woman like her mother," Chiland said. "A girl is assured of her identity, of her belonging to the same sex as her mother. Her mother, her father, let her know it through their feelings and their behavior, even before language reminds her of it constantly. And these verbal and pre-verbal messages from her parents prevail over biological pressures."

She added that "a remarkable point considering penis envy" is that trans-sexualism is much rarer in women than in men, despite the fact that the universality and strength of penis envy might be expected to push girls in that direction. A girl who envies the penis does not necessarily wish to become a boy, she may want to go on being what she is and also have what the boy has, along with the narcissistic, social and "relational" advantages that go with the penis. "To have no penis can be a narcissistic wound, but to be no longer what you are is a total narcissistic failure," she said. "The sacrifice of the sex organ is a defense by delusion against the loss of the limits of the body, against annihilation." She concluded that though we cannot, in the strict sense of the term, "be in the place of another," we can try to "imagine ourselves in his place," helped by what the other person communicates about his experiences: "From one sex to another there will always be something that cannot be experienced in the body."

The second paper on feminine psychology delivered at the

Thirty-First Congress, "Reconsideration of Aggression and Self-Esteem in Women," had four authors: Dr. Joan Zilbach, Dr. Malkah T. Notman, Dr. Carol C. Nadelson and Dr. Jean Baker-Miller. They stated that there is evidence of sexual differences in the development of the nervous system and in hormonal balance between boys and girls, but also cited growing evidence that parents have different expectations of a girl than of a boy and behave differently toward male and female infants, which has a strong psychic effect on the child.

Since the little girl needs and depends on parental love, help and approval, and desires to live up to parental expectations and standards which she accepts for herself, "the state of parental self-esteem and self-image are as critical as are the communications on the part of parents about what attitudes and behaviors are valued." Major influences on the development of self-esteem in a woman include both her original narcissism and feelings of omnipotence that come from her instinctual urges and identifications with her mother and father and the attitudes she absorbs from them.

Little girls are discouraged from expressing the aggressive feelings that are rewarded in a boy, so that when the girls become women they experience and think of aggression as an act of destructive force, "inevitably carrying the implication of the intent to hurt or destroy another. When women begin to recognize their own aggression it is most likely to be experienced as disorganizing and overwhelming, adding to fear and self-condemnation. Women continue to experience their impulses, desires and moves toward action as 'bad'." The result is often depression.

Insistence on their own inadequacy is frequently seen in women and these protestations may cover the desire and ability to use potential strengths, the authors pointed out. Passivity and helplessness, painful as they appear, "may serve to hide the more threatening internal perceptions of aggression." For many women, even to acknowledge the existence of aggression becomes extremely threatening. "The woman who sees herself as aggressive feels she is a failure, inadequate and inferior and her self-esteem is consequently lowered," the authors summed up. "Women's aggression is regarded with horror and dread. The terrifying destructive violence of Medea stands as a symbol of this fear."

They further pointed out that in Freud's early formulation of sexual and self-preservation instincts, each instinct had an aggressive component. The inclusion of aggression in both instincts may be understood as a reflection of the crucial nature of the aggressive instinct, which Freud finally formulated as a separate instinct in 1923. The authors added that the detachment or disentanglement of aggression from sexuality, making aggression "separate and equal" with a full instinctual rationale of its own, is still in progress.

Freud said, "Analysis of children's play has shown our women analysts that the aggressive impulses of little girls leave nothing to be desired in the way of abundance and violence." With the "liberation" of women has come a release of aggressive feelings, some constructive, some destructive. For one thing women are expressing more violence—as shown by crime statistics. They are also more active in making their own decisions and competing with men in careers, the creative arts and the business and political worlds.

At the same time the changing female role has led to increased inner conflicts in the lives of many women. There is the growing independence of the young woman who leaves her parents at an earlier age but is aroused by anxieties over the separation. The sexual freedom accorded women may revive the unresolved Oedipal conflicts. Any crisis facing a woman may reveal the failure of an earlier developmental period. She may then show symptoms Freud described in relation to the thwarting of the sexual drive—promiscuity, lesbianism, frigidity, psychosomatic illnesses—as well as aberrations in the aggressive drive.

Freud has also been taken severely to task for saying that woman's superego was not as strong as man's, that women have less capacity for sublimation than men, and "little sense of justice." He related the latter "to the predominance of envy [for the penis] in their mental life; for the demand for justice is a modification of envy and lays down the condition subject to which one can put envy aside."

Most contemporary psychoanalysts agree with Freud's theories about the sexual development of the woman, including penis envy. But they consider that the latter is part of the phallic stage and becomes a problem in later life only to those women who have had difficult relationships with their mothers and fathers.

If a little girl's first years have been fairly serene, if she has been helped through the normal hazards of childhood by a loving mother aware of her daughter's needs and a father who is protective and caring, the penis envy phase will be accepted, then suppressed and she will proceed to the genital stage with ease.

She will be able to cherish and love a man not only for his physical attributes but out of friendship and respect for what he is, the way he thinks and feels about her, himself and others. She will want him not as an appendage, the desired penis of girlhood, but as mate and father of her child. Her affectionate, tender feelings will merge with her erotic ones.

But what of the special difficulties that face a man? How does his childhood differ sexually from that of a woman, according to Freud's discoveries?

6

The Boy is Father to the Man

A little girl believes she has already lost her penis and all that is left is the clitoris, but a little boy lives in perpetual fear that he will lose his penis whenever his parents accuse him of being "bad" or he feels guilty about his sexual or aggressive wishes.

This terror of castration develops to an intense degree when a boy "desires his mother and would like to get rid of his father as being a rival," said Freud. The Oedipal period, which Freud called a natural development of the phallic stage, starts at about the age of three or four, when a child is "capable of choosing a love object."

It is the fear of castration that "compels" the boy to give up his desire to possess his mother, Freud stated: "Under the impression of the danger of losing his penis, the Oedipus complex is abandoned, repressed and, in the most normal cases, entirely destroyed, and a severe superego is set up as its heir."

Freud published only six lengthy case histories. Two dealt with the fear of castration in boys. The first, known as "The Little Hans Case," published in 1909, runs 134 pages. Freud titled it "Analysis

158

of a Phobia in a Five-Year-Old Boy." It marked the first therapeutic application of psychoanalysis to a child and the first chance of checking by direct observation conclusions Freud had reached about infantile sexuality drawn from his observation of adult patients.

Freud saw the boy only once, when he "took a direct share" in the treatment, which was actually carried out by the boy's father, a physician. Freud had treated the mother before she was married and the father had attended Freud's first lectures. Freud said that it was only because the authority of a father and of a physician were united in a single person, and "because in him both affectionate care and scientific interest were combined, that it was possible in this one instance to apply the method to a use to which it would not otherwise have lent itself."

He said of this case and its importance, "Surely there must be a possibility of observing upon the child at first hand and in all the freshness of life the sexual impulses and conative tendencies which we dig out so laboriously in the adult from among their own débris —especially as it is also our belief that they are the common property of all men, a part of the human constitution, and merely exaggerated or distorted in the case of neurotics."

Little Hans had developed a phobia that became an anxiety state when he was four and three-quarters years old, nine months after the birth of a baby sister. He refused to go out into the street because he was terrified that a horse would bite him.

Freud described the boy as an exceptionally attractive and intelligent child, genuinely fond of his father. Both the mother and father were in the habit of "taking him into their bed, though actually only occasionally, but there can be no doubt that lying beside them had aroused erotic feelings in him," Freud said, adding, "Lying in bed with his father or mother was a source of erotic feelings in Hans just as it is in every other child."

He traces Little Hans' fear of horses to fear of his father, and his belief that the horses would "bite" him to the belief that his father would castrate him because of his erotic feelings for his very seductive mother. Once, when Hans was three and a half, his mother had actually threatened him with castration. She had found him "with his hand to his penis" and had said, "If you do that, I shall send for Dr. A. to cut off your widdler," the name Little Hans gave his penis. Such threats were commonly made by German—and other—women to masturbating sons in those days.

This threat was made three quarters of a year before Hans' phobia about horses appeared. The phobia became intensified after the birth of his sister, when he had a chance to observe that she lacked a penis. Freud said Little Hans was convinced his mother had one and he was afraid of a man's "big penis"—obviously that of his father, whom he had many a chance to observe in his night-clothes since he slept in his parents' bedroom until he was four.

Freud interpreted Little Hans' fear of castration to the father, who in turn was able to reassure Little Hans in a continuous calm way that he was safe from any such act. Gradually the boy lost his fear of horses. Freud said that as a result of the analysis Little Hans recovered—he ceased to be afraid of horses and "got on rather friendly terms with his father."

It was in this case history that Freud made the point that analysis does not undo the "effects" of repression, for the instincts that were formerly repressed remain repressed, but the same effects are produced in a different way. He said analysis replaces the process of repression, an automatic and excessive one, "by a temperate and purposeful control on the part of the highest mental faculties [i.e., suppression by the ego]. In a word, *analysis replaces repression by condemnation*" (italics Freud's). He added: "This seems to bring us the long-looked-for evidence that consciousness has a biological function, and that with its entrance upon the scene an important advantage is secured."

Freud added a note to this case when it was reprinted in 1923, reporting that the study of the castration complex had been further developed in contributions by other psychoanalysts. He referred to the theory that every time a mother's breast was withdrawn from a baby he was bound to feel it as castration, the loss of what he regards as an important part of his own body.

Another contribution, said Freud, was the theory that the act of birth, consisting as it does of the separation of the baby from his mother, "is the prototype of all castration."

"While recognizing all of these roots of the complex, I have nevertheless put forward the view that the term 'castration complex' ought to be confined to those excitations and effects which are bound up with the loss of the penis . . . in the case of little Hans the threat of castration is reported by his parents themselves, and moreover at a date before there was any question of his phobia."

The second case dealing with castration fears, called "From the History of an Infantile Neurosis," published in 1918, was a 132-page essay. The patient was twenty-three years old when he first came to Freud. He was the son of a very wealthy landowner in Odessa, who had died and left him a fortune. But he had become incapacitated and undergone various treatments, including shock and hydrotherapy at several sanitaria. On the advice of a doctor who had accompanied him to Vienna, he went to Freud.

This case became known as the "Wolfman" because of the patient's recurring nightmare in which "six or seven white wolves" sat on the branches of a tree outside his bedroom waiting to eat him. Ernest Jones says the case history is "assuredly the best" Freud ever wrote, that he was then "at the very height of his powers, a confident master of his method, and the technique he displays in the interpretation and synthesis of the incredibly complex material must win every reader's admiration."

It was essentially the study of a childhood neurosis made through the psychoanalysis of an adult neurosis. As he reconstructed crucial scenes of infancy, Freud clearly revealed how early fantasies can influence the course of a life and later mental and physical symptoms.

When the "Wolfman" first came to Freud at the beginning of February, 1910, he was helpless, accompanied by the doctor and a valet because he was unable even to dress himself. His health had broken down in his eighteenth year, after he suffered a gonorrheal infection.

He had lived, according to Freud, an "approximately normal life" during the ten years of boyhood preceding the date of his illness, getting through high school without difficulty. But his childhood was dominated by a severe neurotic disturbance, which Freud said changed into "an obsessional neurosis with a religious content, and lasted with its offshoots as far as into his tenth year."

Freud discussed only the infantile neurosis. He said he was of the opinion that *"the influence of childhood makes itself felt even in the situation at the beginning of the formation of a neurosis, since it plays a decisive part in determining whether and at what point the individual shall fail to master the real problems of life"* (italics Freud's).

He chose the case, he disclosed, to show that neurosis in later life is preceded by a neurosis in early childhood, caused by "instinctual trends which the child cannot satisfy and which it is not old enough to master, and the sources from which these trends arise."

As a child the patient was aware that his father suffered such deep attacks of depression that he often had to live in a sanitarium, where the boy's mother took him and his sister to visit. The mother was not well either, suffering severe abdominal attacks and hemorrhages. She left her two children primarily in the care of nurses and governesses on the family's large estate in Odessa.

The man told Freud that he remembered being four years old and holding his mother's hand as she walked her doctor to the station, lamenting her condition. "I cannot go on living like this," she used to say, making a lasting impression on her son (both his parents were very depressed). His sister, two years older, was lively, gifted and sexually precocious, and he believed that his father, who at first had loved him best, began to show an unmistakable preference for her. Whereupon he felt very slighted. Freud commented, "His fear of his father was the strongest motive for his falling ill, and his ambivalent attitude toward every father surrogate was the dominating feature of his life as well as of his behavior during the treatment."

This man's phobia, first appearing at the age of four, was the fear of a picture in a storybook showing a wolf "standing upright and striding along." Whenever he saw this picture the patient "began to scream like a lunatic that he was afraid of the wolf coming and eating him up." His sister often succeeded in arranging it so he was obliged to see the picture, showing delight at his terror. He was also frightened of other animals, large and small, as well as butterflies, beetles and caterpillars, though he recalled there was an even earlier time in his life when he stepped on beetles and cut up caterpillars. Like Little Hans, the "Wolfman" found that horses gave him "an uncanny feeling." If a horse was beaten, he began to scream, and once had to leave a circus when a horse walked into the ring.

He then became obsessed with religion, going through what Freud called "an easily recognizable attack of obsessional neurosis." When he was four and a half his mother read the Bible to him and he turned pious. Before going to sleep each night he prayed and repeatedly blessed himself with the sign of the cross. He would also make the rounds of holy pictures that hung on the walls of the house, moving around a chair on which he would climb and kiss each picture devoutly.

When he was eight years old suddenly all the obsessional acts disappeared. Freud asked, "What was the origin of the sudden change in the boy's character? What was the significance of his phobia and of his perversities? How did he arrive at his obsessive piety? And how are all these phenomena interrelated?"

Freud answered these questions during the man's four year analysis as he talked of his childhood. He recalled that when he was three and a quarter years old his sister had taken hold of his penis and played with it. At the same time she told him his beloved nurse did the same thing with the gardener, which he did not believe. Freud said the sister's seduction was no fantasy—when the patient was older, a cousin told him he remembered "what a forward and sensual little thing" his sister had been, that "once, when she was a child of four or five, she had sat on his lap and opened his trousers to take hold of his member."

Freud said of his patient that "a hostility toward women, due to his seduction by his sister, found strong expression at this time. And it was destined to disturb him often enough in his later erotic life. His sister came to be the permanent embodiment for him of temptation and sin . . . he was obliged to keep on reproducing the fact of his seduction over and over again."

But during his fourteenth year the "Wolfman" became close to his sister, and from then on they got along like the best of friends. Once he even tried to become sexually intimate, but she rejected him. He then turned to a little peasant girl, a servant in the house with the same name as his sister.

When the sister reached her early twenties she suffered deep depressions and finally, one day far from home, took a fatal dose of poison. Freud said he thought she probably was at the beginning of a psychosis.

When he learned of his sister's death, the "Wolfman" felt hardly a trace of grief, he told Freud. He had to force himself to show signs of sorrow, rejoiced at now being the sole heir to the family fortune. But a few months later he sought out the grave of a famous poet and "shed bitter tears," remembering his father had compared his dead sister's writings with this poet's—thus displacing his grief, Freud said.

The man also recalled that after his sister's attempted seduction he began "to play with his member" in the presence of his nurse. Freud said that in such instances, where children do not attempt to conceal their masturbation, it should be regarded as a kind of seduction. His nurse rebuffed him, said what he did was "not good" and he would be punished by a "wound" in that place—his first threat of castration.

He then started to think of his father, his admired role-model, as a sexual object. He tried, by throwing temper tantrums, to force his father to beat him—he wanted a masochistic sexual satisfaction. Freud said that the father had the not uncommon characteristic of indulging in "affectionate abuse" toward his son and he may have threatened jokingly, as he caressed the little boy or played with him, to "gobble him up." The "Wolfman" was very afraid of his father, at the same time yearning for him erotically.

Shortly after this, the patient watched his sister and a friend of hers urinating but rejected the idea that he saw before him "a confirmation of the wound with which his Nanya had threatened him" by telling himself that what he saw was the girls' "front bottom." As he told Freud this, he then recalled that his father had once come on a snake as they walked together along a footpath, and had beaten it to pieces with his stick. He also remembered a fairy-tale in which a wolf who wanted to go fishing in the winter used his tail as bait but it broke off in the ice. And how in "Little Red Riding Hood" and "The Seven Little Goats" children were taken out of a wolf's body. He had wondered whether wolves were always female and whether men could have children in their bodies too.

Freud said that at the time in this man's early life when he suppressed masturbation, fearing castration, his sexual drive took on a sadistic-anal character as he became cruel to small animals, pulled off the wings of flies and crushed beetles underfoot. Then the sadism disappeared, converted into masochism, as he began obsessive religious rituals to assuage his guilt.

The focal point of the case was the recurring nightmare of wolves. Freud worked hard to uncover its meaning. He reported the exact words of the patient as he described his dream:

"I dreamt that it was night and that I was lying in my bed. (My bed stood with its foot towards the window; in front of the window there was a row of old walnut trees. I know it was winter when I had the dream, and nighttime.) Suddenly the window opened of its own accord, and I was terrified to see that some white wolves were sitting on the big walnut tree in front of the window. There were six or seven of them. The wolves were quite white, and looked more like foxes or sheepdogs, they had big tails like foxes and they had their ears pricked like dogs when they are attending to something. In great terror, evidently of being eaten up by the wolves, I screamed and woke up. My nurse hurried to my bed to see what had happened to me. It took quite a long while before I was convinced that it had only been a dream; I had had such a clear and lifelike picture of the window opening and the wolves sitting on the tree. At last I grew quieter, felt as though I had escaped from some danger, and went to sleep again" (italics Freud's).

In associating to the dream the patient recalled a story his grandfather had told him, in which a tailor was sitting at work in his room when a wolf "leapt in." The tailor caught the wolf by the tail, pulled it off, and the wolf ran away in terror. Some time later the tailor was walking in the forest when a pack of wolves came after him. He climbed a tree to escape. The wolves were perplexed until the maimed one, "a vigorous old fellow" who wanted revenge on the tailor, proposed they should climb up, one on top of the other, until the last one could reach the tailor. The maimed wolf would be the base of the pyramid. The wolves did as he suggested. The tailor recognized the wolf he had deprived of a tail and called out, "Catch the gray one by the tail." The tail-less wolf, terrified by the recollection of his maiming, ran away, and the others all tumbled down. (Germanic fairytales are notoriously grisly, witness the unexpurgated Brothers Grimm.)

Freud said the dream contained an unmistakable allusion to the castration complex, noting that "the *old* wolf was docked of his tail by the tailor." He added that the "fox-tails" of the wolves in the dream were probably compensations for this tail-lessness.

The patient said that two factors in the dream had made the deepest impression on him: the perfect stillness and immobility of the wolves, and the strained attention with which they all looked at him. He also emphasized the "lasting sense of reality" the dream left behind.

Freud commented that from his experience in interpreting dreams such sense of reality showed the dream related to an occurrence that actually took place, was not imagined. Behind the content of the dream lay an unknown scene, one forgotten at the time the dream first occurred when the "Wolfman" was four years old. The dream "belonged to an even earlier period," reproducing material unknown to the conscious of an important scene in some distorted form, perhaps even distorted into its opposite, Freud suggested.

The most "obtrusive thing" in the dream, the wolves on the tree, had led straight to the grandfather's story and its theme of castration, Freud said, bringing to light "the fear of his father which from that time forward was to dominate his life." Freud also reconstructed from the dream what he called "some such fragments as these: *A real occurrence—dating from a very early period—looking—immobility—sexual problems—castration—his father—something terrible*" (italics Freud's).

At one session the patient started on his own to interpret the dream. He said he thought he had awakened and "seen something," that the attentive "looking"—ascribed in the dream to the wolves—should rather be shifted to him. He also mentioned that the wolves sitting on the tree were a transposition of his grandfather's story, where they were underneath a tree and unable to climb up. Freud then asked himself, "What, then, if the other factor emphasized by the dreamer were also distorted by means of a transposition or reversal? In that case instead of immobility (the wolves sat there motionless; they looked at him, but did not move) the meaning would have to be: the most violent motion. That is to say, he suddenly woke up and saw in front of him a scene of violent movement at which he looked with strained attention."

During another session, Freud said, an association suddenly occurred to the patient that "carried us another step forward in our understanding of the dream." The man said, "The tree was a Christmas tree." He now knew the dream had first occurred shortly before Christmas, a day that was also his fourth birthday. He had gone to sleep in tense expectation of the double quantity of gifts he would receive in the morning. Freud commented that in such circumstances a child may easily anticipate the fulfillment of wishes, so it was already Christmas in his dream—the content of the dream showed the presents that were to be his, hanging on the walnut tree. But instead of presents, they turned into wolves. The dream ended by his being overcome with fear of being eaten by a wolf—probably his father, suggested Freud—and by flying for refuge to his nurse.

The knowledge of the boy's sexual development before he had the dream made it possible for Freud to fill in the gaps in the dream and explain the transformation of "satisfaction" into anxiety:

"Of the wishes concerned in the formation of the dream the most powerful must have been the wish for the sexual satisfaction which he was at that time longing to obtain from his father. The strength of this wish made it possible to revive the long-forgotten traces in his memory of a scene which was able to show what sexual satisfaction from his father was like; and the result was terror, horror of the fulfillment of the wish, the repression of the impulse which had manifested itself by means of the wish, and consequently a flight from his father to his less dangerous nurse."

Freud then asked, "But what picture can the nightly workings of his sexual desire have conjured up that could frighten him away so violently from the fulfillment for which he longed?" Freud said the material of the analysis showed there was one condition which this picture must satisfy—it must have been calculated to create a conviction of the reality of the existence of castration. Fear of castration could then become the motive power for the transformation of the emotion from an erotic one into terror: "What sprang into activity that night out of the chaos of the dreamer's unconscious memory-traces was the picture of a coitus between his parents, a coitus in circumstances which were not entirely usual and were especially favorable for observation." He estimated the patient's age at the date of the observation at about one and a half years, at which time he had suffered an attack of malaria that became severe every day at a particular hour. From his tenth year on, he was, from time to time, subject to moods of depression in the afternoon, which reached their height at five o'clock—a symptom that still plagued him. These recurring fits of depression, Freud speculated, took the place of the earliest attacks of malarial fever—five o'clock was either the time of the highest fever, or of the observation of the coitus, or both.

Freud suggested that because of his malaria, the patient had probably been sleeping in his cot in his young parents' bedroom, where they too were taking a siesta on a hot summer's day. When he woke up at five o'clock, the hour later marked by his depressions, he witnessed them in sexual intercourse. He saw his mother's genitals as well as his father's.

In this "primal scene" (a term thereafter used in psychoanalysis to describe the sexual act between parents), he saw the man upright and the woman "bent down like an animal," Freud said, which explained why the patient so feared the picture of the wolf standing upright in the storybook. It had reminded him of what, to him, was the terrifying sight of his father entering his mother sexually from the rear. This was also the only way the patient, as a man, was able to have sex with a woman. Freud commented that it was not only "a single sexual current that started from the primal scene but a whole series of them . . . his sexual life was positively splintered up by it."

At the age of one and a half, the patient had received, in Freud's words, "an impression to which he is unable to react adequately; he is only able to understand it and to be moved by it when the impression is revived in him at the age of four; and only twenty years later, during the analysis, is he able to grasp with his conscious mental processes what was then going on in him." Essentially new to him, as an adult remembering his parents' intercourse, was the conviction of the reality of castration—the terror in the dream. He had seen with his own eyes in his mother's body the "wound" his nurse had threatened him with. One of his associations to the dream was his father beating the snake to pieces with a stick; another was watching his little sister and her friend urinate.

The dream also showed, Freud said, the man's repressed wish as a little boy to be given sexual satisfaction by his father in the same way as he had given it to his mother—the underlying taboo wish of the dream. His wish to be passive sexually toward his father had succumbed to repression, and fear of his father appeared in its place in the shape of the wolf phobia. Freud described the man as having strong repressed homosexual wishes.

In the dream both the father and mother became wolves, the mother taking the part of the castrated wolf who was "maimed" and "let the others climb upon it," the father taking the part of one of the wolves who "climbed," Freud said. He added that the sexual development of the patient was first decisively influenced by his sister's attempted seduction, then diverted by the memory of the scene of coitus, which "in its deferred action operated like a second seduction."

This case contains many other important observations by Freud, including the impact of the fear of death that pervaded the "Wolfman's" life. He told Freud that his mother had said that when he was three months old he had been so seriously ill (with pneumonia, Freud suspected) that his "winding-sheet" had been prepared for him. There was also a dysentery epidemic when he was a boy, and his mother was frightened that her children would die from it. The severe depressions of both his mother and his father provided a morbid atmosphere, a mood of death, as it were, in which the patient and his sister grew up.

This case showed, according to Freud, that in man's prehistory "it was unquestionably the father who practiced castration as a punishment and who later softened it down into circumcision."

Freud also suggested that perhaps the sister, "at a similar tender age," had witnessed the same scene of coitus while sleeping in her parents' bedroom, and that this explained her sexual precocity.

Freud's reconstruction of the psychic life of the child as shown in the "Wolfman" case "is remarkably consistent with modern knowledge of developmental process," according to Dr. Harold P. Blum, addressing the Thirty-First Congress of the International Psychoanalytical Association on "The Value of Reconstruction in the Psychoanalysis of Adults."

In an earlier paper, "The Borderline Childhood of the Wolfman," Blum suggests that in light of current theory, based on an extension of Freud's discoveries, the serious malarial illness the Wolfman suffered at the age of eighteen months might have had a very important impact on his life.

In addition to the parents' deep emotional disturbances, Blum says, the multiple mother surrogates, the inconsistent parenting, the sexual seduction and the malarial infection disrupted the normal developmental process of separating emotionally from the mother and "individuating" during the important "rapprochment phase." This led to disturbances in the establishment of "basic trust," self-esteem and "object constancy." This significantly expands in a modern analytic framework the pioneering reconstruction by Freud of the Wolfman's primal scene experience at eighteen months.

Freud interprets the illness of the patient as "infantile neurosis" but Blum suggests the Wolfman was suffering from a "borderline condition with episodes of infantile psychosis," a more serious illness. He relates the patient's disturbances in "ego, narcissistic disorder and vulnerability to severe regressions" to the disruption in development he suffered in infancy.

This famous case emphasizes how the terror that may be induced by the fear of castration in a boy can haunt his life. It is not unusual to see a little boy's hands fly to his penis as though to protect it when he has been scolded by his mother or father. Men under stress will sometimes unconsciously make this gesture. In these days of televised baseball games, as millions watch, a major league player may, in a moment of anxiety before a big game, touch his crotch as though to reassure himself his penis is still there.

The fear of castration persists if a man has been unable to come to terms with it. It may be the cause, according to Freud, of homosexuality, impotence, bisexuality, sadomasochism, voyeurism.

Freud said that normal genital excitement as such does not markedly manifest itself in a boy during the first two and a half years of life, though there is sensitivity in the genital area. The nearness of the genitals to the excretory organs and the use of the penis for urination provides natural stimulation, as does frequent washing by the mother.

If a boy is sexually aroused by direct overstimulation, as may happen with mothers who "habitually manipulate the foreskin excessively in the process of cleaning" or nurses who may stimulate the boy's penis to keep him quiet (some mothers in primitive tribes do this), then early masturbation may develop in a forced way rather than as part of normal sexual development. This forced masturbation will interfere with a boy's natural sexual development, Freud warned. It is interesting that Lee Harvey Oswald's mother said she had bathed him until he was eleven or twelve, when he "got a little too old for me to look at.")

Through masturbation the boy learns of the pleasure his body can give. The inability to enjoy masturbation may lead to drastic consequences in some cases, especially if there are hateful feelings between parents. A young murderer who had stabbed a woman to death confessed that only in prison had he been able to masturbate, that he had always been too ashamed as a boy, and that to him rape and murder seemed lesser evils. His parents had brought him up with threats of severe punishment if they ever caught him touching his genitals. But in prison, where he saw other men masturbate, he decided there was nothing wrong with it.

The phallic stage for the little boy begins when he discovers, after glimpsing his sister in the bathtub or a feminine playmate urinating in his house, or seeing his mother naked, that girls and women lack what he possesses. Before this he has attributed a penis to everyone, seeing the world in the image of himself, not dreaming that women lack this essential organ. When he first notices the difference between himself and the little girl, he may appear indifferent, as though trying to deny that girls have no penises. He may think the little girl will grow one, even assure her she will, which she is all too willing to believe. But as he grows older and his sexual curiosity becomes greater, he becomes more conscious of his own genitals and starts to investigate those of others in all ways open to him—staring at his mother and father as they undress, begging to sleep with them, practically battering down the bathroom door to watch them urinate. He is interested in whether his mother and father sit or stand to urinate and whether each has a penis.

Some men have difficulty giving up the universal childhood fantasy of the phallic mother, Freud said. The image of a woman with a penis returns over and over in their dreams. Freud referred to the numerous hermaphrodites of antiquity that "faithfully reproduce this once general infantile idea." Actual hermaphroditic formations of the genitals in nature nearly always arouse "the greatest abhorrence," he said.

In discussing the sexual conflicts of boys Freud said that continued "bed-wetting" is "a result of masturbation and its suppression is regarded by boys as an inhibition of their genital activity —that is, as having the meaning of a threat of castration." The relation of enuresis, or bed-wetting, to later sexual difficulty in men was studied by Dr. Karl Abraham, who treated a number of men troubled by premature ejaculation. They reported that at the moment of premature emission they experienced a feeling of shame. The emission took place against their conscious will and they were always surprised at the haste with which it occurred. They tried to hold back but could not.

In such instances the passiveness of the man and his failure to engage in vigorous bodily movements seemed similar to a prior sexual development, the passing of urine in infancy, Abraham said. Unable to attain sexual pleasure through full masculine activity, the men engaged in what, to them, was the only pleasure they knew, the passive one of allowing a bodily product to flow out. In their unconscious, semen equalled urine, and the sexual act was similar to urination. They all described the physical sensation of premature ejaculation as similar to the feeling of being unable to control urination. Just as a small child wets his mother with the urine he cannot contain, so the man with premature ejaculation wets his partner as she becomes a substitute for his mother, Abraham said. For the man, it is an act of defiance, defiance of the woman who symbolizes the mother.

As children, these men had obtained excessive pleasure from urinating. Study of their childhood, according to Abraham, showed that they were difficult to train, bed-wetters until a late age, and as men quickly reacted to sexual excitement with the desire to urinate. Though obtaining the most pleasure of which they were capable from an ejaculation, they were left tormented by the feeling of not being men. Abraham said, "If urethral pleasure is excessively marked we shall find that the 'too much' in this place corresponds to a 'too little' in another." In men where the slightest genital contact with a woman results in a premature flow of semen, over-excitability, thought by some a sign of great masculinity, is rather the opposite, an expression of weakness, said Abraham. For such men the genital zone has not become the leading sexual zone.

Abraham pointed out that in the majority of men he studied premature ejaculation did not occur when they masturbated, but only when they were close to a woman. This was due, he said, to the man's hidden hatred and fear of women. He could only gain sexual gratification if he did not take an active part, if he gave the woman no pleasure. He aroused her, then disappointed her. He felt guilty because of his unmanliness, blamed her for "forcing" him and thus hated her even more.

Unconsciously such men want to kill the woman, Abrahams concluded, and in their fantasy the penis is the weapon. Premature ejaculation removes the danger as they quickly rob the penis of its aggressive thrusts. They over-value the power of the penis almost but not quite as much as a homosexual. They fear and have contempt for the woman because she has no penis, and at the same time her lack of one awakens in them the fear of castration.

The other extreme is the man who cannot ejaculate though he may try for hours. To him the act is also one of urination. He is holding back his urine out of the same fear and hatred of women. To him, the letting go of semen is an explosive act that might harm the woman, which he would like to do.

At first Freud thought it was the repression of sexual desire that caused unhappiness. Then he found that "unrestrained" sexual activity in his patients did not lead to happiness. The Don Juan was no happier than the man who complained of impotence. Both were incapable of combining tender with sensual feelings. To the Don Juan the aim was conquest, not love—eternal and endless conquest. He wanted to possess all women, which, in his unconscious, meant he wanted only one—the unattainable mother of childhood. The Don Juan performed the sexual act without the enjoyment essential to love. He could not bear either himself or the woman after he had ejaculated into her.

Both promiscuity and impotence indicate a strong erotic feeling, unresolved, for the parent of the opposite sex, according to Freud.

He called it a degree of "physical impotence" when a man could not get pleasure from sexual intimacy with one woman he loved.

Promiscuous men are insatiable sexually, their need far exceeding the natural desire, their emptiness a bottomless pit. Insatiability, Freud said, belongs to the time of childhood. A child can never get enough of love, of food, of attention. And insatiability brings frustration, then anger in its wake.

The little boy dares not express anger or hatred for his mother because he cannot run the risk of losing her love, but this hatred may erupt in later life toward a mistress or a wife. This is one reason love in some instances turns so swiftly to hate. A hungry, demanding love may mask the childhood hatred.

Little boys "are *in love,* in the everyday sense of the word," with their mothers, Freud said (italics his). He added that in cases in which a man who had been previously healthy falls ill after an unhappy experience in love, it is possible to show that the "mechanism of his illness" consists in a turning back of his libido on those he preferred in infancy.

The Oedipal conflict lay at the root of Shakespeare's *Hamlet,* Freud pointed out. Shakespeare was propelled by his own unconscious feelings, which he portrayed through the Danish prince. Freud raises the question of how one might explain the hysterical Hamlet's phrase, "So conscience doth make cowards of us all," as well as his hesitation about avenging his father by killing his uncle, though he casually sends Rosencrantz and Guildenstern to their deaths, murders Polonius and later kills Laertes. Answers Freud: "How better than by the torment roused in him by the obscure memory that he himself had meditated the same deed against his father because of passion for his mother—'use every man after his desert, and who should 'scape whipping?'" Hamlet's conscience was his "unconscious feeling of guilt."

Even someone who has been fortunate enough to avoid an incestuous "fixation" of his libido does not entirely escape its influence, Freud said. It often happens that a young man falls in love seriously for the first time with an older woman and "this is clearly an echo" of the earlier phase of his sexual development, since the older woman is "able to re-animate pictures" of his mother.

Why do so many men seek prostitutes and call girls for sex?

What is the need that drives them to illicit sex with women for whom they have no feeling, except perhaps contempt? Freud said this showed a split in their thinking between sex and romantic love. They believe that though they love the "good" woman in a tender, idealizing way they must not express lust for her. It is, however, permissible for them to have sex with the "bad" woman without feeling guilt.

Freud also said that boys are apt to think of their mothers at times as "whores" because they are unfaithful to their sons and have sex with the fathers, which deeply wounds them. Most boys eventually suppress this fantasy and are able to combine sensual and tender feelings toward a woman. It is, of course, far more difficult if a mother actually is a whore, as in the case of Charles Manson and more recently fifty-year-old Joseph Fischer, arrested in Poughkeepsie, New York. He confessed on television that he had murdered more than twenty men and women, including his wife and two seventeen-year-old prostitutes, saying, "Every time a woman did something that reminded me of my mother I killed her." He also said, "My mother was a whore and so were a lot of women I was with. Every time they seemed to be like her, I'd stab 'em or shoot 'em." He killed the men, he said, because they reminded him of his mother's customers.

The prostitute fulfills the fantasy in which a man degrades the woman with whom he has sex, Freud said. If a woman is a prostitute, if any man can have her, *he* is not evil, he is not responsible for taking one woman from one man—his mother from his father.

Having a mistress is a less sordid way of acting out the fantasy of sex with the "bad" or "seductive" mother while preserving tender feelings for a wife. Feelings of lust and tenderness, instead of fusing, are still split into opposing camps. Such a man can feel sensual only when the fruit is forbidden. Such feeling comes from a little boy's over-idealization of his mother, Freud said. He added that the significance "of the factor of sexual over-estimation" can best be studied in men "for their erotic life alone has become accessible to research. That of women—partly owing to the stunting effect of civilized conditions and partly owing to their conventional secretiveness and insincerity—is still veiled in an impenetrable obscurity." This is no longer true, with books such as *The Hite*

Report showing the willingness of women to talk about their sexual feelings and behavior, and recent confessional autobiographies.

There are some men who do not find *any* woman desirable, who are erotically drawn to their own sex. Freud explained homosexuality as due in part to "fixation" on the fantasy that a woman must have a penis. This fantasy, he said, "resists all the influences of later life and makes the man incapable of dispensing with a penis in his sexual object, so that such a person, if otherwise he has a normal sexual life must become homosexual, seeking his sexual object in men who through other physical and mental qualities remind him of women."

Women, as they become known to the homosexual in later life, "are excluded from being sexual objects," Freud said, because "they lack the essential sexual attraction; indeed, in connection with another impression of childhood-life they may become abhorrent to him."

He explained that in masturbating, a child usually produces pleasure by stimulating his penis with his hand, and if he is detected by his parents he may be "terrorized by the threat that his penis will be cut off," like Little Hans. The effect of this "castration threat" is in direct proportion, Freud said, to the value set on the penis, so that the threat may be "quite extraordinarily deeprooted and persistent."

"Sagas and myths testify to the revolt in the childish feelings, to the horror that is then linked to the castration complex, and this later is remembered with corresponding reluctance by consciousness," he said. "The woman's genitalia, seen subsequently and regarded as mutilated, recall this threat and thus awaken in the homosexual horror instead of pleasure."

To a young man the body of a woman should be part of someone he loves and cherishes, not an object of fear and curiosity as was his mother's body when he first discovered she lacked a penis. Instead of feeling threatened by the genitals of a woman, he should accept them as complementary to his own, designed to give him sensual pleasure. Unless he can do this he will feel a hidden hatred toward women, unconsciously fearing they are all out to castrate him.

The homosexual, said Freud, is so fixated on the penis that he refuses to do without it in his sexual partner. The sight of the woman's genitals stirs his anxiety in two ways: the recognition of the fact there are human beings without a penis arouses his fears of castration, and the female genitals are perceived as a castrating instrument, capable of biting or tearing off his penis (he fuses his fears of the oral period, when he wanted to bite his mother, with those of the phallic stage, when he feared castration).

Though the homosexual's acute longing for someone who possesses a penis (the phallic mother) compels him to choose men as love objects, because he has not completely given up his male identity he will choose men who are feminine. Which explains why the men who play the feminine role sometimes dress in women's clothes and have feminine mannerisms. There are two extreme types of homosexual, those who are outwardly effemininate and the super-masculine "macho man" who overcompensates for his inner feelings of femininity in his caricature of masculinity. The man who is truly masculine does not need to be macho.

The homosexual fears that his father, if he knew of his erotic feelings for his mother, would castrate him. So, in a sense he castrates himself—a man who cannot be intimate with a woman is in a sense castrated—he can never produce a child.

During an earlier level of his life the homosexual has identified chiefly with his mother, his wish to be a woman is very strong. The mother of a homosexual is often a domineering, aggressive woman, though she may hide these traits behind an overly sweet and feminine front, and the father tends to be a weak, passive man. The homosexual identifies more with his mother in what Freud called "identification with the aggressor," an identification made out of fear, in the hope that if we become like someone who frightens us we will lose our fear of them.

Some men want to be women so intensely that they literally rid themselves of the penis through sex-change operations, recently much publicized. Far less publicized are those instances in mental hospitals where terrified men castrate themselves in an effort to be rid of the overwhelming fear of castration. This, for them, accomplishes several purposes: They become the woman they unconsciously wish to be, thus avoiding threat of murder by the father.

They say, "Look, I'm no longer a man, I'm a woman, and therefore no rival, so you don't have to kill me." At the same time there is the fantasy they can now take their mother's place as the father's sexual partner—the wish acted out by the homosexual who plays the feminine role.

The homosexual, as Freud saw him, has been unable to successfully resolve his Oedipal conflict. He gives up—it is too threatening. He cannot admit he is in competition with his father, preferring to feel castrated like a woman so he will not be feared as competitor. He defends himself against the guilt of desiring his mother by becoming homosexual. It is less dangerous to risk society's revulsion than to love a woman.

The man chosen by the homosexual as his partner may serve many fantasies. The homosexual may be loving the image of himself, either as he is or as he would like to be, or as he was as a child, Freud said. In homosexual relationships between an older man and younger one, the older man is selecting the image of himself as a youth, and the younger is seeing himself as he would like to be, big and strong, a worthy rival to his father.

The curious platonic alliance sometimes formed between homosexuals and nymphomaniacs fulfills fantasies of each. The nymphomaniac is the seductive mother who tried to win over the homosexual, as she must every man, to defend herself against the unconscious feeling she is frigid. She punishes herself for such promiscuity by choosing a man she knows will be ineffective. The homosexual revenges himself on the seductive mother by saying nay to the nymphomaniac. Where feminine insatiability is pitted against masculine impotence, the relationship lasts as long as there is acceptance of each other's defenses and fears.

Freud's classic work on the nature of homosexuality, *Leonardo da Vinci, A Study in Psychosexuality,* portrays the consequences of deep, erotic attachment between a mother and child. Leonardo was never able to form an intimate relationship with a woman. He was accused, tried and acquitted of homosexuality. From a fantasy Leonardo described in his writings, and from his paintings, Freud made a remarkable deduction about the influence of the artist's mother, Caterina, on his life, later borne out by many psychoanalysts as they studied the early lives of homosexuals. Leonardo was an illegitimate child. Freud considered that the accident of his illegitimacy plus "the pampering of his mother" exerted the most decisive influence on Leonardo's character and later fate. So deep was the attachment between mother and child that ". . . the love of the mother became his destiny; it determined his fate and the privations which were in store for him."

Leonardo's mother, from whom he permanently separated sometime between the age of two and five—no one knows the exact year—must have been a very seductive woman, Freud suggested. He reached this conclusion because of the seductive smile on the face of the Mona Lisa and most of the other women Leonardo painted. Freud speculated that Leonardo remembered "that mysterious smile" as his mother's, which he knew as an infant, then lost, and "which fascinated him so much when he found it again" in the woman who became his model for the Mona Lisa, the wife of a Florentine gentleman, del Gioconda.

The smile of Mona Lisa del Gioconda awakened in Leonardo the memory of his mother in the first years of life, Freud said: "When in the prime of his life Leonardo re-encountered that blissful and ecstatic smile as it had once encircled his mother's mouth in caressing, he had long been under the ban on an inhibition, forbidding him ever again to desire such tenderness from women's lips."

Leonardo succeeded in reproducing in the face of Mona Lisa two things his mother's smile concealed—"promise of unlimited tenderness and sinister threat." The threat was the incestuous desire which made itself known through the smile.

Freud analyzed a fantasy of Leonardo's which, the latter said, he remembered from earliest infancy, and from which Freud concluded Leonardo's mother was very seductive. One day, while writing about the flight of the vulture in one of his scientific papers, Leonardo suddenly interrupted the technical discussion with a personal memory: "It seems that it had been destined before that I should occupy myself so thoroughly with the vulture, for it comes to my mind as a very early memory, when I was still in the cradle, a vulture came down to me, opened my mouth with his tail and struck me many times with his tail against my lips."

Freud connects this image to the mother hungrily caressing her baby. He says that "the impetuosity of the caressing to which the vulture points was only too natural."

According to Freud, Caterina, "the poor, forsaken mother, had to give vent through mother's love to all her memories of love enjoyed as well as to her yearnings for more affection; she was forced to it, not only in order to compensate herself for not having a husband, but also the child for not having a father to love it." Freud adds, ". . . in the manner of all ungratified mothers she thus took her little son in place of her husband, and robbed him of a part of his virility by maturing too early his erotic life."

In addition to the sexual stages of development, Freud posed three stages of love: love of self, then love of members of the same sex, then love of members of the opposite sex. During the stage of self-love, or auto-erotism, one's own body is the object of sexual pleasure. During the second stage one is sexually attracted to the body of someone of the same sex. In the third stage we are erotically drawn to a body different from ours. But love is no simple thing, its shadings develop over the years in processes of complexity involving many feelings.

Homosexuals, according to Freud, regress to the narcissistic or auto-erotic stage. For their love they select a model just like themselves, as though they were "gazing into a pool." As in childhood, the homosexual is his own ideal. He has not developed beyond narcissism enough to give love of a mature nature to another person. He is intensely bound to the mother of childhood in what many of today's psychoanalysts call "a hostile dependency" from which he is unable to free himself. Both the love and hate of the mother are intense, as is the over-idealization of her.

The homosexual man feels feminine, identifying with his mother because he is still psychically attached to her. His femininity also reassures her that he will never leave her for another woman, just as he does not want her to leave him. His femininity reassures his father that he is no rival, and so he never even develops the Oedipal conflict in any serious sense. Over the years Freud added to his theories about homosexuality. Referring to the fantasy of "retiring in favor of someone else," which he mentioned as a motive of the lesbian, he said this also applied to men who gave up women so their fathers could receive all the female adulation and love the sons, now no longer his competition, all the more.

One of Freud's most important theories about homosexuality was that paranoia was a defense against it. He cited four typical paranoiac delusions that, he said, were denials of homosexuality or defenses against it. Starting, in the case of a man repressing his homosexual impulses, with the simple formula, "I love him," Freud pointed out that each of the three words could be denied separately, producing three of the most typical paranoiac delusional ideas. If the verb of the sentence is denied it goes, "I do not *love* him, I *hate* him," an unconscious attitude. By the mechanism of projection, common in paranoia, this is felt as "He hates (and persecutes) me," and then the man feels justified in hating back. Such a feeling—a persecution complex—is the most common delusion of paranoia. If the object of the sentence is denied it becomes, "I do not love *him*, I love *her.*" The projection turns into "She loves me," the delusion of erotomania, the belief that every woman is in love with him. If the subject is denied, the sentence becomes, "It is not *I* who loves him—it is *she* who does," the delusion of jealousy. Here projection does not need to come into play because what two other people do is an external matter, whereas in the first two instances the man is concerned with his inner perception, a painful one, and has to project it. The fourth possibility is that all three words are denied. This signifies, "I don't love at all; I don't love anyone." Since the erotic instinct must find some expression, it falls back on the man himself. The result is the megalomania which in some degree is present in all cases of paranoia, Freud said.

He described "the psychical processes" of the origin of homosexuality in his paper, "Certain Neurotic Mechanisms in Jealousy, Paranoia and Homosexuality," saying that the typical process, established in innumerable cases, started openly a few years after the end of puberty when the young man, who, until this time has been strongly "fixated to his mother, turns in his course," and searches for "love-objects in whom he can rediscover himself, and whom he wishes to love as his mother loved him."

Freud summed up: "Attachment to the mother, narcissism, fear of castration—these are the factors that we have hitherto found in the psychic etiology [cause] of homosexuality; and on them is superimposed the effect of any seduction bringing about a premature fixation of the libido, as well as the influence of the organic factor favoring the passive role in love."

Psychoanalysts today are having some success "treating" homosexuals using Freud's theories of the causes of homosexuality to get at the source of the conflicts in therapy sessions. Masters and Johnson and other sex therapists, however, do not use Freud's discoveries. They focus essentially on the physical, mechanical aspects of sex. It is doubtful in the case of intense homosexual conflicts whether any of their results are lasting.

Contemporary psychoanalysts have been exploring in greater depth how homosexuality develops, linking it to the very early years of life. As Freud pointed, out the homosexual does not try to resolve his Oedipal dilemma. Psychoanalysts have probed the reasons for this and have connected it to the relationship between a boy and his mother. They have found that the mother usually has an unconscious hatred of her son and of men in general, a strong wish that he had either not been born or had been a girl. The mother is apt to use her son to meet all her unfulfilled needs.

"By the age of three, a little boy knows exactly what his mother wants him to be to her," says Dr. Gregory Rochlin, author of *Masculinity*. The homosexual's fear of women is due not just to the threat to his genitals "but, more primordial, the threat to one's being, sense of existing, as is implied in 'separation anxiety'," according to Dr. Robert J. Stoller, who has written extensively on gender identity and has treated homosexuals. Most "feminine boys" result from a mother who, "whether with benign or malignant intent, is too protective, and a father who is either brutal or absent, literally or psychologically," he says.

He distinguishes between two types of homosexuality. The first, which he says is very rare, starts in the earliest years of life and is promoted primarily by the closeness of mother and infant. The mother's avowed purpose is to prevent her son from suffering pain or frustration as she tries to create "a blissful ambiance." The boy's father is not present to drive a wedge that would promote separation between the mother and infant and "allow that individuation we call masculinity to occur." This produces the most feminine of boys, the childhood transsexual, who does not experience the amount and kind of pain and frustration necessary for ordinary psychic development. The second type includes homosexuals, transvestites and most of those who call themselves transsexuals. Their earliest development, however disturbed, allows some commitment to being male and masculine because some separation from their mother has occurred. At the same time, the boy's sense of self as a male and as masculine is threatened by a mother who is "insulted by her son's budding masculinity." There follows "castration anxiety," the precursor of homosexuality, and deep rage and a wish for revenge.

Contrasted with the first type, the main quality of the second is "intrapsychic conflict," Stoller says. The conflicts are between wanting to be merged with, or at least close to, the mother and wanting to be separate, between wanting to be like her and to be different, between wanting to stay with her (to be passive) and to move away (to be active).

Homosexual and transvestite boys are latent heterosexuals, Stoller says. No matter how flawed the process of separation and individuation, they have developed some sense of self as a male who desires females, who senses himself a separate person from his mother and therefore as one who would like to possess her if she, and his father, did not make it too dangerous. However fragmented and primitive, an Oedipal conflict develops.

Dr. Ralph Greenson says the transsexual boy wants to *be* his mother rather than *have* her. The mother has made it unendingly clear that she finds her husband weak and worthless, so the father does not serve as a rival or a danger even if the boy has wished to displace him sexually. The boy has never experienced pride in or need for his genitals, no need for maleness, as Greenson says.

In treatment, when the excessively close relationship to the mother is faced and the boy is encouraged and taught to be masculine, he starts preferring to fight with his sisters and female friends rather than playing with and imitating them. Then his rage at his mother emerges.

In *Beyond Sexual Freedom,* Dr. Charles Socarides, who has treated many homosexuals successfully, says homosexuality is never consciously "chosen" as a sexual preference but is unconsciously determined from the earliest period of childhood. "Man's development of sexual identity occurs when he successfully traverses the separation-individuation phase of human development, normally by the age of three," he says. "This is an *intrapsychic* development dependent on the mother's lovingly and caringly allowing the child to become free of her, form his own identity, while she helps, abets, encourages his strength, independence and masculinity, as differentiated from her own feminine identity."

He also concludes that homosexuality results from developmental failure during the pre-Oedipal period. It involves intense urges to attack and invade the mother's body to ward off personal dissolution by merging with her, accompanied by a murderous fury toward her that is carried into the Oedipal period.

There is a difference between sexual gratification that is "healthy" and sexual gratification that inflicts "destructive insults to sex, to the body, to human relationships, and to the human spirit," says Socarides. He includes as unhealthy gratification: homosexuality, pornography (which he describes as "the rape of the senses"), group sex and bestiality. "Full and passionate sexuality is intensely rewarding but this healthy sexuality cannot embrace any desire for violence, incest, sadism or other acts that extinguish human dignity," he says.

For many years he has studied the origins of homosexuality and the unconscious mechanisms at work. In his books *Homosexuality* and *The Overt Homosexual* he maintains, "There is no question that by now we have sufficient evidence as a profession to demonstrate that homosexuality can be reversed in many cases, or at least its symptoms and suffering greatly alleviated by psychoanalysis."

Homosexuality is not "a way of life" but a form of emotional illness, of sexual immaturity," he says. It represents a "fixation" at the earlier stage of psychosexual development when it was natural to love someone whose body was the same as the self.

Homosexuality is also deeply connected with a death anxiety so strong it threatens to overcome the defenses of the ego, says Dr. Martin Grotjahn in his article, "Ego Identity and the Fear of Death and Dying." . . . "The homosexual person is so afraid of regressing to anything approximating primal love that he will avoid it through the manifest symptoms of perversion. Primary love [love of the mother] and the longing to be dead are symbolically the same. The homosexual denies frantically the death danger of surrendering to the Primordial Mother whom he loves and fears. This motive in the genesis of perversions could explain the homosexual's nearness to psychosis, against which his perversion is a partial defense as it is fulfillment. The homosexual man recreates the terrifying mother in himself after he attempts to destroy her."

Freud's theories have led the way to prevention of homosexuality. Psychoanalysts suggest this can best be achieved by helping mothers understand the son's need to separate emotionally during the first year of life. The next best thing is to help a boy who appears effeminate to develop his maleness through psychoanalytic treatment. The mother of a homosexual boy or man should also be helped to become free of her desire to keep her son close to her and to confront the depression she will inevitably feel as he starts to become more manly—which means he will emotionally leave her. Ideally, the father, if he is on the scene, should also receive help, for he is apt to be a distant, passive man who has allowed his wife to dominate her son's life, or a brutal, selfish man who has inflicted violence on both wife and son.

If they want help, it seems inhumane not to treat boys or young men who appear effeminate, or adult homosexuals; the inability to separate psychologically from a mother produces genuine mental pain.

Most psychoanalysts consider homosexuality the result of the early relationship between a boy and his mother and an "arrest" in psychosexual development. The American Psychiatric Association, however, recently removed homosexuality from the category of deviant behavior in its new diagnostic manual.

Many hazards face a boy as he passes through the stages of sexual development, but there are great rewards when he manages to overcome them with the help of loving parents. Freud described being a parent as one of "three impossible professions"—the others being a statesman and governing and being a psychoanalyst. But his discoveries have made it easier to be a parent, to understand more about the child, as well as about oneself as parent.

The sexual development of both boys and girls may go awry, Freud concluded in his later years, because of the presence of too intense hatred. He spoke of this hatred in a general sense in his early works, not as a separate instinct but as sadism from the oral and anal stages of sexual development which occurred when the sexual drive became frustrated.

But after years of thought, Freud decided hatred was a strong enough feeling to deserve to be called an instinct in its own right, just as important as the sexual instinct.

Dr. Josef Breuer, the first physician
to undertake "listening" to the
words of a hysterical patient, Bertha
Pappenheim, later called Anna O.
in the case report. *(The Bettmann
Archive)* ·

Bertha Pappenheim (the
"immortal" patient whose "talking
cure" inspired Freud) here pictured
in a riding habit. *(From the Archives
of the Leo Baeck Institute, New York)*

Freud, at the age of thirty-five, when he convinced Breuer to write up the case of Anna O., the first publication in the field of psychoanalysis. *(The Bettman Archive)*

As a young doctor, Ernest Jones became Freud's disciple and later wrote the three-volume biography *The Life and Work of Sigmund Freud*. *(The Bettmann Archive)*

Freud in his study, surrounded by his antique collection, gazes at his dog, Yofi, who often sat in on the analytic sessions with his patients. *(Pictorial Parade)*

An etching of her famous father presided over the couch in Anna Freud's consulting room. She was the only one of his six children to become a pyschoanalyst. *(Basic Books, Inc. Photograph by Edward Engelman)*

Anna Freud in 1938, at the age of forty-two a practicing psychoanalyst who had already written her important book *The Ego and the Mechanisms of Defense.* *(Basic Books, Inc. Photograph by Edward Engelman)*

7

Running Second to Sex but Catching Up

For the first thirty years of his professional life—dating from the publication of the article on hysteria that he wrote with Breuer—Freud saw the sexual drive as man's only instinct. He theorized that mental conflicts arose from the clash between unconscious erotic impulses and conscious ego impulses—the latter mainly in the interest of self-preservation.

He ignored all mention of aggression even though Breuer, as early as 1895, had written of "the aggressive instinct" in *Studies on Hysteria*. Breuer said "perception" was impaired by the degree of intensity of sexual feelings during a state of "constant excitement," such as when a normally timid and cautious animal became blind and deaf to danger when sexually aroused. Breuer added, "On the other hand, at least in males, there is an intensification of the aggressive instinct. Peaceable animals become dangerous until their excitation has been discharged in the motor activities of the sexual act." He then described how "people become 'senseless' with anger or fright," as when Bismarck smashed a valuable vase on the floor after suppressing fury in the presence of the king.

Freud spoke of "hate" and "sadism" constantly but attributed them to frustration of the erotic drive, as in the Oedipus complex, where hatred for the parent of the opposite sex was a natural feeling. He also said, in a letter to Fliess on May 13, 1897, that hostile wishes against parents, stemming from childhood, were "an integral part" of the depression that follows a loss.

In some people, he said, these hostile wishes against parents come to light consciously in the form of obsessional ideas. In paranoia the delusions of persecution—the imagined murderous threats by unseen and unknown enemies—arise from the person's wish to kill someone he is close to, someone he feels is threatening his life. Because the wish to kill is dangerous to his own survival, he projects it on others. Freud said there was "a fragment of fact" in the paranoiac's accusation, in that the mother or father of infancy either physically or psychologically threatened his life.

In his self-analysis Freud courageously dealt with his erotic feelings for his mother—he was the first man to do so—but he omitted all mention of hate for her, though not for his father, his rival. The nearest Freud came to facing his early hatred for his mother may have been when he once recalled, as a small boy, "crying my heart out" after she left him alone with a nurse. Such feelings of abandonment always hold both grief and rage toward the deserting one.

In his analyses of patients Freud dealt continuously with their feelings of hate; however, he did not view their hatred as part of an aggressive drive. He did say the roots of war start in the nursery, implying it was the hatred between mother and child that planted the seeds of the child's later destructive tendencies.

In 1909 Freud said that "every act of hate issues from erotic tendencies," still tying hate to sex. In 1914 he introduced the concept of "narcissism," a word so in vogue today that Christopher Lasch and others have applied it to our entire society as a sociological concept. In relation to the individual, Freud said that narcissism included the self-preservation urges. Hate was summoned to ward off threats to life, either physical or psychological.

But the conflict then became one between the narcissistic and the erotic impulses—between two forms of the sexual instinct.

This was "profoundly unsatisfying" to Freud, according to Jones, because Freud thought in terms of "opposing" forces in the mind that created conflict. He had always labeled the force that opposed the sexual drive as "self-interest," and spoke of the self-preservative qualities of the ego.

He was now dissatisfied with this concept. In 1915, in *Instincts and Their Vicissitudes,* he wrote that "hate" was distinct from the sexual drive and a primary part of the ego. This was the start of his concept of a nonsexual part of the ego in opposition to the sexual drive.

Then, in 1919, he wrote the controversial book *Beyond the Pleasure Principle,* in which he established two opposing forces in the mind —the Life Instincts and the Death Instincts (or "the destructive instinct"). He called the former *Eros* but seldom used the term *Thanatos* for the latter except in conversation. He said both instincts were of equal status and in constant struggle with each other, though the latter inevitably won in the end.

The Life Instinct operating under the banner of the erotic drive at times became fused with the death instinct but by and large opposed it. "At times, too, the biological tendency toward destruction is deflected from the self. When directed toward other people or things in the external world it becomes the aggressive instinct, operating constructively as well as destructively," Freud said.

In this way, he differentiated between the terms "death instinct" and "destructive instinct," which at first he used indiscriminately, saying the former was directed against the self and the latter directed outward. He added that the sexual, or Life Instincts, in their struggle against the opponent death, tried to prolong life by diverting the self-destructive tendency outward, against others, as a ruler deflected rebellious or revolutionary impulses against the rest of the world by instigating war.

At first he had described the destructive drive as part of the ego function but now he gave it a more fundamental status, independent of the ego and antedating its formation from the unconscious. He had always regarded masochism as secondary to sadism—a sadistic impulse turned inward against the self. Now he reversed the order and suggested there could be a primary masochism, a self-injuring tendency, indicative of the death instinct, and that destructive and sadistic impulses were derived from it.

In speaking of the two opposing instincts Freud wrote in 1930, "Men have brought their powers of subduing the forces of nature to such a pitch that by using them they could now very easily exterminate one another to the last man. They know this—hence arises a great part of their current unrest, their dejection, their mood of apprehension. And now it may be expected that the other of the two 'heavenly forces', eternal Eros, will put forth his strength so as to maintain himself alongside of his equally immortal adversary, Thanatos."

In the same book he said he could no longer understand how "we could have overlooked the universality of nonerotic aggression and destruction, and could have omitted to give it its due significance in our interpretation of life." He added, as though apologizing for the blindness of others, "I remember my own defensive attitude when the idea of an instinct of destruction first emerged in psychoanalytic literature, and how long it took me before I became receptive to it."

The theory of a "death instinct" has met with a mixed reception among the psychoanalysts of the world. Most analysts do not accept the "death instinct" theory but do accept the aggressive instinct, using what is called the "dual theory of drives." Jones pointed out that an infant has aggressive and cannibalistic fantasies, followed later by murderous ones, but "one cannot infer from them any active will on the part of the cells of the body to lead that body to death." He added that Freud "caused much confusion through the mere play on the word 'death'." The fact that in rare cases of depression death wishes may, through complicated psychic mechanisms such as identification, result in suicide is no proof the wishes arose from "a primary wish for self-destruction on the part of the body," Jones said.

Analysts point out that the aggressive drive is not limited to hostility, that by far the largest and most important of all activity, large and small, is possible only because of aggression, the motor force. We use aggression in moderate form in work and in love—to marry, raise children, take care of them. But when aggressive impulses become excessively tinged with hate and desire for revenge they overwhelm feelings of love and tenderness and may end in psychosis, suicide or murder.

Discussing aggression in a letter to Princess Marie Bonaparte, dated May 27, 1937, two years before his death, Freud said he would try to answer her question about aggression, that the whole topic had not as yet been "treated carefully" and what he had to say about it in earlier writings "was so premature and casual as hardly to deserve consideration."

He told Bonaparte he thought the "instinct of destruction" could be "sublimated into achievements," that all activities "that rearrange or effect changes are to a certain extent destructive and thus redirect a portion of the instinct from its original destructive goal." The sexual instinct cannot be expressed without some measure of aggression and "therefore in the regular combination of the two instincts there is a partial sublimation of the destructive instinct."

He said "curiosity, the impulse to investigate," may be regarded as a complete sublimation of the aggressive or destructive impulse. In the life of the intellect the destructive instinct "attains a high significance as the motor of all discrimination, denial and condemnation."

The turning inward of the aggressive impulse is naturally the counterpart of the turning outward of love when it passes over from the self to others, he said, adding, "One could imagine a pretty schematic idea of all libido being at the beginning of life directed inward and all aggression outward, and that this gradually changes in the course of life. But perhaps that is not correct."

He concluded the letter to Bonaparte by saying the repression of aggression was the hardest part to understand: "As is well known, it is easy to establish the presence of 'latent' aggression, but whether it is then latent through repression or in some other way is not clear." He added, "Please do not overestimate my remarks about the destructive instinct. They were only tossed off and should be carefully thought over if you propose to use them publicly. Also there is so little new in them."

He later said in his book *The Outline of Psychoanalysis,* published posthumously in 1941, "All of psychoanalysis has to be reformulated in terms of understanding the aggressive drive as separate from the libidinal drive."

Freud referred to hate in connection with the ambivalence over the death of a loved one in his 1915 paper "Mourning and Melancholia." He said that the person who feels very guilty and remains unduly depressed after the loss of a loved one does so because, in addition to love, he also feels hate for the lost one, a hate that is denied and thus causes guilt. The feeling of hate for a parent is especially repressed at times "pity for the parent is paramount," such as when he is ill or dies.

Also in this paper Freud explained what he called "the enigma of suicide." He said the suicidal person was able to kill himself because unconsciously he was also killing the one he hated whom he had psychically "incorporated." The ego can destroy itself only if, owing to the power of the loved one as retained within as image, the ego treats itself as though it *were* the loved one and directs against the self all the rage it feels for the loved one who has rejected or abandoned it.

In his later years Freud put great emphasis on the destructiveness of the aggressive urge in man. On July 28, 1929, ten years before his death, he wrote bitterly, "In the depths of my being I remain convinced that my dear fellow creatures—with a few exceptions—are a wretched lot." This pessimistic viewpoint was amplified in *Civilization and Its Discontents:*

". . . men are not gentle creatures who want to be loved, and who at the most can defend themselves if they are attacked: they are, on the contrary, creatures among whose instinctual endowment is to be reckoned a powerful share of aggressiveness. As a result, their neighbor is for them not only a potential helper or sexual object, but also someone who tempts them to satisfy their aggressiveness on him, to exploit his capacity for work without compensation, to use him sexually without his consent, to seize his possessions, to humiliate him, to cause him pain, to torture and to kill him."

One of the results of psychoanalysis is that men become more gentle, more capable of love, more considerate of the feelings of others. When one feels endangered by conflicts within, one has no energy, no time to give to anyone else's needs. It takes all one's strength just to keep going in the world of reality.

Because of Freud's awareness of the role hate plays in the life of the child and the adult, aggression and its many effects on emotional and mental development constitutes one of the main themes of psychoanalytic study. Psychoanalysts have observed in adult patients the aggressive instinct turned on the self. Theodor Reik reported that a man told him, "Instead of knowing that you want to kill someone else, you wipe yourself out." Dr. H. A. Rosenfeld wrote of a severely disturbed woman: "Instead of attacking and destroying the analyst, the destructive impulse had turned against her desire to live, her libido, which left her half dead, as it were, and so in a state of depersonalization [denial of feelings]."

Other psychoanalysts have added to Freud's fundamental theory on aggression. Neither the sexual or aggressive drive is observable in human behavior "in pure or unmixed form" but the two drives are regularly "fused," though not necessarily in equal amounts, says Dr. Charles Brenner in his *Elementary Textbook of Psychoanalysis*. "Thus even the most callous act of intentional cruelty that seems on the surface to satisfy nothing but some aspect of the aggressive drive, still has some unconscious sexual meaning to its author and provides him with a degree of unconscious sexual gratification," he says. "In the same way there is no act of love, however tender, which does not simultaneously provide an unconscious means of discharge to the aggressive drive." He says that Freud accounted for the instinctual aspects of our mental lives by assuming the existence of the sexual and the aggressive drives, though a definition of the two drives is not possible. "We can come somewhat closer to what we mean, if we say that the one drive gives rise to the erotic component of mental activities, while the other gives rise to the purely destructive component."

The hatred of a parent for a child and the effect on the child was mentioned by Freud in 1931 in "Female Sexuality." He described the early attachment of a daughter to her mother as closely connected to the cause of neurosis and speculated that excessive dependence on the mother contained "the germ of later paranoia in women." He described this "germ" as "the surprising, yet regular, dread of being killed (?) devoured by the mother" (question mark Freud's). This dread of the mother may, he said, arise from an unconscious hostility on the mother's part which the child senses.

The greatest hindrance to man's further development is his inability, up to the present, to deal in better fashion with his aggression and destructiveness, according to Dr. Ralph R. Greenson, author of *The Technique and Practice of Psychoanalysis* and *Explorations in Psychoanalysis.*

"I believe that for man to survive he must learn to curb, tame, channelize, and sublimate his aggressiveness and destructiveness," he says. "To do this he must first face more honestly his greed, his envy, his hatred and fear of the stranger, and his hatred and fear of change. Only then can unconscious destructive guilt be changed to conscious guilt which can be controlled and useful. If we do this, man will have made a giant step forward, even if it is not to Point Omega."

Dr. Luis Feder of Mexico refers to a case of Freud's which Feder calls little noted but "of monumental significance." It reads:

> . . . A woman whose dream meant that she would like to see her daughter, now seventeen years old, dead before her eyes, found under our guidance (reconstruction) that she had indeed at one time harbored this death-wish. The child was the fruit of an unhappy marriage which was soon dissolved. Once, while she still bore her daughter in her womb, in a fit of rage after a violent scene with her husband, she had beaten with her fists on her body in order to kill the child inside it.

Freud commented: "How many others, who love their children tenderly, perhaps over-tenderly, today, conceive them unwillingly and wished at that time that the living thing within them might not develop further! They may even have expressed that wish in various, fortunately harmless, actions. Thus their [the child's] death-wish against someone they love, which is later so mysterious, originates from the earliest days of their relationship to that person . . . ."

Feder introduces a new hypothesis with the concept he calls "preconceptive ambivalence," which embodies not only the mother and father's feelings of love but of hate for the expected baby, along with their wishes and fears, their contradictory fantasies and somatic symptoms "that are evidence of conflicts about the anticipated and feared pregnancy." He calls this the child's "prehistory." He asserts the conflicting feelings of the parents continue throughout the child's life, influencing his reactions. "When a child is born, he is saved evidently from abortion, but he is not entirely saved from facing the symptomatic expression of the 'unwanted' portion of the ambivalence repressed."

In this new light, preconceptive ambivalence accounts not only for the maltreatment and battering of children but also for the battering and maltreatment of parents, both tragedies. Maria W. Piers, author of *Infanticide,* says, "Not every brutalized and grossly neglected child grows up to be a Charles Manson. On the other hand, virtually every Charles Manson was once a neglected and abused child."

Excessive aggression is seen in the murderer who is unable to control his hatred and desire for revenge. Freud's theory of sexual and aggressive drives and their developmental vicissitudes is borne out in dramatic form in the penetrating psychological study of the life and crimes of Joseph Kallinger, the Philadelphia shoemaker who murdered a nurse in Leona, New Jersey, as described by Flora Rheta Schreiber in a work in progress. She shows how Kallinger, an illegitimate child, was brutalized as a boy by foster parents. His criminal behavior is portrayed as stemming from his sexual and aggressive fantasies of the oral, anal and phallic stages.

The child's fear that his parents will kill him and his use of fantasy and self-deception to defend himself against that fear is the theme of Dorothy Bloch's book, *So The Witch Won't Eat Me: Fantasy and the Child's Fear of Infanticide.* Equally important in the child's need for defense is the parents' wish to kill the child; this wish may be unconscious, verbalized or acted out.

Bloch reached her conclusion after analyzing children and adults for twenty-five years and finding that all patients, from two and a half years of age to sixty-eight, were struggling to win the love of parents as a primary defense against the fear of infanticide. They were all, in varying degrees that depended on the intensity of love and the violence in their homes and the incidence of traumatic events, afraid their parents would kill them, or that they would kill their parents. They pinned the hope of staying alive on eventually gaining the parents' love.

The core of neurosis, Bloch says, is this fear in children of being killed by parents. It is based on the child's vulnerability as well as on his magical thinking, which leads him to believe he is responsible for everything that happens good and bad. When parents are actually violent towards each other or toward the child, his fear is confirmed and his terror intensified. The parents' violence or violent feelings elicit a similar response in the child and it is that response that produces his feelings of guilt and anticipation of punishment: he expects to be killed.

"Until recently the concept that parents may want to kill their children has been even more carefully buried than the thought that children may live in daily fear of it," Bloch says. "Not only is the wish to kill one of the most deeply repressed feelings, but the general understanding of the nature of feelings is still the subject of considerable misconception. It is usually with a sense of shock, and very often only after a period of agonizing denial, that patients may gradually and reluctantly acknowledge that they not only hate, but that they want to kill those whom they hate . . . It frequently comes as a surprise to patients that contradictory feelings can exist side by side. In any analysis, the startling recognition that love does not exclude hate, nor hate, love, is a milestone on the road to maturity."

Dr. Adelaide McFadyen Johnson took into account not only the individual's strong aggressive drive but how it was shaped and affected in infancy by the attitudes, thoughts and acts of his mother and father. In 1942, exploring the causes of crime and juvenile delinquency, she discovered the subtle ways a parent unconsciously could influence a child into acting out the parent's "own poorly integrated forbidden impulses." She found that delinquent children carried out the unconscious wishes of their parents, both sexual and criminal. Delinquency in a child "is unconsciously fostered and sanctioned by the parents who vicariously achieve gratification of their own forbidden impulses through the child's acting out," she said. "It is possible in every case studied to trace the specific conscience defect in the child to a mirror image of similar type and emotional charge in the parent." She concluded the children were not driven by "constitutionally, unmanageable instinctual drives but had parents who did not set limits to stealing, pathologic sexuality or even murderous intent."

The concept of the "soul murder" of a child by a parent has been described by Dr. Leonard Shengold, referring to psychological destruction in many forms, including the seduction of the child, both overt and subtle, or physical cruelty. Erik Erikson says the impotent anger of childhood is one of life's most traumatic experiences and adult anxiety is a reliving of this infantile rage.

Schizophrenia may be a defense against parental assaultive behavior of such an overwhelmingly destructive nature that its impact leads to malignant distortion of the unfolding of the instinctual life. M. A. Sechehaye was one of the first psychoanalysts to believe the schizophrenic defended against an "eruption" of aggressive emotions by avoiding contact with others. Dr. John Rosen has said that psychosis serves to keep the person from "recognizing consciously the latent source of the terror he experienced with the early maternal environment as he construed it." An angry, raging mother is terrifying enough to another adult but to her baby she becomes such an intolerable threat to his life that he fears annihilation, usually through a feeling she will devour him, Freud pointed out, because at that stage in his life oral feelings predominate.

One result of Freud's theory of the aggressive drive is that psychoanalysts have been developing ways to enable the psychotic to get in touch with his deeply buried rage. Dr. Harry Stack Sullivan, Dr. Frieda Fromm-Reichman, Dr. Harold Searles and others have contributed to the understanding and treatment of the psychotic. Much of the work of the latter two psychoanalysts has been carried on at Chestnut Lodge in Rockville, Maryland.

Fromm-Reichman, author of *Principles of Intensive Psychotherapy*, was one of the first to suggest the therapist pay more attention to the "hating aspects" of the schizophrenic. She said such patients will not be benefited by the doctor's commenting upon the positive manifestations of their relationship with him. Sometimes they may get help, as other patients do, if the hateful or malevolent aspects of their relationship with the doctor are pointed out to them."

One of the first to describe schizophrenia in terms of "rage turned on the self" was Dr. Hyman Spotnitz. He believes schizophrenia to be a "completely reversible disturbance of the psychic apparatus." In his books *Modern Psychoanalysis of the Schizophrenic Patient* and *Psychotherapy of the Pre-Oedipal Conditions: Schizophrenia in Severe Character Disorders*, he describes techniques "to repair the psyche and help the individual become a mature personality." Similar techniques, he says, can be used to help all psychologically reversible pre-Oedipal disturbances be "corrected." His theories and technique in treating the pre-Oedipal conditions are called "modern analysis." If the early emotional background of severely disturbed persons is revealed, it becomes clear, Spotnitz says, that they "suffered a particularly damaging failure in the process of maturation." Aggressive energy, lacking outlets for release in feeling and language, has crippled their egos. "The defense operates unconsciously to protect the person from the release of what is felt as volcanic aggression and thus serves to disrupt his psyche."

By releasing the impulse to love from the "impossible task of blotting out the impulse to hate, and by taming hate into personally and socially desirable forms of human expression," the analyst diminishes the destructive potential of the hate and frees the love urges "for creative service," Spotnitz says.

Freud's theory of aggression as an instinctual drive led into the study of psychosis as well as neurosis. In addition to sexuality and aggression, he pioneered in a third area that stirred up angry discussion as well as skepticism. An area also allied to passionate feelings of the very early years of life—religion.

8

No Promises from Heaven Above

On New Year's Day, 1910, Freud wrote to his close friend Ferenczi, "It's ultimate basis is the infantile helplessness of mankind." He was referring to religion.

His conclusions about the nature of religion and why men were attracted to religious rituals evoked more controversy than perhaps any of his other theories except infantile sexuality.

Freud did not believe in God. He considered God a projection of the child's fantasy of the father who loved him when he was good and would strike him dead when he was bad. And Freud had no use for organized religion, neither its tenets of faith nor its elaborate rituals, which he equated with the superstitions of primitive societies.

In *The Future of an Illusion*, written in 1927, Freud described religion as "the universal obsessional neurosis of humanity." He said that like the obsessional neurosis of children, religion "arose out of the Oedipus complex, out of the relation to the father." Devout believers were "safeguarded in a high degree against the risk of certain neurotic illnesses" in that their "acceptance of the universal neurosis spares them the task of constructing a personal one."

If his view were correct, Freud said, "it is to be supposed that a turning-away from religion is bound to occur with the fatal inevitability of a process of growth." In addition to the obsessional restrictions of religion, it also "comprises a system of wishful illusions together with a disavowal of reality, such as we find in an isolated form nowhere else but in amentia, a state of blissful hallucinatory confusion."

In a letter to his friend, the Swiss pastor Oskar Pfister, who believed in many of Freud's theories and used them with parishioners, Freud said, "In itself psychoanalysis is neither religious nor the opposite but an impartial instrument which can serve the clergy as well as the laity when it is used only to free suffering people."

Freud once told Jones he had never believed in a supernatural world. Jones said in his biography of Freud, "There is no reason to think Freud ever cudgeled his brains about the purpose of the universe—he was always an unrepentant atheist . . ." Jones added, "Having himself dealt in other ways with the needs and wishes that impel people to hold religious beliefs, Freud saw no reason for accepting them. He was simply an unbeliever."

The world of nature seemed all-embracing to Freud, and he could find no evidence of anything outside it. Freud became interested in *why* people had to invent another imaginary "and perhaps illusory" world beyond the one they lived in. "That assuredly," Jones wrote, "was Freud's own view, and it accounts for his lifelong wonderment at the religious beliefs of other people and his ceaseless inquiry into the reason for them." This attitude occurred long before his psychological research, which in no way accounted for it, Jones said.

In discussing religious development from the belief in many gods to the belief in one God, Freud said that if people must believe in supernatural beings, it was preferable they should believe in a single one because this belief revealed "the father nucleus which had always lain hidden behind every divine figure; fundamentally it was a return to the historical beginnings of the idea of God. Now that God was a single person, man's relations to him could recover the intimacy and intensity of the child's relation to the father."

Roman Catholicism, with its Mariolotry and countless saints, pageantry and retention of pagan rituals, appeared to Freud as a regression rather than an advance on Judaism, according to Jones, who said of Freud: "As a Jew he was bound to feel prejudiced against Christianity in general, the religion that had inflicted such untold suffering on his people through the centuries."

Freud was outspoken about his reasons for repudiating religion. In *The Psychopathology of Everyday Life*, written in 1904, he said: "I believe in fact that a great part of the mythological view of the world, which reaches far into the most modern religions, is *nothing other than psychological processes projected into the outer world*. The obscure apprehending of the psychical factors and relationships of the unconscious is mirrored—it is hard to put it otherwise; one has to use here the analogy with paranoia—in the construction of a *supersensible reality*, which science has to retranslate into the *psychology of the unconscious*. One could venture in this manner to resolve the myths of Paradise, the Fall of Man, of God, of Good and Evil, of Immortality and so on, thus transforming *Metaphysics* into *Metapsychology*" (italics Freud's).

A contemporary psychoanalyst, Dr. William G. Niederland, in his book *The Schreber Case: Psychoanalytic Profile of a Paranoid Personality*, extended Freud's analysis of the case of Judge Daniel Paul Schreber, hospitalized nine years for his delusions, mainly religious ones, including his belief God would transform him into a woman, take him as a wife, and that out of this relationship a better and healthier race of men would emerge. Niederland traced this illusion to the relationship between Schreber as a boy and his sadistic, tyrannical father who treated his children as "personal property" and "acted out his ideas and techniques" on their bodies with brutal physical restraints. Niederland also showed that there was a relationship between sexual conflicts in Schreber's life (at one point he bellowed at the sun and called it a "whore") and his "explosive aggression" at his father, much of which was turned on himself as he became delusional.

In Freud's paper, "Obsessive Acts and Religious Practices," published in 1907, he compared "the sense of compulsion" accompanying the ritual acts in religious observances, such as praying and kneeling, with that of the private ritual acts of the obsessional neurosis (such as washing hands compulsively a certain number of times a day, or returning several times to make sure a door is locked). He pointed to the part played by fear and the sense of guilt if the acts are omitted. Such acts are designed to ward off "certain temptations," often unconscious, together with the punishment that yielding to these temptations might bring. In the neurosis, these were essentially sexual temptations, Freud said, whereas religious observances were more concerned with aggressive and anti-social ones—with conduct in general. Freud summed up the comparison by stating the obsessional neurosis may be regarded "as a pathological counterpart" to religion and individual piety, and religion might be called a universal obsessional neurosis.

Freud had great respect for Dr. James Jackson Putnam of Boston, his first staunch supporter in America, whom he knew personally. After reading Putnam's book *Human Motives*, which emphasized the importance of religious beliefs as well as psychoanalytic theories, Freud wrote Ferenczi, "It is a good and loyal book but filled with the sense of religion which I am irresistably impelled to reject. From the psychical reality of our ideas he directly infers their material reality, and therefore God."

Freud wrote Putnam, on July 8, 1915, of his thoughts on the book, saying he had read what were for him the most important sections on religion and psychoanalysis and had "yielded to the impulse to write." He told Putnam, "It is pleasant to think that it will make an impression on your fellow-countrymen and with many of them break down their deeply rooted resistance [to psychoanalysis]." Then he added, referring to the religious section, "The publicity with which moral demands are made often makes an unpleasant impression on me. What I have seen of religious-ethical conversions has not been very inviting."

He mentioned one point on which he could agree with Putnam, that "an impulsion toward the ideal forms an essential part of our constitution." He added, "If only more of this valuable constitution were to be observed in others!" He also told Putnam, ". . . when the knowledge of the human soul is so imperfect that even my poor abilities have managed to make such rich discoveries it is evidently premature to decide for or against such assumptions such as yours."

In his study of Leonardo da Vinci in 1910 Freud stated unequivocally his conclusions about the source of religious beliefs—Jones calls this Freud's main contribution to the psychology of religion. Freud said: "Psychoanalysis has made us aware of the intimate connection between the father complex and the belief in God, and has taught us that the personal God is psychologically nothing other than a magnified father; it shows us every day how young people can lose their religious faith as soon as the father's authority collapses. We thus recognize the root of religious need as lying in the parental complex."

Freud began to investigate the sources of primitive religion in 1911, the results appearing in *Totem and Taboo* two years later. He saw his study as primarily about the origins of religion but it also delved into the origin of civilization itself. He traced religion, civilization, law, morality and the start of community life to man's conflict over the primordial Oedipus complex.

In a preface to a book by his friend Theodor Reik on the psychology of religion, Freud stated in 1919 what he called "an unexpectedly precise conclusion: that God the Father once walked upon earth in bodily form and exercised his sovereignty as chieftain of the primal human horde until his sons united to slay him. It emerged further that this crime of liberation and the reactions to it had as their result the appearance of the first social ties, the basic moral restrictions and the oldest form of religion—totemism." The later religions, which had the same content, tried to obliterate the traces of that "crime" or expiate it by bringing forward other solutions of the struggle between father and son, even as they kept repeating the theme of the elimination of the father.

In *The Ego and the Id*, written in 1923, Freud said that the "ego ideal" was a substitute for the early longing for a loved father and as such contained the kernel out of which all religions are constituted. He held that religion, morality and social feeling were originally one. In the same year he published a study, "A Seventeenth Century Demonological Neurosis," showing how in earlier centuries repressed impulses could be projected on "imaginary demons" whereas today they are internalized as bodily suffering.

He said the repressed impulses were connected to conflicting emotions about the father and these were reflected in religious ideas. He accepted the historical view that originally God and the Devil were one figure which later split into two, one holy, the other evil.

In his controversial work, *The Future of an Illusion*, Freud dealt head-on with the nature of religion and what he thought its probable future. He explained in what sense he was using the term "illusion" as distinguished from "error": "An illusion is not the same as an error, it is indeed not necessarily an error . . . We call a belief an illusion when wish-fulfillment is a prominent factor in its motivation." He gave the example of "a poor girl" indulging in the illusion that a prince would appear to rescue her, adding, "It is possible; some such cases have occurred." There are no rational grounds for the girl accepting this as a "belief," any more than there are rational grounds for religious beliefs—it is a hope derived from certain wishes and needs, he said.

Freud believed knowledge of the inner self was the most important knowledge of all. But he also understood there was a need in everyone somehow to come to terms with the complicated emotions involved in the father-child relationship, a need that led people to construct and carry out religious beliefs. He concluded that the need stemmed from the helplessness of man in face of the many dangers with which he had to cope—from the outer world, from within himself, and from his relations to his fellow man. Religion, myth and morality may be regarded as attempts to compensate for the gratifications lacking in reality, Freud said.

"Man's helplessness remains, and with it his father-longing and the gods. The gods retain their threefold-task: they must exorcise the terrors of nature, they must reconcile one to the cruelty of fate, particularly as shown by death, and they must make amends for the sufferings and privations that the communal life of culture has imposed on man."

In dealing with the future of religion Freud suggested that perhaps mankind could find it possible to endure the hardships of life without needing the consolation of religion. He admitted he himself might be indulging in an illusion, but nevertheless ventured "the opinion and the hope" that in some distant future it might be possible for man to face life without the help of religion.

He mentioned two factors he thought might bring this about: 1) If childhood and youth were no longer subject to the teachings of religion, "conditioned" to its beliefs and also liberated from some of the sexual restrictions society imposed so the intelligence freed might prove to be more effective than in the past 2) The belief that religion, like the earlier mythologies, might turn out to be nothing more than a necessary phase in human evolution, one comparable to adolescence.

Every child has to learn gradually to distinguish between the ideas and wishes of his fantasies and the facts of the outer world and to learn to do without the protection of parents; perhaps the same might be true of mankind as a whole, Freud suggested. "In the long run nothing can withstand reason and experience, and the contradiction religion offers to both is only too palpable," he said.

In *Civilization and Its Discontents,* written three years after *The Future of an Illusion,* Freud was even more outspoken. He said that in the earlier book he was concerned much less with the deepest sources of religious feeling than with what the ordinary man understands by his religion—that system of doctrines and pledges which on the one hand explains the riddle of this world to him with "an enviable completeness," and on the other hand assures him that "a solicitous Providence is watching over him and will make up to him in a future existence for any shortcomings in this life." And then: "The ordinary man cannot imagine this Providence in any other form but that of a greatly exalted Father, for only such a one could understand the needs of the sons of men, or be softened by their prayers and placated by the signs of their remorse. The whole thing is so patently infantile, so incongruous with reality, that to one whose attitude to humanity is friendly it is painful to think that the great majority of mortals will never be able to rise above this view of life. It is even more humiliating to discover what a large number of those alive today, who must see that this religion is not tenable, yet try to defend it inch by inch, as if with a series of pitiable rearguard actions."

And: "At such cost—by the forcible imposition of mental infantilism and inducing a mass-delusion—religion succeeds in saving many people from individual neuroses. But little more. There are, as we have said, many paths by which the happiness attainable for man can be reached, but none which is certain to take him to it. Nor can religion keep her promises either. When the faithful find themselves reduced in the end to speaking of God's 'inscrutable decree', they thereby avow that all that is left to them in their sufferings is unconditional submission as a last-remaining consolation and source of happiness . . . And if a man is willing to come to this, he could probably have arrived there by a shorter road."

Freud raised the question in 1933 as to whether there was a world outlook peculiar to psychoanalysis, and answered it with a decided negative. He had said before, "No, science is no illusion. But it would be an illusion to suppose that we could get anywhere else what it cannot give us."

For religion, Freud wanted to substitute the primacy of the intelligence, the solutions of science as it applied to mental functioning. "I know how difficult it is to avoid illusions; perhaps even the hopes I have confessed to are of an illusory nature," he said. But his illusions about science were not like religious illusions—science was "not incapable of correction" nor were its findings "delusional." On the other hand, he granted his substitution of knowledge for religion might be inadequate, its application to the human race unjustified and his optimism about its inspirational power without foundation.

He then said that though we may insist as much as we like that the human intellect is weak in comparison with human instincts, and be right in doing so, "Nevertheless there is something peculiar about this weakness. This voice of the intellect is a soft one, but it does not rest until it has gained a hearing. Ultimately, after endlessly repeated rebuffs, it succeeds."

Freud saw religion as the chief opponent of science and contrasted the suppositions and aims of the two. He denied the claim of religion to be concerned "with a different sphere of truth," one that science had no right to invade. This "hands off" attitude had been endorsed by Francis Bacon in *The Advancement of Learning* (1605) and respected by most empirical scientists ever since. But Freud declared that religious beliefs were just as legitimate an object of psychological investigation as any other mental phenomena.

He again criticized religion in *New Introductory Lectures,* saying it was an attempt "to get control over the sensory world in which we are placed by means of the wish-world, which we have developed within as a result of biological and psychological necessities. But it cannot achieve its end. Its doctrines carry with them the stamp of the times in which they originated, the ignorant childhood days of the human race. Its consolations deserve no trust. Experience teaches us that the world is not a nursery."

The ethical commands to which religion seeks to lend its weight require some other foundation, since humane society cannot do without them and it is dangerous "to link up obedience with religious belief," Freud said. "If one attempts to assign to religion its place in man's evolution, it seems not so much to be a lasting acquisition as a parallel to the neurosis which the civilized individual must pass through on his way from childhood to maturity."

In the last book he ever wrote, *Moses and Monotheism,* published in 1939, the year of his death, Freud discussed the question of why religious emotion reaches a greater sublimity, profundity and majesty than any other human emotion. He accounted for this by saying it represented a re-emergence from the very depths of man's unconscious, after a long period of latency, of extremes of feeling that are inaccessible except in religious transformation.

Moses and Monotheism is both a study of the origins of the Jewish religion—and to some extent of the Christian—and a consideration of the significance of religion in general. Freud considered Moses, who bore an Egyptian name, as an Egyptian and his real mother as an Egyptian princess who, like many of the royal ladies of that era, had to deny an illegitimate child. Freud made the original suggestion that Moses was faced with the choice of either becoming a renegade or an exile after a counter-revolution following the death of Akhenaten, who had believed in one God.

Convinced of the truth of Akhenaten's concept, Moses, on being rejected by his Egyptian compatriots, created a people of his own who would carry on this religious belief. Freud said the retinue accompanying Moses out of Egypt later became the Levites, thus accounting for the Egyptian names some of them bore.

Freud quoted his previous opinion about the nature of religion, then added another important idea—that of the latency period, the years between six or seven and adolescence, during which sexual drives become less urgent and interest is centered on school, friends and new activities, but then is followed by "a return of the repressed." Freud equated this "return of the repressed" with the profundity of religious feeling. He compared the latency period in the individual and the race, and said both represented the emergence of emotions from the unconscious. "Something unique and commensurate with that which has grown out of it" had to first suffer the fate of repression "before it could produce such mighty effects on its return and force the masses under its spell, such as we have observed—with astonishment and hitherto without understanding—in religious tradition." What re-emerges, he said, are the emotions that at the beginning of life were "attached to the idea of the Father." Infantile feelings are far more intense and inexhaustibly deep than are those of adults and only religious ecstasy can bring back that intensity, he added: "Thus a transport of devotion to God is the first response to the return of the Great Father."

Referring to the religious experience on Mount Sinai when Moses presented the Ten Commandments from God, Freud said, "The first effect of the reunion with what men had long missed and yearned for was overwhelming ... There was admiration, awe and gratitude that the people had found favor in His eyes . . . The conviction that His power was irresistible, the subjection to His will could not have been more absolute with the helpless, intimidated son of the father of the (primal) horde than they were here; indeed they become fully comprehensible only by the transformation into the primitive and infantile *milieu.*"

What brought the figure of Moses so much to the forefront of Freud's mind in the years 1933 to 1938? According to Ernest Jones, the reason Freud's interest in mankind and its religions had narrowed to the more specific question of the Jews and their religion "could only have been the unparalleled persecution of his people that was getting under way in Nazi Germany, with the likelihood of this spreading to his native country [Austria]." Jones added, "Freud was once more forced to wonder what it was in his people that evoked such horrible reactions, and how they had become what they were."

Freud wrote Pfister in 1918: "From a therapeutic point of view

I can only envy you the possibility of sublimation that religion affords. But the beauty of religion certainly does not belong to the domain of psychoanalysis. Naturally our ways part at this point in therapy; and it may stay so. By the way, how comes it that none of all the pious people discovered psychoanalysis; why did they have to wait for a quite godless Jew?"

Pfister answered: "In the first place you are not a Jew, which my endless admiration for Amos, Isaiah, Jeremiah, with the men who composed Job and the Prophets, makes me greatly regret; and in the second place you are not so godless, since whoever lives for the truth lives in God and whoever strives for the freeing of love 'dwelleth in God'. If you would fuse your own contribution with the great world harmony, like the synthesis of notes in a Beethoven symphony into a musical whole, I could say of you, 'There never was a better Christian'."

In an earlier letter to Pfister on February 9, 1909, Freud had said, "I have been very struck at realizing how I had never thought of the extraordinary help the psychoanalytic method can be in pastoral work, probably because wicked heretics like us are so far away from that circle."

He went on to say that psychoanalysts do not see in sexual gratification anything forbidden or sinful but recognize it as a valuable part of a person's "vital activity." He added, "You know that our word 'erotic' includes what in your profession is called 'love' [in the Augustinian sense of *caritas,* or charity] and is not at all restricted to gross sensual pleasure. Thus our patients have to seek in people what we are not able to promise them from the Land Above and what we have to refuse them personally."

Freud wanted to substitute the science of human behavior for religion. Reason for ritual. Freedom of choice for obsessive faith. But there were those who questioned, and still question, how much of a "science" psychoanalysis was, charging it lacked the validity of a "true science."

They asked how either the analyst or the patient could "prove" the effectiveness of the treatment on the couch? How could the results of psychoanalysis possibly be "measured"?

9

The "Proof" of Psychoanalysis

Someone in the audience at a lecture given by Dr. Franz Alexander in Chicago once rose to insist psychoanalysis was *not* a science since it could not prove its principles "through experiments." Alexander was so upset that he wrote to Freud at once.

Freud suggested Alexander ask the audience at his next lecture "whether they considered astronomy and paleontology real sciences, since one cannot experiment with the stars or with fossils."

Psychoanalysis is not a science in the sense of chemistry or biology. The "natural" scientists study substances or germs that can be seen or measured or whose effects (like those of bacteria on human cells) can be measured. They deal with something that is tangible.

Psychoanalysis deals with the intangible. What a person *thinks*, *feels* or *daydreams*. His dreams at night, his fear of the dark, of crowds, of high places. Or a man's inability to get an erection. Or a woman's fear of letting go in the act of sex. Or a child's inability to stop wetting the bed or throwing temper tantrums.

In dealing with human emotions there is nothing concrete to measure in a statistical way. But one knows when anxiety is present. Its effect can be seen on the individual if he is depressed and commits suicide or if he is angry and kills someone. An individual's impact on a nation may be visible, as in the case of Hitler or Idi Amin, where a leader's aggressive, hostile impulse is powerful enough to sway—and slay—millions.

Psychoanalysis is the scientific approach to man's inner life. The substance with which it deals is of a *qualitative* not a *quantitative* nature. As Freud put it: ". . . psychoanalysis is not an impartial scientific investigation, but a therapeutic measure. Its essence is not to prove anything, but merely to alter something. In a psychoanalysis the physician always gives his patient (sometimes to a greater and sometimes to a lesser extent) the conscious anticipatory images by the help of which he is put in a position to recognize and to grasp the unconscious material. For there are some patients who need more of such assistance and some who need less; but there are none who get through without some of it."

Freud used the word "metapsychology" (originally the study of the relation between mind and body) as meaning the psychology of the unconscious. Psychoanalysis is a "depth" psychology, a psychology of the unconscious aspects of the mind and "its novelty, its great and special contribution to the science of the mind was precisely what it had to say about what does go on unconsciously," said Dr. Charles Brenner in his paper, "Metapsychology and Psychoanalytic Theory," given at the Thirty-First International Congress.

Referring to Freud's view that psychoanalysis is a branch of science and that it has no philosophy of life except the pragmatic, materialistic one it shares with the rest of science, Brenner pointed out that psychoanalytic theories depend for their support on observational data derived from the application of the psychoanalytic method.

"Those data are not accessible in any way other than by applying that method," he said. "They were essentially unknown before Freud developed the analytic method and would still be so today without it. No one could have predicted that instructing a patient to say whatever is on his mind without editing—the basis of the psychoanalytic method—would have proved to be fruitful of new and unexpected knowledge about human psychology. Yet it turned out to be so. This method of investigation has yielded more significant knowledge of human mental functioning and development in a few decades than anyone could possibly have predicted. For the first time, man is in possession of a technique for studying the psychic life of his fellow men."

Freud created "the science of psychoanalysis—not only a new science but a new *type* of science," according to Dr. Samuel Atkin, former president of the New York Psychoanalytic Institute and Society. He says Freud established "an exquisitely psychological science solidly established on a biological foundation."

"Psychoanalysis is a tool for understanding not only the patient but mankind itself," in the words of Dr. Jacob Arlow, past president of the American Psychoanalytic Association. "The early psychoanalytic pioneers were keenly aware of the broad humanistic significance of psychoanalysis, of psychoanalysis as a body of knowledge transcending the purpose of individual therapy."

Psychoanalysis operates according to a scientific method and a scientific theory, based on the laws of unconscious thinking and its interaction with conscious thinking. In psychoanalysis there evolved for the first time in human history a scientific technique for the study of man himself. As Dr. Lawrence Kubie said: "At long last the ancient Socratic precept, 'Know thyself', has become a scientific process instead of a vague and naive aspiration . . . Man himself is armed for the first time with tools to penetrate below the surface. Knowledge of the self is the forgotten man of education. It is the newest and the youngest of the sciences, and like all young sciences it is far from precise . . . Our very survival, as human beings and as a culture, hinges upon self-knowledge." Declaring man's unsolved psychological problems "are derivatives from the lusts and hates and heartaches of the human nursery," he said, "one dares to ask, therefore, whether modern psychoanalytically guided research can for the first time in human history discover how to make human infancy and human childhood a breeder of health and love instead of illness and hate. Psychoanalysis itself is just beginning to face this challenge."

Psychoanalysis is unique in that it is both a science *and* an art. Havelock Ellis said Freud's art was "the poetry of psychic processes" that lie in the deepest and most mysterious recesses of the human being. The psychoanalyst must be both scientist and artist. Unless he is skilled in establishing trust and empathy between the patient and himself, and in giving interpretations at the proper moment, the science will not be effective.

As early as 1909 **Dr. Ernest Jones** wrote: "Apart from technical knowledge, the physician must possess not only unimpeachable integrity but also a considerable measure of tact, patience, and sympathetic understanding; without these qualifications he is unlikely to gain the patient's confidence. The demands made on the patient are no less great. The results of the treatment will vary with the intelligence, courage, honesty and perseverance he shows."

Jones spoke of the "intricate task" in psychoanalysis of converting "an intolerable existence into a happy life, and a person paralyzed by doubts, fears and suffering into an active and useful citizen."

Psychoanalysis is a search for the truth within. Freud declared ". . . we must not forget that the analytic relationship is based on a love of truth; that is, on a recognition of reality, and that it precludes any . . . kind of sham or deceit."

Marie Bonaparte once said to Freud, "Those who thirst before everything for certitude do not really love truth." To which Freud replied, "That is so true. I have said that too somewhere, in another way. Mediocre spirits demand of science a kind of certainty which it cannot give, a sort of religious satisfaction. Only the real, rare, true scientific minds can endure doubt, which is attached to all our knowledge. I always envy the physicists and mathematicians who can stand on firm ground. I hover, so to speak, in the air. Mental events seem to be immeasurable and probably always will be so."

As Dr. Luis Feder says, "When you walk into the analyst's office, the only instrument you both have is truth. It becomes a link, it becomes a process, it becomes a goal."

Dr. Edward Joseph, president of the International Psychoanalytical Association, said at the Thirty-First Congress that analysis is a never-ending undertaking, that the tremendous realm of unconscious life is never exhausted: "Alteration of any one portion of the inner world leads to a readjustment of the relationships between other unconscious portions of the mind, a process that goes on silently. In line with this thought is the well-known phenomena reported by many psychoanalysts that patients will report the disappearance of problems and difficulties that have never been analyzed during the course of an analysis."

What is "truth" in analysis? Psychoanalysts define it as the gaining of insight. In addition to the conscious understanding of the unconscious processes, insight involves the fundamental concept of lasting changes in the personality. Through the gaining of insights, patients reach what Freud called "the goal of psychoanalysis . . . to transform neurotic misery into normal human suffering." Insight makes possible the bringing into awareness the distortions and projections that are rooted in the past and the defenses that have kept the conflicts of earlier years repressed. This awareness is achieved as the ego becomes stronger. "The business of analysis is to secure the best possible psychological conditions for the functions of the ego; with that it has discharged its task," Freud said.

Hanns Sachs defined the goal of analysis as "relative anxiety-free and guilt-free communication with the unconscious." The patient becomes acquainted with the unconscious fantasies that have dominated his behavior and learns to tolerate the feelings that are part of them, instead of being unconsciously possessed by those feelings. He accepts what has happened in the past, no longer blaming himself or others.

Dr. Walter A. Stewart points out that psychoanalysis offers troubled people the unique opportunity "to repeat the unfinished business of childhood, discover the conflicts that are repeated in adult neurosis, and to re-experience childhood events without feeling rejected or humiliated in any way, provided instead with insights." He warns that the psychoanalyst must give the insights "at an emotional, not intellectual level."

The gaining of insight is a very complex process; it does not happen all at once. "The pretense of assumption on the part of the psychiatrist or the patient that intellectual understanding due to one single interpretation may help is a dangerous block against real change and real cure," said Dr. Frieda Fromm-Reichmann. "Any understanding, any new piece of awareness which has been gained by interpretative clarification has to be reconquered and tested time and again in new connections and contacts with other interlocking experiences, which may or may not have to be subsequently approached interpretively in their own right."

Margaret Brenman-Gibson has put it: "An interpretation emerges as the joint [analyst and patient] experience of a truth which relieves and restores as it enlightens."

How can the achievement of analytic goals be measured? The usual kinds of scientific measurement will not show how much happier a person feels after several years of analysis. Changes in heartbeat or blood pressure can be measured but the efficacy of couch treatment is of another nature though, as a result, headaches disappear, the heartbeat slows down, sinus conditions and ulcers vanish, even cancer can be halted and reversed, according to Dr. Selwyn Brody in his article, "Psychoanalytic Treatment of Cancer Patients."

Inasmuch as the mind has conscious and unconscious fantasies and conflicts, the study of those fantasies and conflicts and how they affect mental functioning may be called a science. Inasmuch as human beings have feelings, those feelings and their effects may be observed. As Freud said, ". . . the only subject-matter of psychoanalysis is the mental processes of human beings and it is only in human beings that it can be studied."

Mental health, or the lack of it, is difficult to measure unless a person is violent, suicidal or lives in the world of hallucinations. Freud "defined mental health very simply, succinctly, almost naïvely," says Rudolf Ekstein, of the Reiss-Davis Clinic for Child Guidance in Los Angeles, as "nothing more or less than 'the capacity to love and to work'."

A reporter once asked Jones, "What is your definition of a normal man?" Jones replied, "Don't know. Never saw one."

But there are definitions. Dr. Karl Menninger in his classic work *The Human Mind* says: "Let us define mental health as the adjustment of human beings to the world and to each other with a maximum of effectiveness and happiness. Not just efficiency, or just contentment—or the grace of obeying the rules of the game cheerfully. It is all of these together. It is the ability to maintain an even temper, an alert intelligence, socially considerate behavior and a happy disposition. This, I think, is a healthy mind." The lack of what is called "mental health" may range from someone with a slight degree of emotional difficulty to someone so severely disturbed that he may have to spend months, even years, in an institution for the protection of himself and society.

In discussing the difference between the "normal" person and the "neurotic," Freud said the only difference was that "the healthy know how to overcome these complexes (which make them fall ill) without great and practically demonstrable harm; while the suppression of these complexes in nervous people only succeeds at the price of costly substitute-formations, thus in practice proving unsuccessful."

The choice of a specific "costly substitute-formation" has always been a puzzling question. Why is one person terrified of crowds? Why does another develop an ulcer? A third become addicted to alcohol? A fourth obsessed by overwork? A fifth seized by depression?

Psychoanalysts say the only answer is to examine the inner life of that particular person and discover his specific fears and repressions and traumas. Only the observance of his life in depth will yield the reason he has unconsciously chosen a certain illness or form of aberrant behavior.

How measure the depth of relief felt on the couch as a patient becomes free enough to release a tear? Or gives partial outlet to a buried wish in the emotions aroused by a dream? How measure the intensity of fury at a frustrated desire? Or the degree of guilt at a murderous wish?

How measure the decrease in the struggle against awareness? The breaking down of defenses erected against the pain of earlier experiences whose repressed memories have shattered confidence in the self?

How measure the effect of the distortion of childhood experiences when parents were considered gods or cruel giants?

How measure the process of making conscious the unconscious

—"Where there is id, let ego be," as Freud puts it—so one is no longer under the control of destructive wishes?

How measure a new sense of identity that is recognized slowly, for change on the couch takes place imperceptibly?

All this is measured with a different kind of evaluative tool than that of the natural sciences. The proof of the success of an analysis lies in the opinions of both analyst and patient. Each knows, as a rule, whether the patient has changed for the better, though the words they use to describe the change differ.

First, from the analyst's point of view, what causes change in a patient—what cures? This question was raised recently by Dr. Leo Rangell, former president of the American Psychoanalytic Association and the International Psychoanalytical Association in his article "Contemporary Issues in the Theory of Therapy." Many factors combine to "cure" a patient, said Rangell, author of *The Mind of Watergate,* but one that has not been sufficiently explicit is that "an active role on the part of the patient is necessary and must be continuously enlisted." The patient should care about an interpretation after it has been given by asking, "Why?" wanting further knowledge, instead of feeling, "So what?"

A combination of feeling and knowledge constitutes "the means and ends of analytic cure," he said. "Intellectual and emotional insight together, to be effective, by undoing unconscious structuralized conflicts release psychic energy for the pursuit of healthier activities and more appropriate channels for discharge."

Saying that "analyzing the unconscious is at times like shining a flashlight into the Grand Canyon," Rangell pointed out that traumatic experiences are repeated in memory and in unconscious fantasy "countless, even infinite" numbers of times—they have lasted a lifetime in the adult. The original traumas have been broken up "in small, chronic-release doses in an attempt to overcome their traumatic effects." Microscopic and spread out, these result in what analysts call "the strain trauma" that occurs from ongoing traumatic conditions. It is against this chronic strain, not the limited times of the original occurrences, that the "analytic battle is pitted," Rangell says.

What takes place as a direct result of analysis is an "intrapsychic change during the microdynamic sequence" which is a routine part of thought, he said: "Intrapsychic trial actions, which still go on routinely, result now less in signals of danger, the latter being more limited to realistic fear. The result is a wider choice for the ego of what it can safely do. What the patient with his newly expanded ego possibilities unconsciously chooses to do next is then his own."

The second of the two-step process at the core of therapy, "a last link necessary in the therapeutic chain without which change cannot occur," has, in Rangell's opinion, remained virtually unspoken in the theory of therapy. Yet its failure to take place can "vitiate" the entire work. "The nature of the activity to which I am referring is the unconscious roots of the decision-making process, the ego's 'actions' in routine life following the results of 'trial actions' in the unconscious," he said. What has been emphasized in the past as the peak events "are the liberation of the ego by the solution of conflict, after which changes spontaneously occur. Energy is liberated, new channels found, all more or less in a passive patient." But, more important, he said, is how the patient now unconsciously uses his new strengths to choose a more rewarding way of life.

There is no "cure" in emotional illness in the sense a toothache or a broken arm is "cured." We are all beset by infantile fantasies, many of them distorted in terms of reality, and they never disappear. But we are able to accept them as they spring into our conscious and lose their destructiveness.

The person who "finally has the intelligence, courage, and honesty to be what he has to be—himself—is the free person, the existential man," says Grotjahn. "Nobody can call him sick anymore, even when he happens to be different from anyone else. I no longer think in terms of healing. Nobody leaves my office or the group 'cured' from being human. I hope everybody leaves it with a little more courage to go on, to climb the mountain, to be more himself, and to understand and accept himself and his neighbors."

There are both short-term and long-term aims in psychoanalysis, said Dr. John Klauber of London, addressing the congress on "Formulating Interpretations in Clinical Psychoanalysis." "The short-term aim is to relieve the anxieties and conflicts the patient keeps in the forefront of the analysis. The long-term aim is to

foster his development by means of a process, started in the consulting room, which will help him in the much longer period of
his life after he has left the consulting room for the last time."

The interpretations the analyst directs at the resolution of immediate anxieties must be consistent with achieving the long-term
developmental aims, added Klauber, author of *Difficulties In the
Analytic Encounter.* What he called "some internalization of the
analytic process, perhaps in a modified form, accompanied by an
increased capacity for instinctual satisfaction," provide practical
and logical criteria of analytical success. Such an outcome implies
"the patient has enjoyed the analytic process and has formed a
trusting enough relationship with his analyst to internalize him as
a function, just as a child, according to Anna Freud, internalizes
a mothering function with perhaps only a loose connection with
the actual person of the mother."

A warning against what he called "the myth of perfectability,"
as applied as a goal of analysis by either patient or analyst, was
sounded by Dr. Herbert S. Gaskill at the congress. Even patients
who had "profited greatly" from their analyses showed "areas of
incompleteness" falling short of idealistic or perfectionist goals, he
said. The continuation of the "self-analytic function offers the
optimum for permanence."

Among the profound changes analysts may look for are whether
the patient is able to develop a new capacity for loving another
person more freely and fully, taking into account the needs of the
other person as well as his own. Does he enjoy his work more? Is
he more creative? Can he accept frustration more easily? Has his
anxiety decreased? Has his need to overwork, or not work enough,
disappeared? Has there been a diminuation of his headaches, sinus
condition, ulcers, alcoholism, insomnia, accident-proneness—"the
heartache and the thousand natural shocks that flesh is heir to"?
Has the understanding of what the symptoms masked been
achieved—the wishes and fears against which the symptom was
defending? Has he been able to separate from the analyst, indicating he has achieved the developmental separation from the mother
of childhood? Has he been able to express his underlying anger, his
long held-back grief and sadness? Is his capacity for pleasure and
reflective self-awareness greater?

Analysts have conducted a number of follow-up studies, five and ten years after the analysis ended, which describe the ways in which patients have changed. The majority found new solutions to conflicts that had only achieved neurotic resolutions prior to analysis.

The patient has *his* personal measurements of the success of the analysis as well. Is he more comfortable within himself? Does he feel more self-confident? More thoughtful, more capable of affection, of compassion, of understanding others? Does he feel freer sexually with someone he loves? Freer about his own body? Does he feel more optimistic about his life as a whole? Can he connect the past and the present and understand how the past has influenced the present?

A woman of thirty-nine went to an analyst because of migraine headaches so severe she was almost incapacitated. She lay in bed most of the day, got dressed in the evening to have dinner with her husband. At first she protested to the analyst she was happily married. But as the analysis progressed she spoke of her fear and anger at a husband who often got drunk and struck her, accusing her of being "no good" and a "parasite."

She said she had accepted his abuse for several years because of their six-year-old daughter. But as she was able to be more honest with herself she realized she was concealing deep fury at her husband and had been accepting his cruelty as punishment for her unconscious guilt at her anger—anger related to the repressed anger of childhood at her mother and father.

Within two months her headaches had vanished. After a year in analysis she was able to leave her husband, find an apartment for her daughter and herself, start a new life. She had artistic talent and found work in a commercial art firm. As she continued her analysis she discovered many inner conflicts stemming from a childhood with a tyrannical father and a depressed, masochistic mother whose self-inflicted suffering she had unconsciously copied.

A man of forty who had many affairs but had never married went into analysis wanting to find out why. As he slowly recollected experiences of the past in which he had felt humiliated and rejected, he realized how closely tied he was emotionally to a mother who had always hated her husband and criticized him as man, obviously preferring her son. He had thought that to marry meant being unfaithful to his mother.

He also realized that his image of masculinity was molded on his perception of his father, a passive man dominated by his wife. As he, the patient, became aware he did not have to be like his father, his image of himself changed. After three years in analysis he met a woman of thirty-three, a divorcée, with whom he fell in love. He asked this woman to marry him, saying to his analyst, "I'm no longer tied to the crazy fantasies of childhood. I understand that part of myself I tried to keep in prison."

A woman of forty woke up screaming from a nightmare, so terrified that she turned on the light to reassure herself her life was not in danger. At her next analytic session she described the nightmare in which a white-clad figure approached her as she lay on her bed, intending to murder her. The analyst asked her to tell more about the shadowy figure in white. She said it was "sturdy and plump with long, flowing black hair." Then she recalled that her mother had long dark hair when she, the patient, was a little girl. Then talked of her deep fear of the dark and how her mother would come into her room every night, sometimes in a white nightgown, to make sure she was all right, sometimes waking her.

"I was so mad I couldn't fall asleep for hours," she said. "It was like she wanted to possess me even in sleep. I spent the days fighting her domination and that was hard enough. I felt I could never escape her." She mentioned how her mother made up for her possessive manner by overfeeding her—her mother's solution for all ills was food. She said, "No wonder it's so difficult for me to lose weight. Last night I ate like a pig! I hated myself." At that point she gritted her teeth as though in pain.

The analyst pointed out that the dream had stemmed from stuffing herself "like a pig" the night before. This led, in memory, to her childhood, when her mother had stuffed her to quiet all outbreaks of rage. But in the nightmare her rage was permitted partial expression in her scream of terror, caused by the fear her mother wanted to devour her ("It was like she wanted to possess me even in sleep") and fear of her own overwhelming ("piggish") wish to devour her mother because of her repressed childhood anger. The wish to devour the mother occurred in the oral stage when she became angry because her mother unnecessarily frustrated her. She was also angry because her overpossessive mother had made it difficult for her to separate from her emotionally.

Understanding some of these facts of her early life enabled her to live more happily. She had a husband who openly taunted her about his many affairs and when, through analysis, her self-esteem increased, she left him.

The person on the couch changes far more deeply and effectively than if given doses of lithium or a series of electroshocks whose administration and results can be chemically and biologically measured and observed. Under the latter so-called "scientific" treatment, the observation that after the dosage a person's excessive anger or depression diminishes so he no longer threatens to kill himself or others is accepted as "proof" of cure. But what the drug or shock has achieved is only the temporary removal (further repression) of the symptom. More and more, larger and larger dosages may be required and there is always the danger of crippling side-effects. Memory may be temporarily lost after sustained electro-shock treatments. Studies show that large doses of certain drugs cause muscle impairment as well as other bodily defects.

In the far more delicate, difficult and subtle process of psychoanalysis, an "emotional experience" takes place *within* the person rather than being physically inflicted *on* him. A "relationship" develops between patient and analyst. And as a result of this relationship, one that allows the patient to trust the analyst, he is able to reconstruct much of his earlier life, remember scenes in which he felt humiliated, angered or threatened in some way, scenes that lowered his self-esteem. Most important, he is able to express the emotions connected to these experiences—fear, rage, grief, erotic desire, shame, jealousy, rejection. He slowly starts to accept the fact he is on the couch to get help in understanding his conflicts, and that he will receive empathy, understanding and compassion —not the anger, hurt looks or rejection of the past. He realizes he is being accepted as a human being, faults and all, by someone willing to listen to his most intimate thoughts. Someone whose love and admiration he wants with the childish desperation with which he wanted the love and admiration of his parents.

There is an eight-way communication going on at all times. The patient is communicating to himself and also to his analyst on a conscious level. He is also communicating to himself and to his analyst on an unconscious level. The analyst is communicating to himself and to the patient on a conscious level. And he is also communicating to himself and to the patient on an unconscious level. As a result of this communication of words and feelings, as Freud said, "The transference thus creates an intermediate region between illness and real life through which the transition from one to the other is made." During this transference the patient projects all his erotic and aggressive desires onto the analyst as he did as a child onto his mother and father.

Perhaps one of the most important "facts" of psychoanalysis is that the patient slowly realizes he has an "unconscious" that, both day and night, is trying to get important messages through to him, if he will only listen. He senses this dimly at first as he explores his hidden feelings and accepts the interpretations of the analyst. Then, gradually, he himself feels more in touch with his unconscious emotions and thoughts and wishes and conflicts.

Dr. Abraham Brill said he had difficulty at first reading *The Interpretation of Dreams.* But he forced himself to go on, "and it was not until I found the Freudian mechanisms in my own dreams with the help of my more experienced colleagues that I became, as it were, a Freudian by conviction."

He noticed the same reaction occurred when he presented the theories of psychoanalysis to others: "They accepted and adhered to it only after they had found the Freudian mechanisms in themselves and in others. For nothing is as convincing as finding something in one's self which is common to all."

Both patient and analyst explore what Freud called "psychical reality"—the realm of childhood fantasies that still possess us. This is the stuff of psychoanalysis . . . "in the world of the neuroses, it is psychical reality which is the decisive kind," Freud said.

This world, one the imagination rules, is the world often called "crazy." It is the world of dreams, of the "mental underground." From it spring creative urges as well as the urges Freud and society call "taboo."

Entering the world of the past, a world that, as long as one refuses to face it, may make the present and the future tormented, one discovers oceans of buried grief and rage connected with the losses of life. There may have been real losses—the death of a parent or a brother or sister, or a beloved grandparent. Or the loss suffered when a parent leaves the house, in the case of separation or divorce. There are also the real and imagined losses experienced as part of growing up—losses of a mother's love every time she gets angry or at the birth of another baby, or at weaning, toilet training, separating emotionally from the mother. After each loss comes a feeling of anger at the mother, who is bound to frustrate us as she civilizes us. Then guilt at the anger. All this must be faced and resolved.

The proof of psychoanalysis lies essentially in the patient. He knows whether he has gained insight. He is aware of how much his self-destructiveness has lessened. Whether his life is based more on reality, less on fantasy. If at long last he can feel and verbally express anger in the presence of the analyst—maybe nothing more world-shaking than calling him a "bastard" when he is late or goes on vacation. If he feels less torn apart. If he can now make his own decisions, refusing to give way to the emotional conflicts of others. Whether he has come out of the psychoanalytic experience feeling he has reached a place where he can go on by himself in the search for the truths about his life. If he has more of a sense of self. Recognition of a sense of self comes out of a growing awareness of greater self-esteem. "Recognition is accepting instead of denigrating and accusing oneself," as Paul Ricoeur says. "This movement from misunderstanding to recognition is also the standard itinerary of analytic experience, and it designates what might be called the veracity of truth in psychoanalysis," he states in his article, "The Question of Proof in Freud's Psychoanalytic Writings."

"This sort of truth involves above all the subject's capacity for *selbstreflexion* [self-reflection]," he says. The "truth claim" of psychoanalysis is primarily its claim to increase this capacity by helping the person "overcome the distortions which are the source of self-misunderstanding."

Freud said that psychoanalysts should never *suggest* solutions to patients. The analyst was not to repeat the parental behavior of the past that had helped create the conflicts. To do so was to fly in the face of analytic technique and could only cripple the patient further. When an analyst suggests or orders (patients take suggestions as orders), this is not psychoanalysis. It throws the understanding of the mind back to primitive days.

The analyst helps the patient face his defenses and buried feelings in order to achieve, in Ricoeur's words, "self-recognition, recognition of the other, and recognition of the fantasy."

The patient is "both the actor and the critic of a history which he is at first unable to recount. The problem of recognizing oneself is the problem of recovering the ability to recount one's own history, to endlessly continue to give the form of a story to reflections on oneself. And working through is nothing other than this continuous narration."

Many changes occur in the years after analysis. The effects of treatment do not end when the door to the analyst's office closes for the last time. Insights and changes in mental functioning and bodily feelings continue to take place. As Dr. Lawrence J. Friedman says, "One day you may suddenly become aware you are doing something differently, less destructively." For example, you may walk down the street at a slower pace, no longer driven by the old urgency, now taking delight in savoring a new sense of serenity. Or you may say "no" in situations where you always believed you had to give in so that someone would love you. Or you may now refuse to get involved sexually with someone, knowing it will only prove another disappointing affair, wanting to find a more mature person with whom you can try to establish a permanent relationship. Or you may have acquired the ability for self-reflection—far different from obsessive introspection. In self-reflection you stand at a distance from your self, at the same time feeling more integrated.

There is still another intangible "fact" of psychoanalysis. Analysts know technique is never enough. Surgery may be performed perfectly but the patient dies. There may be missing in psychoanalysis, as well as in surgery, one unmeasurable factor by the usual scientific standards—hope.

Hope plays a large part in the success of the therapy, as Dr. Karl Menninger once pointed out in an article on the need for hope on the part of the analyst, as well as the patient. Some believe this feeling of hope and belief in the patient's progress is *the* most important quality—presuming the competence of the analyst. If he does not believe he can ease the torment in a patient and convey this feeling to the patient, if he feels the patient "too sick," "too uncooperative," "too stupid" or "too unappealing," he cannot help. The patient will sense the analyst's discomfort and lack of trust in him. Trust is a two-way street, so to speak, when it comes to the couch.

Why does the analyst sit behind the patient? Freud said no analyst who felt himself under constant close observation by a patient, aware his slightest move would be interpreted by the patient as some sort of signal, can give himself over to the "free gliding attention" needed for the assimilation of unconscious material. The position enabled the analyst to relax as well as to maintain the anonymity needed for the transference to be effective.

Does everyone need analysis? Obviously many do not—those functioning well at their jobs and in their personal lives, who are neither conscious of undue stress nor show physical or psychological symptoms of neurosis. Others who might need psychoanalysis may lack the willingness to probe deeply into their minds, to face harsh, painful realities about the past and present. They lack the "ego strength" to undergo the psychic distress inherent in facing up to feelings such as fear, anger, jealousy, erotic desire, all repressed and contained since childhood.

For those who do undergo analysis, there is the opportunity of genuine reward in facing the pain. Instead of wandering the earth crying out helplessly, "Why me? Why me?" they become aware of *"Why me."* They understand how the "me" was formed in part out of the fantasies and experiences of the past. And as they realize how the battle was waged between their childhood passions and those of their parents, they lose the need to cry out, "Why me?"

In spite of the fact that "proof" of the effectiveness of analysis is offered through new and unusual methods of measurement, methods it has taken a long time to convince both other professions and the public are as scientific as those of the natural sciences, psychoanalysis has indeed come a long way since its introduction in America.

When did psychoanalysis first appear in the United States? What are its roots in a country that has accepted it more wholeheartedly than any other, in spite of Freud's darkest forebodings?

IO

The Land of the Psychically Free

An event of historic importance took place in September, 1909, not only for Freud but for America. He was invited to this country to speak—the first public recognition anywhere in the world of his new science.

Freud visited America for the first and only time in his life when he spoke at the twentieth anniversary ceremonies of Clark University in Worcester, Massachusetts. The founder and president of Clark, psychologist G. Stanley Hall, had asked Freud to give five lectures and receive an honorary doctorate of law.

Ironically, psychoanalysis was introduced into America in the most puritanical of all the colonies. Massachusetts was the birthplace of Calvinist theologians Increase and Cotton Mather, the scene of the infamous seventeenth-century witch hunts, the colony that condemned, more cruelly than any other, indulgence in sexual desires—a condemnation memorably depicted by Nathaniel Hawthorne in *The Scarlet Letter*. Nor was the Bay State celebrated for its openness to new philosophical ideas—Roger Williams, Anne Hutchinson and Ralph Waldo Emerson were among those forced to abandon their pulpits because of religious intolerance.

But in spite of its repressive and parochial atmosphere, Massachusetts also possessed men of intellectual curiosity who seemed eager to champion a new kind of freedom in this home of the brave —emotional freedom.

A few psychologists and neurologists had become intrigued by the startling discoveries about the mind of man wafting westward from Vienna, devised by a doctor who had once been a neurologist but was now forming a psychology of his own. A number of physicians in Boston had received their graduate medical training in Europe, where the latest scientific advances were being made.

In a remote way the first link between Freudian formulations and American attitudes was made at the end of the eighteenth century. Benjamin Franklin, then United States ambassador to France, sat on a committee appointed by Louis XVI in 1784 to judge whether Dr. Franz Anton Mesmer's use of hypnotism as a cure for what was called hysterical illnesses was a valid medical practice, or whether Mesmer should be banished from Paris as he had been from Vienna. The medical profession won—the committee decided Mesmer was a charlatan and he had to leave Paris. Though unaware of it, Mesmer had discovered the powerful effect of transference—the feelings of love and desire to please that a patient showed for his doctor (mirroring his childhood feelings towards his mother and father).

A century later, what is believed to be the first allusion to Freud's work in America was made in 1894 by William James, Professor of Psychology at Harvard University. Giving a lecture on psychopathology James said, "In the relief of certain hysterias, by handling the buried idea, whether as in Freud or in Janet, we see a portent to the possible usefulness of these new discoveries. The awful becomes relatively trivial." Pierre Janet, professor of psychiatry at the Collège de France, supported Charcot's theory that the nervous system of the hysteric had a psychic weakness, which Janet called "psychasthenia," saying it might follow excessive fatigue or shock.

That same year James also published a short abstract of Freud and Breuer's "Preliminary Communication" in the *Psychological Review*, telling the story of Bertha Pappenheim ["Anna O."]. And when the elaboration of that "communication" came out in the book *Studies on Hysteria*, James reviewed it.

The first long citation of Freud's work appeared in a paper by Dr. Robert T. Edes, "The New England Invalid," given as the Shattuch Lecture before the Massachusetts Medical Society on June 11, 1895. He said: "It is held by Breuer and Freud that the essential part of the action of mental or moral shock in the production of hysteria lies in the absence of the appropriate motor reaction, as for instance, when a lower official received from his superior an insult which he could not resent. The correctness of this view seemed to be demonstrated by the result that when the history of the affair was completely elaborated by hypnotism and fully talked over, the hysterical symptom disappeared . . ."

One of the first landmarks of psychoanalysis in America was the publication in April, 1906, of a paper by Dr. James Jackson Putnam, who taught at Harvard University, describing how he used Freud's new psychoanalytic method with patients. This paper, "Recent Experiences in the Study and Treatment of Hysteria at the Massachusetts General Hospital," appeared in the *Journal of Abnormal Psychology*.

Putnam, a neurologist who was America's first "Professor of Diseases of the Nervous System," holds the honor of being the first doctor in America to apply the principles of psychoanalysis to treatment. A pillar of Boston cultural life, at the age of sixty-three he took up the cause of psychoanalysis, becoming America's original psychoanalytic missionary. Like Freud, but a decade earlier, Putnam had studied with Charcot in Paris and Meynart in Vienna. Putnam had also been influenced by William James, his close friend ever since they were fellow students at Harvard Medical School in 1866.

And so in 1904, at a time when Freud's theories were being denounced as ridiculous or obscene or both in Europe, Putnam was applying them to three cases—two women and a man—in a small outpatient clinic for the treatment of nervous diseases he had started at Massachusetts General Hospital. This famous hospital was founded by, among others, his mother's father and his name-sake, Dr. James Jackson.

Quoting Freud in his article, Putnam focused on the importance of the repression of the sexual drive and the new technique for helping to reach the unconscious. He warned, "The strict application of the analytic method is very difficult, and implies a degree of skill which few physicians can attain."

The year after Putnam's article appeared, Dr. Richard Cabot, who established the country's first hospital social service department at Massachusetts General, referred to "Freud's psychoanalysis" as one of the methods of treatment at the hospital.

Putnam was one of the first editors of the *Journal of Abnormal Psychology,* which he helped establish in 1906 along with Dr. Morton Prince, noted for his study of multiple personalities. In 1913 Prince was threatened by the Boston police with prosecution for the "obscenities" he was publishing in the *Journal,* referring to Freud's sexual theories. But Prince, who had been a former mayor of Boston, knew how to take care of official harassment without appearing in court. The *Journal* continued to publish Freud's work, the first periodical in this country to offer psychoanalytic papers. The second was the *Psychoanalytic Review,* started in 1913 by Dr. William Alanson White of Washington, D.C. and Dr. Smith Ely Jelliffe of New York City.

The historic role of the *Journal* was more than the recording of early psychoanalytic thinking. It became a forum for the discussion of the new art-science. The unconscious, the meaning of dreams and slips of the tongue and Freud's other provocative ideas were extensively described in the early volumes by Putnam, Prince, Jelliffe, Dr. Isador Coriat of Boston, Dr. Adolph Meyer of New York, and by Dr. Ernest Jones, at that time "Demonstrator of Psychiatry" at the University of Toronto and pathologist at the Toronto Hospital for the Insane.

Putnam met Jones in 1908, when the latter was only twenty-nine and visited Boston to present Freud's theories. Jones later described Putnam as possessing "extraordinarily high ethical standards, uprightness, honor, fairness and loyalty . . . modesty, amiability, persistence and tenacious adherence to convictions."

One of William James' students at Harvard was G. Stanley Hall, the son of a farmer and a graduate of Williams College. Dr. Henry P. Bowditch, the historian, called Hall a kind of "queer genius." He had studied psychopathology in Berlin and Leipzig and in 1884 at the age of forty was appointed Professor of Psychology and Pedagogy at Johns Hopkins University. Three years later he became founder and president of Clark University. This was a small institution compared to Harvard, where his former professor, William James, now taught. At Clark, Hall quarreled publicly with his erstwhile mentor, deriding what he called James' "armchair" psychology as contrasted to the "strictly scientific" psychology of Freud.

Since Hall read widely in German, he was aware of everything Freud wrote. Apparently sensing that the autumn of 1909 was the right moment to upstage James and make a major intellectual coup —both for Freud and for himself—Hall invited Freud to America. He also invited Dr. Carl Jung to speak and receive an honorary degree.

Freud accepted the invitation, asking his close friend, Dr. Sandor Ferenczi, to accompany him and Jung. Ferenczi was concerned about whether to bring a silk top hat. Freud said he intended to buy one in America—and toss it into the sea on the way home.

On Monday, September 4, 1909, and the following four days, Freud delivered his lectures, speaking extemporaneously in German. The first lecture was historical, describing Breuer's work in the case of Anna O. The second outlined the roots of psychoanalysis and its emergence from the period when hypnotism was used, and also discussed resistance and repression.

The third lecture detailed the technique of psychoanalysis, including the interpretation of dreams and free association. The fourth dealt with infantile sexuality and the Oedipus complex, and the fifth with fantasy, transference and sublimation.

A dramatic moment occurred at the close of the ceremonies. Freud thanked Clark University for the doctorate—the only honorary degree he ever received. Then, visibly moved, he said, "This is the first official recognition of our endeavors."

He later commented that he found, to his surprise, that members of the faculty not only knew of his writings but taught them in class, and "in prudish America it was possible, in academic circles at least, to discuss freely and scientifically everything that in ordinary life is regarded as objectionable."

He also noted: "In Europe I felt like an outcast, here I saw myself received by the best men as their equal. It was like the realization of a fantastic daydream . . . Psychoanalysis had ceased to be an illusion, it had become a valuable piece of reality."

On a visit to Niagara Falls Freud's feelings were hurt when a guide at the Cave of the Winds pushed other visitors aside and, referring to Freud, said, "Let the old fellow go first." Freud was only fifty-three. In New York City, Dr. Abraham Arden Brill, who was to become a leading advocate of psychoanalysis in America, took Freud on a tour of Chinatown, Coney Island, the lower East Side, Columbia University and Central Park. Freud also visited the Metropolitan Museum of Art to see the Grecian antiquities he so loved.

One of his few recorded remarks about New York was made to Brill, who lived on Central Park West. Looking out the window over the sea of trees, Freud advised, "Don't ever move from this park." But he criticized American cooking—bland next to the rich Viennese fare—and the lack of public toilet facilities (a criticism still valid today).

A postcard the three European visitors sent Hall from Grand Central Station on their way home has been unearthed by Dr. Arcangelo R. T. D'Amore, former chairman of the Committee on History and Archives for the American Psychoanalytic Association and current chairman of the History, Library and Museum Committee of the American Psychiatric Association. The postcard, written in German and postmarked September 21, 1909, says: "Goodbye and sincere thanks from three homeward-bound travelers." It was signed:

> Freud
> Jung
> Ferenczi

Freud had formed a definite opinion about America as very religious, superficial and faddish before his visit. His sister Anna had married Ely Bernays in 1888, and Bernays had gone to live in the United States in 1891. Anna followed her husband a year later but her heart seemed to have remained in her native Vienna; from 1901 to 1912 she returned there with her children almost every summer for a reunion with the Freud-Bernays families. Freud learned from his sister and his American nieces and nephews about American customs.

While he was grateful because the Clark University reception meant a triumph for psychoanalysis, Freud left America after his two weeks stay believing the country would "dilute" and "distort" his psychoanalytic theories, as he was to warn several times in the future.

For the next seven years Freud and Putnam exchanged letters discussing the nature of man and problems of ethics. Putnam wrote Freud after he returned to Vienna, "Your visit was a more significant event to me than you can easily imagine, for it helped to change radically the whole course of my life and thought." Not to mention the whole course of psychoanalysis in America, which might have been delayed many years had Freud not made the trip.

On September 29, 1910, a little over a year after his visit to America, Freud wrote to Putnam: "You convince me that I have not lived and worked in vain, for men such as you will see to it that the ideas I have arrived at in so much pain and anguish will not be lost to humanity. What more could one desire?"

Hall thereafter spoke of Freud as representing "the psychology of the future." But for William James, who though suffering from heart trouble traveled to Clark University to hear Freud, initial respect for psychoanalysis seems to have lessened. He wrote his friend Theodore Flournoy, the Swiss psychologist, on September 28, 1909:

"Speaking of 'functional' psychology [as the new dynamic psychoanalysis was called] Clark University had a little international congress the other day in honor of the twentieth year of its existence. I went there for one day in order to see what Freud was like. I hope that Freud and his pupils will push their ideas to their utmost limits, so that we may learn what they are. They can't fail to throw light on human nature; but I confess that he made on me personally the impression of a man obsessed with fixed ideas. I can make nothing in my own case with his dream theories; and obviously 'symbolism' is a most dangerous method. A newspaper report of the congress said that Freud had condemned the American religious therapy (which has such extensive results) as very 'dangerous' because so 'unscientific'. Bah!"

But in contrast to the skepticism of James, Putnam was convinced even more deeply of the validity of psychoanalysis. In an article he wrote in the December, 1909–January, 1910, issue of the *Journal of Abnormal Psychology* entitled "Personal Impressions of Sigmund Freud and His Work, With Special Reference to His Recent Lectures at Clark University," he said: "Freud's therapeutic method is his method of analysis into the structure and working of the whole mind, the whole man, carried out with a searching and merciless rigor that is in the end fully justified by the fact that it brings at last a sense of freedom and of manhood." Alluding to Freud, Jung and Ferenczi, Putnam commented, "We owe their visit, and the gathering of the intelligent audience who came to hear them, to the energy of the officers of Clark University in Worcester, which recently celebrated with intellectual sumptuousness the twentieth anniversary of its founding." He then took to task those who criticized Freud's theories: "The detective novel is welcome at every fireside, but the scientific student of human acts and motives is considered a disseminator of morbid tendencies."

Speaking of those who showed contempt for the study of man's inner life, he said: "A fool's paradise is a poor paradise. No investigation is wrong if it is earnest. Knowledge knows nothing as essentially and invariably dirty. It is a piece of narrow intolerance, cruel, in its outcome, to raise the cry of 'introspection' in order to prevent an unfortunate invalid, whose every moment is already spent in introspection of the worst sort, forced on him by the bigotry, however well meant, of social conventions, from searching even to the death, the causes of his misery and learning to substitute the freedom, liberality, tolerance, and purity that comes from knowledge for the tyranny of ignorance and prejudice."

Also in 1909, Dr. Frederick Peterson, Clinical Professor of Psychiatry at Columbia University, wrote in the *New York Medical Journal*: "Freud is perhaps extreme in attributing so great a role to the sexual basis of neurosis, but we might grant him half, since roughly speaking fifty percent of the trends, wishes, desires that inspire our activities are for the preservation of the species and fifty percent for self-preservation."

The following year Putnam presented a laudatory paper on "Personal Experience with Freud's Psychoanalytic Methods" at the annual meeting of the American Neurological Association, of which he was past president. The organization was unsympathetic to Freud but the daring endorsement by Putnam carried with it the weight of the high professional esteem in which he was held. From then on, no matter how scornfully the reactionary neurologist or psychiatrist in America might sneer at Freud (as a number still do), he could not afford to ignore the challenge to examine the new theories placed squarely before him by one of his most respected contemporaries.

From 1913 to 1918, when he died, Putnam held informal weekly meetings at his home to discuss psychoanalysis, following Freud's pattern in Vienna. In his obituary of Putnam, Freud called him "the great support of psychoanalysis in America." Dr. Karl Menninger, in his talk "Footprints," delivered at the twenty-fifth anniversary of the Boston Psychoanalytic Institute on November 30, 1958, also paid tribute to Putnam, describing him as "the great, elegant, powerful Putnam who never abandoned his courageous stand in favor of the unpopular, the proscribed and ridiculed new truth discovered by his Viennese colleague." Dr. Menninger also praised Putnam's "great vision, which permitted him to detect a precious truth in its incipiency and become a great leader in the midst of unpopularity."

Psychoanalysis in America was promulgated primarily by three men: Putnam, who introduced its theories and defended it ardently; Jones, who was the tie between Freud and American psychoanalysts, and Brill, who became a leader in promoting psychoanalysis among physicians and the public.

The trio was a strange one. The shy, eminent, respectable Boston professor-physician. The doughty little Welshman, educated as a neurologist at London and Cambridge and so dedicated to Freud he later became Freud's biographer. And the immigrant from a small town in Austria, who sailed alone to the United States at the age of fifteen to become one of America's missionaries in the cause of psychoanalysis.

Arriving without a cent in his pocket and without a friend or relative, Brill learned the language as he worked in a saloon in exchange for the privilege of sleeping on the floor. He completed his elementary and high school education in three years, acquired a medical degree from Columbia University College of Physicians and Surgeons in 1903, working at many jobs to support himself and pay his tuition. Then he spent four years in Central Islip Hospital, Long Island, treating patients suffering from mental disturbances.

Peterson, one of Brill's professors at Columbia, advised him to go abroad for postgraduate work in neurology, and Brill went to Paris, where he worked under Dr. Pierre Marie at the Hospice de Bicêtre in the spring of 1907. This was the institution where Dr. Philippe Pinel, in the autumn of 1893, became one of the first to cast the chains off the insane, who were then still shackled to posts.

"At the time I frequented all the other clinics, where I hoped to learn something about borderline cases of mental diseases or psychoneuroses," said Brill in "The Introduction and Development of Freud's Work in the United States," which he wrote for a special issue of the *American Journal of Sociology,* November, 1939.

Next Peterson suggested he go to the Bürgholzli Clinic of Psychiatry in Zurich . . . "They are doing the Freud work there, and I think you will like it." At the clinic, Brill said, he became "inspired" by Jung, second in command under Dr. Eugen Bleuler, the director, who coined the word "ambivalence." This was the turning point in Brill's life. He was appointed a regular assistant in the clinic, where "I worked with heart and soul in the pioneer work of testing and applying the Freudian mechanisms to psychiatry."

He described Freud as having "taken away the stigmata of degeneration" from the neuroses by showing they were "distorted continua of past experiences . . . Before the advent of Freud everything psychiatric was considered something *sui generis,* something alien from so-called normal behavior. In my pre-psychoanalytic life it had never occurred to me to associate obsessions, phobias, or delusions with the patient's past or so-called normal state." He said of Freud's work: "Every case showed the pleasures and woes of mankind; they really held up the mirror, as it were, to nature."

He visited Freud in Vienna, where Freud and he would take long walks, tell each other their dreams, analyze them. Brill returned to New York in 1908, filled with admiration of and devotion to Freud. He entered private practice and between 1908 and 1910 was the only analyst in New York City. He soon became the semi-official spokesman for psychoanalysis in America. He translated *Studies on Hysteria, Three Contributions to the Theory of Sex* and *The Interpretation of Dreams.* By 1924 he had translated ten of Freud's works from the original German, thus bringing to the American public an awareness of psychoanalysis. With typical generosity, Brill turned over all royalties to Freud.

Dr. Bertram D. Lewin said of Brill, "Favorably known to his psychiatric colleagues and of great personal charm, more than he realized, he created an atmosphere of benevolence toward psychoanalysis in the local community."

Several of Brill's articles contributed to psychoanalytic thought. In "Unconscious Insight: Some of Its Manifestations," written in 1929, he described neurosis and psychosis as "fortresses" erected to protect the person from pain. In his work with schizophrenics he concluded they feared and resisted their feelings of helplessness and frustration but denied their fear to themselves and the world.

Freud's visit to America, plus Brill's translations of his books, accelerated interest in psychoanalysis. A headline in The New York *Times* on March 2, 1913, accompanied by a photograph of Brill, read:

DREAMS OF THE INSANE HELP GREATLY IN THEIR CURE
Theories of Dr. Freud Are Put in Practical Use at Ward's Island and in Other Institutions in the City That Care for the Mentally Disturbed

America was becoming "the proving ground of practical psychoanalysis," according to Dr. Clarence Oberndorf in *History of Psychoanalysis in America:* "The new theories of Freud, supported by facts if one were trained and sufficiently alert to observe them, supplied new keys to open wide doors that afforded vast new, amazing and inspiring vistas into human conduct." Observation of the extreme degree of mental illness seen in a mental hospital gave the physician a perspective of the likelihood for success with the patient less profoundly disturbed and living in the community. "The study of the psychotic is probably the best means of convincing the novitiate in psychiatry of the truth of psychoanalytic mechanisms," he wrote. "In working with deteriorated psychotic patients, the postulates of Freud become so obvious and undeniable that one who like myself in 1909 still doubted the diagnostic as well as the therapeutic value of psychoanalysis will be forced to admit the validity of psychoanalysis."

In the 1920s and 1930s a number of neurologists journeyed to Vienna for a personal analysis with Freud or one of his colleagues, which lasted only a few months in those days. To pay expenses, they took along patients or sought grants from the Commonwealth Fund. They returned to lecture to medical and lay groups and treat patients who could afford the couch six days a week.

Freud's popularity in America continued to grow. In April, 1935, *Fortune* devoted an article to him. He appeared on the cover of *Time* on June 26, 1939. Literary critic Bernard De Voto wrote in the *Saturday Review* of October 7, 1939, on "Freud's Influence on Literature."

Meanwhile in Europe Freud had organized psychoanalysis on a broad basis. The First International Congress of Psychoanalysts was held in Salzburg in 1908, the second in Nuremberg in 1910, when the International Psychoanalytical Association was founded with Jung as president. Branch societies were recognized in Vienna, Zurich and Berlin. Putnam and Jones attended the Third Congress at Weimar in 1911.

No psychoanalytic organization was necessary in the United States, Putnam and Jones thought, because there were so few practicing psychoanalysts. But Freud, eager to preserve the integrity of his theories and technique, told Jones in 1910 that he believed a branch of the International would be desirable in America. An official relationship with European psychoanalysts would offer some protection in America against "amateurs and charlatans," he said.

Jones wrote Putnam on September 9, 1910: "I strongly feel the necessity of some such formal move to counteract the numerous amateurs who already are beginning to spring up and who will do the cause much harm. Membership will constitute some kind of guarantee in a general way that the person has at least some actual knowledge of the subject."

The American Psychoanalytic Association was founded May 9, 1911, in Baltimore. Jones persuaded a reluctant Putnam to be president and he served as secretary. Though listed as a sponsor, Brill was not present. Three months before, on February 12, 1911, the New York Psychoanalytic Society had been formed when Brill invited fifteen physicians to his home. Fourteen of the twenty-seven members who joined by October, 1912, had been or still were on the staff of the Manhattan State Hospital on Ward's Island, New York. There, under the leadership of Dr. Adolph Meyer, they were using psychoanalytic theories in the diagnosis of psychotic patients.

Brill became the first president of the New York Psychoanalytic Society, the first such society in America. Meetings were held both at his and Oberndorf's homes, where study groups, after discussing the topic of the evening, talked late into the night about problems of technique.

Close ties were maintained between the psychoanalytic and the psychopathological associations that had first sponsored psychoanalysis. In 1905 Dr. William Alanson White, superintendent of the Government Hospital for the Insane in Washington, D.C., (later renamed Saint Elizabeth's), and Jelliffe had translated Paul Dubois' *The Psychic Treatment of Nervous Disorders,* which sparked medical and popular interest in psychoanalysis. In 1917 White appointed two full-time psychotherapists at Saint Elizabeth's—the first to be employed by a mental hospital. White was among the first doctors to try psychotherapy with psychotic patients.

White believed that the psychoanalytic and psychopathological associations should be merged. But Brill, Oberndorf and their colleagues wanted to keep the two groups separate even as they discussed a possible merger. White and Jelliffe, a leader in psychosomatic medicine, quarreled with Brill, who insisted the constitution should not permit women members after Jelliffe had proposed

Louise Brink, his assistant. Brill won the battle to keep the two groups apart.

The constitution of the American Psychoanalytic Association was later revised to admit women, and Dr. Lucile Dooley of Washington and Dr. Marion Kenworthy of New York, who brought psychoanalysis into the field of social work, in 1926 became the first women members. Dr. Kenworthy in 1958 became the first woman president. There have been two women presidents since, Dr. Grete L. Bibring and Dr. Rebecca Z. Solomon, the current president.

The American Psychoanalytic Association in 1930 had fifty-six members, half of whom lived in New York. The object of the Association was stated as "the study and advancement of the Psychoanalytic Science and its application to the study and treatment of nervous and mental diseases, as well as to pure psychology."

The New York Society became more and more an educational group, like the European psychoanalytic societies, which insisted the training of psychoanalysts include a personal analysis by an approved training analyst. On September 14, 1931, the New York Society formed the New York Psychoanalytic Institute. Dr. Sandor Rado, who had been organizer and teacher at the Berlin Psychoanalytic Institute, was the first paid educational director. The Institute served as model for the twenty-six institutes accredited by the American Psychoanalytic Association that have followed.

The three main functions of a psychoanalytic institute as stated by Freud at the inauguration of the Berlin Institute are: the training of psychoanalysts (a three-year course plus a personal analysis), the conduct of research and service to the community. The growing number of psychoanalysts in America led to the founding of other societies—Boston and Washington-Baltimore in 1930, and Chicago in 1931. The national association was converted into "A Federation of American Psychoanalytic Societies" in 1935. Brill's long tenure as president ended when Oberndorf was elected first president of the Federation.

The midwest became acquainted with psychoanalysis through Chicago's first practicing psychoanalyst, Dr. N. Lionel Blitzsten, who was analyzed by Abraham. Blitzsten was a founding member and first president of the Chicago Psychoanalytic Society. In a tribute to Blitzsten after his death, Dr. Minna Emch praised his patience, his wisdom, his interest, "which gained him so many friends that someone once said, 'If Lionel were set down in Borneo, a monkey would drop from the nearest tree and say, 'Why Lionel, fancy meeting you here!' "

Blitzsten's fundamental tenet in psychoanalysis was "that each person has within him the miracle of his capacity for living, to which we as analysts can only act as *accoucheurs,*" Emch said. "He taught of psychoanalysis: That it adds nothing to the capacity of a person that is not already there; and that it takes away nothing that is *really* there. It can remove only the doubts, the confusions, the unreal—the window dressing of a personality." She reported that Blitzsten was delighted when his first analytic patient, an illiterate German workman, toward the close of his analysis said, "Ah doctor, now I know you for what you are. You are the Apostle of the Obvious!"

Though Blitzsten was a founder of the Chicago Institute for Psychoanalysis, its first director was Dr. Franz Alexander, who came from Berlin to be Professor of Psychoanalysis at the University of Chicago, the first such title bestowed in this country.

The American Psychiatric Association formed a special Section on Psychoanalysis in 1933 to introduce psychoanalytic thinking more fully into the field of psychiatry. A comparison of the programs of the annual conventions of the association in 1948 and 1979 shows the widespread extent to which psychoanalytic thought had permeated psychiatry. In 1948 almost every paper dealt with drugs, electroshock or lobotomy. The 1979 meeting offered such topics as "The Child in His Family," "Psychoanalytic Theory and Practice," "Aggression and Violence," "A Philosophy of the Psychotherapy of the Psychoses" and "College Suicides."

The interest in psychoanalytic thought among intellectuals led large foundations dedicated to health and medical research, like the Commonwealth, the Josiah Macy, Jr. and Rosenwald funds, to support mental health projects. National organizations interested in mental health developed, some representing professional organizations, others, volunteer groups. The Mental Health Association today speaks for the nation's volunteers, with headquarters in Arlington, Virginia. Among its recent interests is the promotion of research on depression. . . .

Greater emphasis on the prevention of emotional disturbances in children by bringing to parents and all those who deal with the child an understanding of what a child needs for healthy emotional development is urged by Dr. Robert L. Stubblefield, current president of the American Academy of Child Psychiatry and past president of the American Orthopsychiatric Association. In a report to President Carter's Commission on Mental Health, the Academy estimated that 10 million of the 67 million children in school need help for psychological disturbances: 2,200,000 children require long-term intensive care and 30,000 are so seriously ill they require in-patient or residential care. Two million severely distrubed adolescents are housed in state hospitals and correctional institutions, receiving little or no psychological help.

When the President's Commission on Mental Health made its final report on September 15, 1978, it estimated that one-quarter of the population suffered severe emotional stress, that "between 20 and 32 million Americans need some kind of mental health care at any one time," in addition to the six million who are mentally retarded. Officials who compiled the report said even these numbers are "conservative," that probably about 40 million Americans had diagnosable mental disturbances and were in need of professional care.

While the problem is an immense one, at least in this country efforts are being made to solve it. In Europe all concern with mental health ceased temporarily when Mussolini and Hitler rose to power. The philosophy of psychoanalysis, with its inherent respect for the individual, clashed with the fascist philosophy under which individual rights were sacrificed to the will of a dictator. Psychoanalysis was forbidden as contrary to the state's political policies in Germany and Russia. The Russian Psychoanalytic Society faded away in 1930 and the Institution for Children in Moscow, where psychoanalytic principles had been used in therapy, was closed by the government on grounds of "immorality."

Psychoanalysis in America was enriched by the many prominent European psychoanalysts who came to this country fleeing the Nazis. The American Psychoanalytic Association appointed a committee to aid them financially and professionally. Though the majority remained in New York, a number went to live in Boston, Chicago, Los Angeles, Topeka and Detroit, and their knowledge and abilities resulted in many important contributions to the field as they joined the teaching staffs of the institutes.

Several secessions from the parent organization, the New York Psychoanalytic Society, took place in the 1940s. A number of analysts, including Rado, Dr. Abraham Kardiner, Dr. George E. Daniels and Dr. David M. Levy, with the assistance of Dr. Nolan D. C. Lewis, director of the New York State Psychiatric Institute, formed the nucleus of the Association for Psychoanalytic Medicine and the Psychoanalytic Clinic for Training and Research at Columbia University. Dr. Sandor Lorand, former president of the New York Psychoanalytic Society, established the Division of Psychoanalytic Education at the State University of New York, Downstate Medical Center, and became the first director of the Psychoanalytic Institute there. These two training centers became member institutes of the American Psychoanalytic Association. But a few other institutes were formed outside the Association.

On April 29, 1941, Dr. Karen Horney was disqualified as an instructor and training analyst at the New York Psychoanalytic Institute. She had, in 1937, written *The Neurotic Personality,* which minimized the role of infant sexuality in personality development, and she differed with Freud on other theories, including penis envy. During a business meeting of the New York Psychoanalytic Society, when she learned she was not allowed to teach at the Institute, Horney and four colleagues, among them Dr. Clara Thompson, walked out. Horney had been one of the guiding spirits of the Berlin Psychoanalytic Institute, where she formulated her own "feminine psychology," ascribing the inferior status of women to cultural factors rather than biological inferiority and countered Freud's concept of penis envy with the evidence that men as well as women suffered from feelings of sexual inadequacy.

With the Nazi takeover of Germany, Horney emigrated to the United States where she became a training analyst at the New York Psychoanalytic Institute. But here she aroused antagonism as she stressed social and cultural factors, challenging the Freudian belief "in the primacy of instinct and genetics as the basis of human behavior."

After leaving the New York Psychoanalytic Institute, Horney became the leading founder of the Association for the Advancement of Psychoanalysis, which publishes the *American Journal of Psychoanalysis*, whose editor is Helen De Rosis, author of *Women and Anxiety*. Horney also became the first dean of the Association's training institute, the American Institute for Psychoanalysis.

Horney was one of the first psychoanalysts to distinguish between the need for intimacy and the drive for sex. "A great part of what appears as sexuality has in reality very little to do with it, but is an expression of the desire for reassurance." Horney believed sex was the expression of general emotional needs. She stressed the rewards of pregnancy and motherhood as a supplement to and not a substitute for other areas of fulfillment. She also considered that human beings were basically creative and always capable of change, and that social and cultural factors influence personality and behavior as much or more than biological instincts. This theory, which takes into account all the forces that contribute to personality, is known as "holistic" psychology. Horney is considered its originator.

In 1946, Horney's former colleague, Dr. Clara Thompson, with the support of Dr. Harry Stack Sullivan, Dr. Frieda Fromm-Reichmann, Erich Fromm, Dr. Janet Rioch and Dr. David Rioch, started the William Alanson White Institute. It accepted psychologists as candidates for training in 1948, one of the first medical institutes to do so.

Also in 1946 Theodor Reik, a lay analyst, came to America, and after disputes with the New York Psychoanalytic Institute, formed the National Psychological Association for Psychoanalysis, whose current president is Elizabeth Thorne, psychoanalyst and lawyer. A graduate of this group, Reuben Fine, author of *The Healing of the Mind*, in 1964 founded the New York Center for Psychoanalytic Training, and a number of other graduates started the Center for Modern Psychoanalytic Studies.

The American Academy of Psychoanalysis was organized in 1956, outside of the American Psychoalnalytic Association. Its purpose was to develop communication among psychoanalysts and their colleagues in other disciplines in science and the humanities. An annual conference provides a forum for inquiry into individual motivation and social behavior. The Academy advocates acceptance of what it believes relevant and responsible psychological views of human behavior, rather than adherence to any one particular doctrine.

The growth of psychoanalysis in the United States may be measured by the fact that in the past thirty-five years the number of psychoanalysts belonging to the American Psychoanalytic Association has increased tenfold. In 1944 there were 247 members. In July, 1979, there were 2,642, including associate and affiliate members.

Why has the United States, relatively speaking, accepted psychoanalysis so wholeheartedly? Freud attributed the generally cordial reception his theories received in America to "the absence of embedded scientific tradition and the slight weight of official authority." Geoffrey Gorer in *The American People: A Study of National Character* singled out as the most prominent characteristic of Americans their tendency to reject authority, particularly that of foreign-born parents.

The United States was founded in a pioneer spirit. This is a nation that fought for economic and political freedom from a tyrannical and oppressive "mother" country. America welcomed the idea there was still another freedom beyond those of economic, social and political—emotional freedom. There were more shackles to be cast off—the psychic chains of childhood. More frontiers to be won—exploration of inner space, which held repressed memories and feelings that caused emotional crippling.

America, with its philosophy of "saving" the world, proved receptive to the idea of "saving" the emotional life of the individual. The savior unconsciously wants to save himself, projecting this wish onto the saving of others.

America's wealth has also enabled more persons to afford psychoanalysis. More psychoanalytic clinics have been established to provide treatment for those who can pay little. Publishers have kept Freud's works in print, even selling paperbacks on subway stands, so that millions have become aware of his thinking.

In 1909, Freud, on his only visit to America, is pictured (front row, left) at Clark University in Worcester, Massachusetts, with G. Stanley Hall, president of Clark (center) and Dr. Carl Jung (right), who became Freud's disciple in 1907 but broke with him in 1912 after formulating his own theory of the collective unconscious. In the back row, from left to right are Dr. A. A. Brill, Freud's translator, Dr. Ernest Jones, Freud's biographer, and Dr. Sandor Ferenczi, one of Freud's earliest disciples. *(The Bettmann Archive)*

Over the years, Freud presented his closest colleagues with a special ring, copies of an antique Roman seal in the shape of a carved head of Jupiter—hence the nickname, "The Seven Rings Committee." Standing left to right are Otto Rank, Dr. Karl Abraham, Dr. Max Eitington, and Dr. Ernest Jones. Seated left to right are Freud, Dr. Sandor Ferenczi, and Hanns Sachs. They are pictured here together in 1922. *(Keystone Press Agency)*

Freud at the age of seventy-two takes his first airplane flight in 1928, boarding a plane at Tempelhof Field in Berlin. *(Wide World Photos)*

Forced to flee the Nazis in June, 1938, Freud takes a train to Paris. On his left is Marie Bonaparte (Princess George of Greece), his close friend and colleague, who gave the Nazis money so Freud could leave Vienna. On Freud's right is U.S. Ambassador to France William C. Bullitt, his former analysand, who helped arrange his escape. *(Keystone Press Agency)*

Headed for London, Freud passes through Paris in advance of the Nazis. *(Keystone Press Agency)*

Safe at his new home in Hampstead, England, 82-year old Freud
takes a walk with his daughter, Mrs. Mathilde Hollistschek. Less
than a year later, Freud died. *(Pictorial Parade)*

So America, scorned by Freud even though it was the first country to give him official recognition, has attained the leadership of the world, challenged only by the English and the Dutch, in perpetuating the work of Freud and extending it into the new provinces he urged his followers to explore.

What are these new territories—what have been the contributions of psychoanalysts since Freud, how have they elaborated on his theories?

II

More than "A Greek Chorus"

The giant is Freud. In his works are found the fundamentals of everything in psychoanalysis that has since developed. Psychoanalysis was his creation, molded by his discoveries and eloquent explanations. His lifelong struggle was to have his theories and techniques accepted as a method of helping the troubled mind. His continued exploration, investigation and constant revision of his work, the pattern of his daily life—all was aimed at perfecting and expanding psychoanalysis.

Knowing the art-science of psychoanalysis offered unlimited psychic expanse, Freud said, "I am not an artist; I could never have depicted the effects of light and color, only hard outlines."

Successors have added "light and color" to psychoanalytic theory. Depending on individual preferences, they have chosen different areas of research. Freud's daughter Anna, close to him all his life, became dedicated to the study of the development of children. Her *Normality and Pathology in Childhood*, written in 1965, traced personality development and relations between the child and

248

mother from direct observations of the mother-child unit starting at birth. She founded the Hampstead Child Therapy Clinic in England, where child psychoanalysts are trained and where at this writing she still works.

Anna Freud also contributed to her father's study of homosexuality. In "Studies in Passivity" she reported that her treatment of homosexual men showed that analysis of different kinds of homosexuals' fear of women, or fear of their own aggression toward women, "had a limited value" in helping the passive male homosexual. Her most effective interpretations, she said, concerned the equation she made between the passive homosexual and his active partner. She said, ". . . the active male partner, whom these men are seeking, represents to them their lost masculinity, which they enjoy in identification with him. This implies that these apparently passive men are active according to their fantasy, while they are passive only so far as their behavior is concerned."

What these patients dreaded was that the analyst would try to deprive them of the masculinity represented by other men. "The promise of a cure turned into a castration threat," she said.

The representation of a boy's masculinity by another man is a normal process in childhood, Anna Freud pointed out; it is the young boy's attitude toward his father. While admiring his father's masculinity, the boy at the same time has a part in it, shares it in fantasy, "borrows it from the father occasionally, even if he borrows it only in the form of a piece of clothing, a penknife, a fountain pen."

This attitude, overcome in latency (the years between six or seven and eleven), recurs normally in adolescence in the form of hero worship. But in adulthood the admiration of the masculine partner in a sexual way does not lead to an increase in masculinity but, on the contrary, "we see the homosexual become insatiable in his wish for the partner's masculinity."

Melanie Klein focused on the very early months of a child's life, postulating certain fantasies and psychosexual development during this period. Anna Freud disagrees with Klein's findings, saying, ". . . this darkest of all ages has never been my predilection. I have always preferred as my subject those phases of development where assumptions can be checked against verbalized material recaptured from the unconscious by the analytic method, or against facts which are open to view in the direct observation of infants . . .

"Whenever we break through the barrier which divides articulate life from the preverbal period, we find ourselves on uncertain ground, left with conjectures, reconstructions and interpretations which of necessity have to remain unconfirmed by the individual with whom they are concerned. In no other realm of psychoanalysis does speculation need to run quite as free, as far, and as wild."

One of Anna Freud's most important contributions has been the study of the ego. Freud frequently mentioned the role of the ego in conflict and how it mediated between the demands of our instinctual drives and the demands of parents and society that we become civilized. He did not systematically explore that role, concentrating more on the unconscious, believing in treatment it was important to make conscious the unconscious fantasies determining destructive behavior.

Then in 1923 he wrote *The Ego and the Id.* He no longer thought of the mind as divided into conscious and unconscious, equating the unconscious with the instinctual drives. Instead he proposed a new formulation of the mind, or "mental apparatus." He called it "the structural theory." He divided the mind into *id, ego* and *superego.* The id was totally unconscious. But the ego and superego not only had conscious aspects but unconscious and preconscious ones, the latter easily accessible to the conscious. This made the ego and superego far more complex than formerly visualized. In proposing this conceptual change Freud ran the risk that his followers might interpret it as displacing the unconscious from its original position of primacy, especially in their practice with patients. Some have done this, even to the extent of paying scant attention to the interpretation of dreams.

Referring to her father's new structure of the mind in *The Ego and the Mechanisms of Defense,* Anna Freud wrote that inquiry into the workings of the ego did not mean the abandonment of fundamental convictions about unconscious processes. This book appeared in 1936, three years before her father died. She said the only way to "reconstruct the transformations" undergone by the sexual and aggressive drives was to analyze the ego's defensive operations, "most of which lay below the threshold of consciousness."

What has become known as "ego psychology" centers on the way the ego protects itself against what it believes dangerous emotions—fear, hate, wishes for revenge, lust, selfishness, greed—and during a personal analysis these defenses are pointed out to the patient at an appropriate time.

In 1927 Dr. Heinz Hartmann, who had become a member of the Vienna Psychoanalytic Society at the same time as Anna Freud and who had been analyzed by Freud, read a paper, "Ego Psychology and the Problem of Adaptation." His purpose, he said, was to stake out the *"general* psychology," the *"general"* theory of mental life. Hartmann ventured beyond both Anna Freud and her father in the role he ascribed to the ego. In expanding what Freud called the "organizing" system of ego function and characterizing its work of adaptation as "reality of mastery," Hartmann markedly reduced the classic psychoanalytic emphasis on "inner conflict," according to the many analysts who heralded this as the single most influential article since Freud. "Not every adaptation to the environment or every learning and maturation process" need be thought of as derived from conflict, Hartmann said. There were many processes in the development of the individual—perception, intention, object comprehension—that went on in what he called the ego's "conflict-free sphere," the particular domain of "ego strength." He said he hoped the study of this conflict-free sphere would "open up the no-man's land between sociology and psychoanalysis" and extend the contribution of psychoanalysis to the social sciences.

Fleeing from the Nazis in 1941 Hartmann journeyed to New York with his wife Dora, a pediatrician. In the next three decades, until his death in 1970, he published a series of papers, some in collaboration with Ernst Kris and Dr. Rudolph M. Lowenstein, that constitute the basic theoretical work on ego psychology. The term "ego," Hartmann said, was "often used in a highly ambiguous way, even among analysts." He described the ego as emerging from what Freud called "the matrix of animal instinct," or the id. The ego developed as the result of three factors: inherited ego characteristics and their interaction, influences of the instinctual drives and influences of outer reality. Its functions were more numerous than those of the id or the superego. Among the most important ego functions were adaptation to reality, action and thought. Beyond, and less tangible, lay the set of functions commonly called "a person's character." At a still further distance from observable experience occurred the work of psychic "synthesis" or "organization."

Freud's concept of an *unconscious* part of the ego and superego, determined in part by relationships in reality, was a vital step in setting the stage for establishing psychoanalysis as what is now called a "developmental psychology." Many analysts have worked to cast new depths on Freud's thinking, which clearly encompassed the effect of painful experiences at various levels of development (the younger and thus more vulnerable the child, the more traumatic the experiences). In his own life Freud reconstructed what he called the "prehistoric period" of childhood—the forgotten years—via dreams and memories. He always spoke in terms of development but usually that of "psychosexuality"—the oral, anal, phallic and genital stages and how they were affected by "vicissitudes." The main contribution of his successors has been to apply this "developmental" concept to other factors in relation to the sexual.

Freud, as seen, mentioned the "hate" of a parent for a child. He spoke in one case of the wish of the mother to devour or kill her small daughter. Another time he cited a mother's wish to abort a baby because she did not want it and the effect this had on the child's life. He referred to a little girl's fear her mother would kill her, "a fear which, in turn, justifies her death-wish of her mother, if that becomes conscious." He also predicated that a woman's "bad relations" with her mother could influence her to choose a husband so similar to her mother that she would not be able to tolerate him. But he left it to his followers to explore in depth what the hate of a parent, both conscious and unconscious, might mean to the ego of the child, affecting later life. A strong or weak ego depends on the *quality* of the child's first human relationship. It has nothing to do with intelligence; he may have a superior I.Q. but become emotionally stunted if he feels unloved or too harshly treated.

There is a reason why Freud may not have explored in more

depth this early time of life. His chief fear, according to his biographer Ernest Jones, was the "haunting thought that he might die before his mother." Jones attributed this fear to Freud's belief the news of his death would be "terribly painful" to his mother. But, adds Jones, "it would seem also to imply a separation from her," a separation Freud perhaps did not wish to contemplate because the thought was so painful.

Freud did, however, note the way in which a child attempts to cope with the first separations from the mother. He cited the example of his grandson of eighteen months, who, he said, was a normal child of average intelligence and generally well-behaved. He never cried when his mother went out and left him for hours, though they were very close. His father was absent, fighting at the front in World War I. But occasionally when his mother left the house this quiet little boy would fling all his toys into the corner of his room or under the bed, then emit a loud drawn-out "o-o-o-oh." Both Freud and the mother judged this meant "gone away." Freud thought the child, as he flung the toys around, was using them to play at "being gone." One day this was confirmed as he watched the little boy maneuver a wooden reel with a piece of string tied around it. The boy kept throwing the reel over the side of his cot, holding the string as the reel disappeared. He cried his symbolic "o-o-o-oh," then drew the reel by the string back to the cot where he greeted its appearance with a joyful "da." The little boy was re-enacting his mother's disappearance and her return. First he threw the reel out of sight, symbolizing her going away, then eased his pain by pretending he had her on the string and could pull her back any time he wanted. He enjoyed, in fantasy, the satisfaction of controlling her coming and going.

In similar fashion in our play as children we act out real, unpleasant experiences to lessen their danger by imagining we are in control. As we exchange the role of a passive, innocent victim to whom something harmful is being done for the experience of being the one to act we start to become masters of our fate, independent of the whims of others.

Recent psychoanalytic studies have brought important new knowledge about the early years of life and how a child separates emotionally from his mother. These studies show that the child may be crippled sexually and psychically if his mother, out of her obsessive needs, cannot allow him to become independent but considers him an extension of herself. Other studies show the effect on a child who lacks a father in the home. Still others reveal to what degree a child will consciously and unconsciously imitate the defenses and try to carry out the wishes of his parents.

Without Freud's findings, the interactions between parent and child would be meaningless. There has to be awareness of the causes of sadism, masochism, aggression and the purpose each serves in the interest of self-preservation. There has to be awareness of the fantasies that may cripple the mind at each stage of psychosexual development. There has to be understanding of what an individual feels at each stage of his development as threatening to his integrity and self-esteem.

If a child does not successfully separate emotionally from his mother, he may throughout life have trouble feeling a sense of independence or self-esteem. It is never all or nothing—no one achieves *complete* emotional separation. The longing for the mother remains with one to some degree until death. But the degree to which one can attain a sense of independent identity may well make the difference between being reasonably happy or tormented.

The new developmental theory is called "object relations"—the "object" being the mother or her substitute. The term "object relations" was first used by Freud; he introduced the concept of "object choice" in 1905 in *Three Essays on the Theory of Sexuality*. He discussed in detail the reciprocal relations between mother and child, "object" and "subject." He spoke of "object cathexis," of "object choice," of the "discovery of the object" and of "object relations," all related to the mother. He called her the first "libidinal object" of life. He was very aware of the crucial part a mother played in the first months and years of her child's life as she fed, fondled, disciplined and created a mood of either optimism or pessimism that would carry through life. Freud acknowledged the power of "the hand that rocks the cradle." He also said that an infant's experience with feeding was a "crucial factor" in personality development.

On January 17, 1918, he wrote to Lou Andreas-Salomé, ". . .

people are so apt to forget in life . . . what has recently been obscured by the theories of Jung—namely, to what extent the child is already a finished product by the time he is confronted with life, let alone the doctor [psychoanalyst]." In another letter to Andreas-Salomé, this one written on January 28, 1925, he commented on a woman patient he had sent to Andreas-Salomé whose "prognosis for cure" he did not think very good, saying that "though the patient has had a mother, she has never had any proper relationship to her. The prospect of a cure is founded on this fact." Freud also said the relationship to a mother could be destructive for a child, "the depressive mother" drawing her child into the depression.

The term "object relations" includes ways of regulating the instinctual impulses in relation to objects (the mother first, then the father, brother and sisters) and the internal representations of those objects—the fantasies about them and the identification with them. What Dr. René Spitz calls the "dialogue" between mother and child enables the child gradually to build a coherent image of his world. The reciprocity between mother and child, a special form of interaction, creates for the baby a unique world of its own, with a specific emotional climate. For the newborn, the environment consists of a single person—mother or her substitute. She is the world. The way it sees the world of the future will be shaped by the way it sees her, whether she is tender, loving and caring or angry and irritable, whether she conveys the wish she wants the baby or that it had never been born, or vacillates between the two. She gratifies needs or frustrates them, feeds amply or starves or overfeeds. The importance of this first year of life cannot be overestimated in understanding human behavior. "The infant cannot tell what he suffers; but that does not imply that he does not suffer," said Spitz in *The First Year of Life*. "Indifference, lack of empathy, and lack of imagination have resulted in unbelievable cruelty to infants." Thoughtless brutality, he added, had consequences beyond its immediate effects, referring to surgery on infants without anesthesia because physicians actually believed they could not feel.

"Absence of mothering equals emotional starvation," Spitz said. Mother has "an all-encompassing role in the emergence and unfolding of the infant's consciousness" and a vital part in his learning processes "in the emotional climate she creates."

Spitz was among the first to define object relations: "Perhaps one might say that object relations which gratify both mother and child are relations . . . that not only . . . offer gratification to both partners, but the very fact that one of the partners achieves gratification will produce a gratification for the other also . . . This last statement would be an equally fitting description of a love relation and even of the mutual feelings between man and woman in the sexual act. But then . . . what is the love relationship, if not the crowning fulfillment of object relations?"

Initially analysis had to depend on patients to dredge up memories of their childhood traumas. On such memories the analyst would "reconstruct" the early years. But recent observations of the development of infants and children, including the early defenses and adaptations used to ward off fear and anger and how these defenses and adaptations affect a child's development, are enabling analysts to better understand what is normal and what contributes to future abnormality.

"We can assume that what we call object relationships represent the fulfillment of important needs in the developing child as well as in the adolescent and adult," says Dr. Joseph Sandler of London. "Such needs may show themselves in the form of wishes, which may or may not be predominantly instinctual. The wish may be motivated by the need to restore feelings of well-being and safety. Wishes are aroused by changes in the object world as much as by internal pressures."

The treatment of psychosis has become another focal point of research by Freud's successors in the psychoanalytic movement. Freud himself distinguished between what he called a "transference neurosis" and a "narcissistic neurosis." A "transference neurosis" applied to the neurotic patient who could, through his "transference" of feelings to a psychoanalyst during treatment, be helped to face his conflicts. A "narcissistic neurosis" as seen in psychosis, was more severe, the person more involved with himself, unable to relate to another human being. Brill reported, after he had gone to Vienna from Bürgholzli, where he saw psychoanalytic principles applied to the treatment of psychotics, that

Freud told him he felt that "in time we would develop a psychoanalytic therapy for the psychoses."

In his 1924 paper "Neurosis and Psychosis," Freud stated that the difference between the two lay in the strength of the ego. The pathology depended on whether, in the tension of a conflict, the ego "remains true to its allegiance to the outer world and endeavors to subjugate the *id*, or whether it allows itself to be overwhelmed by the *id* and thus torn away from reality."

He defined neurosis as *"the result of a conflict between the ego and the id,"* and psychosis as *"the analagous outcome of a similar disturbance in the relation between the ego and its environment [outer world]"* (italics Freud's).

There always remains as a common feature in both neurosis and psychosis "the factor of frustration—the lack of fulfillment of one of those eternal uncontrollable childhood wishes that are so deeply rooted in our composition . . ." Freud said. In the last resort this frustration always comes from the outside, provided by the environment or the individual's conscience, "which has taken over the part played by the demands of reality."

The outcome depends on the strength of the forces striving with one another. ". . . It is always possible for the ego to avoid a rupture in any of its relations by deforming itself, submitting to forget something of its unity, or in the long run even to being gashed and rent."

The ego of the psychotic is "gashed and rent." And in the neurotic, at times, bent and battered. Neurosis and psychosis are moving nearer and nearer, there is no longer a clear-cut line between them as far as treatment and theory goes. Dr. Sydney Klein of London told the Thirty-First Congress that in recent years there has been increasing awareness among analysts that behind the "mask" of the neurotic patient there lies hidden "a psychotic problem which needs to be dealt with to ensure real stability."

He compared this to what Dr. D. W. Winnicott called "the false self." Klein said, "I do not think this term quite does justice to what may be described as an almost impenetrable cystic encapsulation of part of the self which cuts the patient off both from the rest of his personality and the analyst." This encapsulation shows itself "by a thinness or flatness of feeling accompanied by a rather desperate and tenacious clinging to the analyst as the sole source of life, accompanied by an underlying pervasive feeling of mistrust, and a preoccupation with the analyst's tone of voice or facial expression irrespective of the content of the interpretation." There is a constant expectation of hostility and a tendency to become quickly persecuted at the slightest hint of the analyst's irritation or disapproval. Consciously the analyst is idealized as an extremely powerful and omniscient figure who also occurs in this guise in the patient's dream. As a concomitant, the patient denies his persecutory feelings in spite of the evidence subsequently given by dreams and other analytic material."

Another feature of the analysis is the patient's tendency, when the analyst brings up some topic, to seize upon it with obsessional rigidity but never work it through because of the inability to deal with the problem. This shows a striking similarity to the behavior of autistic children, who play with a ball or toy in a compulsive repetitive way and who scream and resist any attempt to interfere with or change the pattern of play. Sooner or later, though, the patient's personality structure is made clearer by references in projected form. One of Klein's patients said, "I can never get through to my mother. She seems to have an encapsulated relationship inside herself." Another described herself in the analytic session as "drifting away" from the analyst, even though she was interested in what he was saying, "in exactly the same way autistic babies are described as drifting away from their mothers." A patient's sensitivity to the analyst's tone of voice, partly due "to the need to hang on to something for life and support," and partly due "to the expectation of hostility," requires the analyst to be alert to his own reactions, Klein said. While there is no doubt that the visual deprivation caused by lying on the couch plays a part in the patient's ascribing such importance to the analyst's voice, it also has its roots in the patient's early infancy.

All Klein's patients in this group experienced their mothers as "anxious, insecure, controlling, overprotective and hypochondriacal," while their fathers were either physically absent in their childhood or emotionally absent in the sense of being remote intellectuals "heavily invested in academic or professional interests outside the family." In such patients "we have to recognize that although the patient appears to communicate at one level there is also a non-communication corresponding to the mute phase of the autistic child, and that what is not communicated are not only the aggressive but also the loving feelings which accompany the growth of the sense of separateness and the associated sense of responsibility for the self and objects." The recognition of the existence of the "encapsulated part of the personality" reduces "considerably" the length of the analysis and may prevent further breakdowns in later life.

A number of psychoanalysts are working with what is called the "borderline" (on the border of psychosis) patient—a controversial term that some analysts say is not clear-cut—and the "narcissistic personality," a nonpsychotic syndrome. In his book *The Analysis of the Self* Dr. Heinz Kohut describes some of his cases in these areas and the developmental disturbances he found interfering with establishing a sense of self-esteem.

Kohut noted that many patients suffered a deep disturbance of self-esteem, manifested in feelings of inner emptiness, lack of initiative and various malfunctions in the sexual and social spheres. He called this syndrome "narcissistic personality disturbance." He defined it as a defect in the person's sense of inner cohesion and continuity: "an insufficient consolidation of the self." He traced the syndrome to an earlier phase of personality development and claimed that understanding of the cause of the malfunctions opened the door to successful treatment of those whose disturbances were formerly thought inaccessible to psychoanalytic insights. Such patients can now understand the nature of their disturbances and gain mastery over them. In Kohut's words, they are able to "convert their archaic grandiosity into healthy self-esteem."

In working with the severely mentally ill, Dr. Harry Stack Sullivan was one of the first psychiatrists in America to apply psychoanalytic theories to their treatment. Dr. Ralph Crowley, past president of the American Academy of Psychoanalysis, says of Sullivan: "Almost everyone respected him as someone who had something to teach and who was a model in terms of his profound respect for patients, which was not only evident in his teachings but in his practice and in his relationships with students. With him, the psychotherapeutic treatment of schizophrenics became a reality."

Dr. Frieda Fromm-Reichmann was noted for using psychoanalytic theories with psychotics. She was the analyst in Hannah Green's moving book *I Never Promised You a Rose Garden*. Of Fromm-Reichmann, Crowley says, "She emphasized the positive aspects of the person who became mentally disturbed. Her humanity, her interest in the severely mentally ill, came through in her teaching."

Today Dr. Harold F. Searles, whose *Collected Papers on Schizophrenia and Related Subjects* describes his work with deeply disturbed patients, is known not only for his success in the treatment of such patients but for his observation of the qualities in an analyst that are required to help the very mentally ill.

An impetus to the study of the severely disturbed has been given by the large number of psychoanalysts who have contributed to the deeper understanding of the mind and emotions of the child, including Dr. Albert J. Solnit, past president of the American Psychoanalytic Association, Dr. Samuel Ritvo, Dr. Edith Jacobson, Dr. Phyllis Greenace and Dr. Margaret Mahler.

Mahler's original research over a period of years on what takes place emotionally between mother and infant as her child tries to separate physically and emotionally from her has focused attention on the vital need of a child to slowly gain psychic independence. She calls this process "separation-individuation." She divides it into three phases: the "differentiation and practicing" phase, the "rapprochement phase," in which the child gradually and painfully gives up his delusion of his own grandeur, and the phase she calls "on the way to object constancy." If all three phases are passed through successfully, the child is able to survive without undue anxiety in the absence of his mother. He can tolerate being alone because he is able to hold both the image of himself and his mother within, trusting her to be there when he needs her. Crucial to the healthy resolution of all the conflicts in each stage is the continued emotional availability of the mother.

The greater a child's dependency on his mother at a time he should be striving for independence, the more hatred he will feel.

Overdependency produces the sensation of being in someone else's power. It is experienced as an oppressive influence that must be overcome. This relation between overdependency and aggression accounts in part for the particular aggressiveness of the human species, according to some analysts, since man's dependent state is relatively longer than that of other animals. A number of analysts observe that it is erroneous to compare man with the other animals since their mental functioning is so very different, and suggest that excessive aggression is caused, not by the duration of the dependency period, but by the fact that mothers make it difficult for their children to separate from them. It is no accident that many murders occur when a lover, wife or husband threatens to leave. The murderer has never managed to separate emotionally from the mother of childhood. He or she erupts with the fury of a child suddenly abandoned by its mother.

A mother should accept a child's need to become increasingly separate and independent. She must set the child off on the way to freedom, not depend on him for the fulfillment of her needs. At this time the father, as a familiar but different love object, can help the child resist his powerful attraction to the mother in his move toward increasing independence, as Mahler points out. If a child has not been able to go through the "rapprochement" phase successfully but insists on clinging to or clutching at his mother excessively, this failure may more or less affect him throughout life. He may, as an adult, be helpless, passive and inhibited on the one hand and demanding, coercive, possessive, envious and given to temper outbursts on the other.

Freud's work, except in the case of Little Hans, was chiefly "reconstruction" of the infantile past, whereas today many analysts observe directly the behavior of children. But the reconstructive or retrospective view from the couch "cannot be equalled through attempting to predict the future results of currently known trauma in the developing child," Dr. Calvin F. Settlage told the Thirty-First Congress. On the other hand, he said, the analytic situation is unable to pinpoint the precise nature and timing of the original trauma and the details of the normal developmental progression as shown by direct observation. "The approaches are complementary to rather than in conflict with each other and both are valuable and essential to a full psychoanalytic understanding," Settlage said.

Reconstruction is central to classical analysis, Dr. Harold P. Blum told the congress. The referred to Freud's statement, "What we are in search of is a picture of the patient's forgotten years that shall be alike trustworthy and in all essential respects complete." (Freud also said, "If the analysis is carried out correctly, an assured conviction of the truth of the construction . . . achieves the same therapeutic result as a recaptured memory," and, still another time, ". . . a sense of conviction is only attained after the patient has himself worked over the reclaimed material.")

Dr. Eric Brenman of London gave an eloquent and apt example of the new developmental theory and how it applies to the individual. He chose as his "individual" no less a figure than Oedipus. Brenman began by saying that what is past environment and what is instinct "is always a complex problem in reconstructing" the patient's past. He said he would consider this question by venturing some further "reconstructions" of the Oedipus myth. "I am starting from the assumption that Oedipus failed to resolve his Oedipus complex."

Freud, he said, used the Oedipus myth to give profound insights into the sexual and aggressive nature of the child, which was "an epoch-making construction of a genius. If we take note of the early history of Oedipus, we see he was abandoned as a baby by a frightened murderous father (a baby basher)." Lacking a loving mother or father to whom he could relate, Oedipus grew up with a "murderous rage that could not be contained and modified." We could trace the tragedy of Oedipus, Brenman went on, to the belief of his father, King Laius, due to his worship of primitive, omnipotent gods, that no human intervention could prevent his own death at the hands of his son, as the oracle predicted. "Had Laius held the belief that love and understanding could modify the murderous incestuous wishes, it is possible that a different story might have followed," Brenman said. "If there was a belief in the milk of human kindness and a good object-relationship had been established, the tragedy might have been averted."

The whole background of the Oedipal tragedy was the failure

of Oedipus to establish a good pre-Oedipal relationship "with the breast mother. The intervention of the gods at all stages of the story, insisting that nothing could change their omnipotent pronouncements or modify relentless, harsh superego revenge and initiate forgiveness, is basic to our understanding of the myth (the persecuting primitive superego). But again, if we follow the Oedipus story, the superego was unmodified and reinforced by Laius' behavior. We could argue that the good later experience of Oedipus, brought up by the loving King of Corinth, was not enough to avert tragedy and likewise, however good an analyst may be, he may be powerless against the forces of the past . . . We could put forward the view that Oedipus' determination to find out the truth was the tragedy and that had he not been so determined to analyze the origins of the sickness (the plague) he would have been spared facing the unbearable. By the time Oedipus conducted his analysis it was too late.

"Considered from the point of view of what equipment Oedipus had to meet his Oedipus complex, it is difficult to imagine that any analyst would believe that he was furnished with a good enough environment or objects to deal with his problems at the start of life. His later good experiences were not enough to save him, perhaps because he could not reconstruct links and work through his early experiences with later experiences.

"What then can we say of the value of reconstructions? The more we delve into the problem, the more complicated it becomes, and the intricate problem of what is constitutional and what is environmental and their interactions is infinite. We can construct a trauma theory that Oedipus was the victim of circumstances or an instinct theory that he was totally responsible for his crime. If we are to be more than a Greek chorus, then effective interventions are required. Psychoanalysis is based on the belief that the patient can be helped by knowledge and analysis of his own propensities. He also needs to know what modifies these propensities and what exacerbates them in the present, and how this operated in the past."

Settlage, in his speech at the congress, also raised the question whether psychoanalysis as a treatment was at one and the same time a therapeutic process and a developmental process (serving to help the patient at long last separate successfully from the mother of infancy). Settlage said that he believed psychoanalysis was both. He added that the new concepts as well as work with patients supported this view, that "the undoing of psychopathology and the furtherance of development proceed hand in hand."

Dr. Hans W. Loewald has suggested that more attention be paid to the development of the id, ignored in this "ego" era. At the congress, Dr. Jonathan Cohen, in "Trauma, the Ego and the Id: A Note on the Theoretical Problem Posed by Freud in *Beyond the Pleasure Principle,*" said that the id was not just "a region of chaos in the mind," but subject to complex development. When psychic trauma occurs during the earliest years of a child's life, it not only interferes with the development of the ego but also the id, Cohen pointed out. Referring to Freud's theory that the ego develops out of the id, Cohen added that "the differentiation of the id from an undifferentiated id-ego matrix is not a single maturational step but a process involving innumerable discrete steps all through the developmental period." He suggested trauma be defined "as a developmental event or pattern that interferes with id differentiation at whatever stage." He gave as an example of traumatic interference with the developmental tasks of the anal stage "intrusive enema-giving, which overrides and renders ineffectual the biological mechanisms of reflex bowel activity, depriving the child of its most important biological ally."

Secondary to such interference with id development, the ego also suffers to the extent that its normal development depends upon adequate structure and regulation within the id, he said. As a result, both id and ego are "faultily formed." There is "inadequate laying down of memory traces of satisfaction to constitute an established mastery of a given stage and zone."

During a personal analysis, "in the re-living and structuring into memories of faultily mastered trauma, not only the ego but also the id is re-educated and the proper balance between the two domains of the personality is established," he said. "This requires a complementary dictum to be added to the classic one: 'Where ego was (and id belongs) shall id be'."

In addition to the new developmental theory of psychoanalysis, Freud opened up many other areas for his successors to explore.

One followed from his discovery that there was a difference between the "natural" mourning after the loss of a loved one and what he called "unnatural melancholic" feelings that became part of a lasting depression. He explained the difference in his paper "Mourning and Melancholia" written in 1915.

Freud described mourning as the normal emotion of grief at the loss of a loved person. Then he noted that some people, instead of grieving naturally over the loss of a mother or father or some other loved one, sank into a deep depression, or melancholia, in which their feelings of self-esteem plummeted.

Freud said that if what he called "the work of mourning" remained unfinished—if it were not possible for the bereaved person to bestow his love on someone else and the depression lasted for years—the person was denying his feelings of hate (partly because of desertion) for the lost loved one. This repressed hate was causing him to feel guilty and the guilt caused the depression.

A son or daughter always has feelings of ambivalence toward a parent, Freud said. This ambivalence "casts a pathological shade on the grief, forcing it to express itself in the form of self-reproaches, to the effect that the mourner himself is to blame for the loss of the loved one, i.e., desired it."

Mourning the loss of a loved one is a normal emotional process. It has "a quite specific psychical task to perform; its function is to detach the survivor's memories and hopes from the dead. When this has been achieved, the pain grows less and with it the remorse and the self-reproach."

Freud raised the question about when loss led to anxiety and when to mourning. In 1926, in *Inhibitions, Symptoms and Anxiety* he referred to a "peculiar painfulness" that followed a loss, saying, "Thus the problem becomes more complicated: when does separation from an object produce anxiety, when does it produce mourning and when does it produce, it may be, only pain?"

He answered by describing "the one situation which we believe we understand—the situation of the infant when it is presented with a stranger instead of its mother. It will exhibit the anxiety which we have attributed to the danger of loss of object . . . but the expression of its face and its reaction of crying indicate that it is feeling pain as well. Certain things seem to be joined together in it which will later on be separated out. It cannot as yet distinguish between temporary absence and permanent loss. As soon as it loses sight of its mother it behaves as if it were never going to see her again; and repeated consoling experiences to the contrary are necessary before it learns that her disappearance is usually followed by her re-appearance. Its mother encourages this piece of knowledge which is so vital to it by playing the familiar game of hiding her face from it with her hands and then, to its joy, uncovering it again. In these circumstances it can, as it were, feel longing unaccompanied by despair."

Because the infant cannot understand the reality as yet, the situation of missing its mother is not a danger-situation but a traumatic one, Freud said, if at the time she is absent the infant feels a need which its mother should be the one to satisfy. It becomes a danger situation if the need is not present. There is little in this view to give satisfaction to millions of working mothers, which is not to say that it is wrong—just unpopular—and for very understandable reasons . . . with many women, inside and outside the women's movement.

The first determinant of anxiety introduced by the ego is loss of the perception of the object—which is equated with loss of the object itself, Freud points out. This explains why an adult who falls "madly" in love cannot bear being away from the loved one. The loss of sight of the loved one equals the actual loss.

In the infant, there is as yet no question of loss of love, Freud said. Later experiences teach the child the object can be present but angry, and then loss of love "becomes a new and much more enduring danger and determinant of anxiety." A state of mental helplessness arises that has the specific character of pain when a child is separated from his mother or when she rages at him and he feels unloved because of his deep dependence on her for his safety, his very life.

The traumatic situation of missing the mother differs in one important respect from the traumatic situation of birth, Freud explains. At birth no object exists and so no object can be missed. Anxiety is the only reaction. But after birth, repeated situations of satisfaction with the mother have created an object, and towards this object, whenever the infant feels a need, he experiences intense "longing." It is in connection with this new reaction that pain may appear when the object is lost. Pain is thus the reaction to the danger which that loss entails and, by a further displacement, a reaction to the danger of the loss of the object itself, Freud says.

Three stages of the mourning process, as seen in children deprived temporarily of their mothers, were delineated by Dr. John Bowlby of the Tavistock Child Development Research Unit in London—protest, despair and detachment, during which restitution was sought.

Dr. George Pollock asked the question: Is Bowlby's description of a young child's reaction to loss of his mother the same as the mature, fully developed mourning process in adults? He concluded there was a mourning process that started in infancy and reached maturity after adolescence when the psychic apparatus was fully developed. This mourning process, he said, had evolved through the evolution of man as "an adaptive means of dealing with loss, disappointment and change." The earlier and more primitive stages of the mourning process are seen in the infant. The process is initiated by the first experiences of separating from the mother. If these experiences include excessive anxiety, fear, sadness and anger, these intense feelings are apt to be part of all future reactions to loss.

This mourning process is a "normal, universal, adaptive" one found in all people and throughout history, Pollock stated in the article, "Process and Affect: Mourning and Grief." He believes that "all change involving 'the loss' of something and 'the gain' of the new, entails a mourning process that may be brief, non-conscious and in telescopic fashion including affects associated with the process." The word "affect," used originally by Freud, means an emotion and the thoughts, both conscious and unconscious, associated with the emotion.

The mourning process is clearly seen during psychoanalytic treatment, Pollock points out. The work of analysis is similar to, at times identical to, the mourning process, as the process of detachment and separation occurs. This is experienced during analysis not only at times of separation or termination, but in the unfulfilled mourning for childhood losses, a mourning that must be fulfilled with the help of the analyst before the analysis can proceed.

A special kind of depression in infancy after a loss was named "the anaclitic depression," by Spitz. It followed an infant's separation from his mother at a time he could not cope emotionally with the separation. This depression was seen in babies deserted by their mothers, who spent the first months of their lives in hospitals or other institutions. If there is a complete absence of mothering, the loss is usually so devastating it equals "emotional starvation," in Spitz's words. It "leads to a progressive deterioration engulfing the child's whole person." The child becomes like the infant monkey who, deprived of his mother, sits huddled in a corner of the cage refusing to move, a starved, pitiful look on its pinched face.

Spitz made the distinction that we feel one kind of loss as a child when a mother dies or abandons us and another kind of loss when she sinks into a depression. The depressed mother gives her child the feeling of an "emotional loss." He explained: "The mother, in changing her emotional attitude . . . radically changes the signals which identified her as good object for the child. Physically, she remains the same mother she was. Emotionally, the good mother . . . the person whom the child loves, is lost."

Every infant sees his mother in two images, the "good" and the "bad." The two images remain separate until, fusing good and bad, the infant can consider her a total human being. The depressed mother, ineffectually coping with her own losses, blocks this normal development, Spitz said. He added that every child will "follow the mother into the depressive attitude."

Dr. Edith Jacobson advanced the theory that too early a disappointment or loss of faith in parents will cause depression. She described "disappointment" as an experience that occurs when promises and expectations of gratification are not fulfilled. She said that oral frustration, in particular a state of severe and lasting hunger, seems to be the earlier forerunner of profound disappointment "such as comes about later by being hit by the loss of a most valuable object."

If a mother fails to feed a hungry baby on time, she theorizes, the baby will become depressed and in later life a minor disappointment may revive this feeling of severe depression, "the feeling of blank, empty hopelessness, of nothingness, often accompanied by the sensation of physical emptiness."

The child who has been disappointed too early cannot use his disillusionment for the development of his self-respect. On the contrary, he "must get involved in the collapse of his world of magic," in Jacobson's words. Instead of acquiring a realistic picture of the world, the child may swing from optimism to a pessimistic illusion which distorts reality.

Both the quality of a mother's care and the infant's capacity to accept frustration set an emotional tone that influences how the infant accepts his losses, psychoanalysts agree. Though childhood may be remembered as a time of innocence and happiness, no period in life compares to it in the number of losses and the intensity of day-by-day disappointments. "As a period of disappointment and renunciation, childhood has no parallel, nor is there a richer source of frustration, unrequited wishes, or expectations that fail," says Dr. Gregory Rochlin, author of *Griefs and Discontents: The Forces of Change.*

The concept that losses start early in life and have a profound effect on our emotions led Rochlin to originate the phrase "the loss complex." The loss of a loved one "in fact or fancy" refers not only to a mother's absence or death but the loss suffered by a child when, for instance, mother speaks sharply or punishes. The child feels a loss of self-esteem, or self-confidence.

During the early years the fear of loss, the dread of abandonment and the thought of dying constitute "our three major conflicts," says Rochlin. Each conflict acts "in concert with the others as the loss complex." These conflicts are based on three convictions: 1) that relationships are tentative 2) that stability is threatened by change from within and outside the self 3) that there exists a deep and necessary dependence on others.

Everyone fears dying, whether they admit it or not, but there is one thing more feared, according to Dr. Martin Grotjahn: the loss of ego identity "is felt with more horror than death itself . . . to lose mastery of oneself, to become a victim of one's own unconscious drives and impulses, is living death. Such total annihilation is the prototype of the worst anxiety the ego is capable of experiencing." The great anxiety of the child at the early oral level is the primordial anxiety of annihilation, he says. It is the child's fear of being left by the mother, an act the child believes will lead to his death. "It is felt as a double threat: one coming from the deserting mother, the other coming from within as murderous rage against her for having deserted her child. Repeated threats of such danger can probably stimulate in a child death anxiety, and murderous hostility of immense intensity. Against this the infant has only one defense, and that is complete—meaning psychotic—denial. We can assume that this is the trauma which, if reactivated in later life, may lead to insanity."

At the next stage, the anal level, the symbolization of death is less obvious, Grotjahn says: "It seems that children begin to deal consciously with the fear of death at the time of their toilet training. At that time children realize there is something alive in them; then all of a sudden, at the request of mother, it is outside of them in the little pot. Now it is dead and must be flushed away. At this realization children begin to fear death or to recognize it as a possibility. Preoccupation with feces in dreams is frequently a symbolization of death anxiety. In primitive burial rituals, this connection was often expressed by defecation at the funeral rites."

Love alone "is not the answer to all existential problems," Grotjahn states. "The mother must also offer her authoritarian strength to help the child to win in his struggle to fight the inner enemy" —his destructive impulses.

"Normal people know how to deal with their instincts and their introjected bad objects," he continues. "Neurotics and psychotics do not know how to struggle with these split-up objects; therefore they have to regress to a time when this struggle was still raging.

"Death fear is directed against a realistic threat from the outside. Death anxiety is a warning sign against the longing for death coming from the inside of our unconscious." Grotjahn describes the unconscious as "the eternal pleasure seeker and also the last destroyer, the instrument of the death instinct. It is represented by the incorporated dead or destructive mother."

Freud began the search, and latter-day psychoanalysts have contributed to a deeper understanding of the processes of mourning, especially ways in which to help a child face his grief and anger so it will not become destructive in his later life.

Freud's theory of dreams and their relation to the unconscious has inspired countless articles and books. Grotjahn's *The Voice of the*

Symbol explains how dreams use symbols to disguise their threatening meanings—the stuff dreams are made on is incest, murder, castration, revenge. Full awareness would be too dangerous to the conscious self, but during sleep, which is an altered state of consciousness but not complete absence, one thinks on a deeper level of the mind, a more primitive level.

A red hat may, in the dreamer's mind, be associated with menstrual blood. A ghost may represent the nightgowned mother of childhood. "To understand the symbol is to understand the unconscious," says Grotjahn. "The word *symbol* implies throwing together, bringing together, integrating. The process of symbol formation is a continuous process of bringing together and integrating the internal with the external world, the subject with the object, and the earlier emotional experiences with later experiences."

Ancient man accepted the symbol as reality—the sun was a god driving his chariot across the heavens. The symbol was a magical means of dominance over reality, even though illusional. Through use of the symbol, anxiety about the unknown was postponed and time could be won to prepare to master reality. For schizophrenics, the symbol is still the way of relating to what they believe a hostile world.

The first popular explanation of Freud's interpretation of dreams is contained in Dr. Walter A. Stewart's *The Secret of Dreams*. "Through the study of dreams an entire new continent of awareness has been forced upon mankind," Stewart said. "Dreams show that at night, when our rational controls are reduced, a hidden world of feelings and memories fleetingly dominates our lives, only to be rejected or ignored as crazy or foolish or obscene by our waking consciousness. Yet the understanding of a dream can open a window into a level of our mental life observable in no other way. When we say, 'I would never think of such a thing in my wildest dreams', we are wrong. It is exactly in our dreams that our deeply buried impulses appear. The dream, like hypnosis, can bring back to consciousness deeply repressed memories and impulses which we would never otherwise permit into consciousness. The dream is the unique normal experience which allows us to open this closed door to greater self-understanding. Dreams offer a route to insight about ourselves not available any other way."

The Secret of Dreams explains how Freud discovered what he called "the royal road to the unconscious" and the varous disguises used by the dream to conceal the hidden meaning from the dreamer. It also emphasizes the importance of knowing what a dream—a message to the self—reveals about a conflict that may be affecting the dreamer in a destructive way and which, if he becomes aware of it, he is then able to resolve.

Dr. Charles Fisher has done outstanding research on dreams, both in corroborating Freud's theory of the dream as a partial outlet for repressed sexual wishes and in establishing new data on dreams. For instance, Freud spoke of the "day residue" which sparked the dream, saying the residue consisted of something we saw or experienced—or even an image of which we were not conscious—the day before the dream. As part of a demonstration Fisher flashed a slide on a screen for one-hundredth of a second, then asked each of twenty-four subjects to draw what he had seen and to record his dreams that night. On the following day each subject was asked to describe and draw the images of his dreams. The results showed the dream "developed" more of the picture than the dreamer's conscious mind had taken in. Details not re-called appeared in the dream, woven into the action. The drawing of the dream scene seemed "to come out of the pencil, almost like automatic writing—the pencil draws by itself. Along with the automatic quality there is a compulsive need to put in or omit certain items."

Fisher collaborated with Dr. William Dement on the original "dream deprivation" experiments, which showed that dreaming is essential to well-being. When people are deprived of dreaming they tend to feel exhausted and depressed the next day, and try to make up for it by added dreaming time the following night, as experiments showed.

Previous experiments in 1953 by Dr. Nathaniel Kleitman and Dr. E. Aserinsky revealed a universal dream cycle. They found that everyone, aware or not, dreams four or five times a night in a regular cycle, spending twenty-five percent of the night in dreams. This was substantiated by rapid eye movement, or REM periods, which occur at intervals of ninety minutes and average twenty-five minutes in length. They increase regularly in length during the night from ten to twenty-eight minutes. By awakening the subjects each time the eye movements occurred, the researchers were able to correlate the rapid eye movements with dreaming. More than seventy percent of the subjects awakened from REM periods reported dreams—only seven percent from non-REM periods. These findings have been verified by the thousands of subjects investigated in numerous laboratories.

Fisher and Dement also confirmed Freud's theory that all the dreams in one night are related to the same unconscious wish by waking the subject right after the REM period, then asking him to tell the dream and his associations to it.

The discovery of a major biological cycle involving alternating phases of the building up or conservation of energy in the mind and discharge of that energy during sleep and dreaming has important implications for the instinctual drive theory of psychoanalysis, Fisher says: "It would appear that we are here at the very heart of the mystery of the mental apparatus and basic motivational forces."

Fisher points out that Freud spoke of dreams as preserving "more mental antiquities than we could have imagined possible; so that psychoanalysis may claim a high place among the sciences which are concerned with the reconstruction of the earliest and most obscure periods of the beginnings of the human race." Among the antiquities preserved by the dream "we may now add the activated REM periods of archisleep, which are regulated by old parts of the brain and which carry us back not only to man's archaic heritage but even further into the phylogeny of prehuman species."

In 1965, at the Mount Sinai School of Medicine in New York, Fisher and his co-workers, Dr. Joseph Gross and Dr. Joseph Zuch, showed that one of the important aspects of the physiological activation accompanying REM dreaming sleep in ten males was "a massive excitation of the sexual drive in the male as manifested by a cycle of penile erections synchronous with the REM periods." They used the mercury strain gauge, about the size of a small rubber band, for measurement, looping it around the base of the penis. "We were able to show that about ninety-five percent of the

REM periods are accompanied by some degree of erection; more or less full erection in sixty percent of instances and partial erection in thirty-five percent," Fisher reported. "Erections are found to occur in temporal relationship to onsets and terminations of REM periods, so that there may be approximately as much erection during a night as there is dreaming, that is, from one-fifth to a quarter of sleep in the young adult male may be spent in a state of full erection."

Initially, he said, he was reluctant to believe such extensive erections could be related to the content of dreams and decided to investigate further. In collaboration with Gross and Dr. Joseph Byrne, he studied the relationship between REM period erections, their fluctuation and dream content.

They found that dreaming was accompanied by erection if the dream had manifest erotic content—sexual images or feelings in the story. But the majority of REM erections were not associated with such manifest sexual content, which meant the erections were stimulated by unconscious sexual thoughts and feelings.

If, in the presence of an ongoing erection the story of the dream shifted to an episode arousing marked anxiety or other negative emotion, rapid detumescence followed. The anxiety involved the danger situations related to castration, loss of love or loss of the loved one.

If aggressive content associated with anxiety or other negative emotion was present in the dream from the onset of the REM period, erection would not occur or would be markedly inhibited. "Whether or not erection occurs appears to depend upon the particular balance in any given dream between aggressive and sexual content and the accompanying anxiety or other negative affect," says Fisher.

Fisher and Dr. Edwin Kahn also carried out an investigation on the erection cycle in a group of relatively healthy men over seventy, recruited from various old age clubs around New York City. They found that both the erection cycle and sexual desire and activity can endure into extreme old age, though considerably diminished.

These observations have demonstrated something not heretofore known, that dreaming in the male is accompanied on a physiological level by massive sustained genital excitation if no anxiety exists in the content of the dream. From a psychoanalytic point of view, Fisher says, this sexual excitation may be considered "a periodically insistent physiological concomitant of instinctual drive arousal. The excitation is importantly involved in the sexual nature of dreams, and I have demonstrated that the fluctuations and inhibitions of erection, which represent waxing and waning of this sexual excitation, can to a considerable degree be correlated with dream content." He also said that the erection cycle as a physiological phenomenon was primary, and that more or less full erection will occur during every REM period in the absence of inhibitory factors. The chief inhibitory factor appears to be anxiety aroused by dreams with aggressive content especially related to castration wishes and fears, loss of love or the loved one, feelings of jealousy and rejection.

Manifestations of the aggressive instinctual drive appear only in connection with the sexual drive—that is, there are always fusions of libido with aggression, Fisher points out. He adds that it may be assumed that from the neonatal period on, REM-period sexual excitation begins to organize memory traces of penile sensations of frustration and gratification, pleasure and unpleasure, pain and anxiety.

Fisher's results attest to what he calls "the irrepressible force of the sexual drive." There is every reason to believe that during REM periods of dreaming sleep, there is a release from inhibition of the drive centers and circuits located within the so-called limbic system, which includes the hypothalamus of the brain, and which flood our consciousness with all our emotions—love, hate, fear, guilt. These same areas and circuits are also implicated in the triggering of REM sleep. The functions regulated by the limbic system have in the broadest sense to do with self-preservation and racial preservation. There are areas within the hypothalamus necessary for the integration of copulatory behavior in the male and mating and maternal behavior in the female, and other areas and circuits, stimulation of which produces erection and ejaculation or oral and feeding behavior.

These findings corroborate Freud's formulation of the relationship of instinctual drives to dreaming, "one of the great products of his genius," Fisher says. Freud said in 1900 that the majority of dreams of adults deal with sexual content and give expression to erotic wishes, and that this is not surprising since no other instinct has been subjected since childhood to so much suppression as the sexual instinct with its numerous components: "From no other instinct are so many and such powerful unconscious wishes left over, ready to produce dreams in a state of sleep."

Fisher says it is likely that repressed erotic unconscious wishes are activated each night during the periodic waves of REM period excitation, which are "instrumental in lifting such wishes and their derivatives from repression." He adds, "I do not believe that we will ever have a complete understanding of mental functioning without breaching the mind-body problem. Psychoanalytic theories can lead us to hypotheses about the workings of the central nervous system, and neurophysiological findings can have an impact on our views of psychic functioning. I do not wish to imply that psychology will ever be *reduced* to neurophysiology but only that one can be *translated* into the other. As Dr. Seymour Kety has said, there may someday be a biochemistry of memory but never of memories. The same can be said of dreaming and dreams, which will always require psychological interpretation."

Fisher also made discoveries about impotence. He found that in psychogenic impotence the nocturnal REM erections were normal in amount and degree and an excellent indicator of erectile potential. In these cases a marked discrepancy existed between the amount and degree of nocturnal erection and the person's daytime performance level attained during attempted intercourse or masturbation. In organic impotence no such discrepancy existed. Instead, the maximal nocturnal erection attained corresponded closely to, and mirrored, the man's impaired waking performance. This new method may be useful in the diagnosis and decision about the type of treatment for impotence, especially in the more difficult cases.

No similar experiments have been performed to measure sexual excitation in women, obviously because as yet there is no such visible way to measure this. But some analysts believe it may be assumed that women, just like men, use their dreams to express repressed sexual desires. Both women and men have been known to have orgasms while dreaming.

Freud introduced the term "countertransference" in 1910 to describe "what arises in the physician" as a result of the patient's "influence" on the physician's "unconscious feelings," an influence that might interfere with treatment. He urged analysts to become aware of these feelings and suggested that after their first analysis they return every five years for further analysis to make sure they were in touch with the feelings and thoughts induced in them by patients. He also said that only through knowing his own "personal suffering" could an analyst hope to help others.

Psychoanalysis is different from other scientific disciplines because the investigator is also the healer. He is not the detached scientist whose personality and emotions have no effect on the subject of his study. The so-called "exact" sciences do not require the one conducting the work to be aware of his feelings. But the "psychic apparatus" of the psychoanalyst must be known to him because he uses it as an instrument both of investigation into the patient's life and in the healing process.

During the course of treatment every psychoanalyst experiences "many shades and degrees of love, hate and indifference toward each of his patients" and "this range of feeling is necessary for doing psychoanalytic therapy," as Dr. Ralph R. Greenson says in his book *Explorations in Psychoanalysis.* "One ought to determine whether a reaction or attitude is predominantly countertransference or therapeutic," he says, or "if it was unnecessarily hurtful or unexpectedly helpful to the patient." It is often helpful to find out what it was the patient said or did "that triggered our reaction," he adds. "Then we have to analyze in ourselves, by introspection and free association, the unconscious source of the countertransference reaction and our unconscious motives for hurting or helping the patient."

Greenson called the ability to empathize with the patient an "absolute prerequisite ... it is our best method for comprehending the complex, subtle and hidden emotions in another human being." He also stressed the analyst's ability to be aware of his own erotic and hostile fantasies.

Dr. Lawrence J. Friedman, past president of the Los Angeles Psychoanalytic Institute and former dean of training, has called attention to what he says is a "long overdue discussion of the personality of those attracted to psychoanalysis and the difficulties that arise out of their personalities."

He refers to "the majority of medical doctors," who, he says, "have certain specific conflicts about human violence" and for whom becoming a physician "represents an attempt to find a satisfactory solution." He adds, "Some find the solution, others don't." When the training of psychoanalysts in America became restricted by the American Psychoanalytic Association to doctors of medicine, psychoanalysis limited itself in this choice "to people who choose the medical profession in the first place on account of unconscious conflicts about violence."

Friedman goes on: "I have seen a number of applicants for psychoanalytic training whose interest was based on the conviction, even if totally unconscious, that being a psychoanalyst means being passive; it would help them avoid their conflicts about violence. They want to become psychoanalysts because the medical profession did not solve their conflicts, regardless of whether they tried it in various branches of physical medicine or within the framework of general psychiatry." If these physicians are accepted and their training analysis "is unequal to dealing successfully with their conflicts, they will be passive and anxious. Their passivity, instead of minimizing, increases their conflicts, forces them to do things that may be unwise. Instead of recognizing their difficulties, more often than not they will find theoretical explanations for their behavior; they will insist that whatever they do is motivated by the need of the patient and not of their own need."

Friedman points out that the analyst is forced to physical and emotional passivity. He has to sit quietly for most of the hours of the day and give up full emotional participation in the exchange that takes place between him and the patient. This physical inactivity, day after day, is an occupational hazard. Dr. Luis Feder in his paper "Prometheus Chained: Masochism in Psychoanalytic Practice," compared the psychoanalyst to Prometheus, with the analyst "chained in postural, positional, attitudinal, ethical, technical, professional, ideological, societal, social and family restrictions and paradoxes . . . What price we pay for the Promethean privilege of partaking in the glory of the daily discovery of the unconscious and the treatment of the neurosis! To boot, sexual and hostile transferential and countertransferential buzzards gnawing at our entrails are still no open theme, exposing all details, read and discussed at congresses."

Searles, in his discussion of countertransference and the important part it plays, speaks also of "the patient as therapist to his analyst." The therapeutic striving in all of us may be "warped" by relationships to the mother and father in the early years and other environmental factors, he points out, warning that "the analyst's failure to discern that long-repressed striving in the patient accounts, more than does any other interpersonal element in the treatment situation, for the patient's unconscious resistance to the analytic process." He adds, "Despite the acknowledged complexities involved in our departing from classical psychoanalytic theory and technique in this regard, it is essential that we do so . . . The classical analytic position, containing an element of delusion to the effect that the analyst is not at all a real person to the patient but simply mirrors the mother and father of the past to whom the patient relates as a child, simply will not do." He asks analysts to pay attention to their own feelings of rage in relation to the patient and how it affects the treatment, as well as to the many ways patients tell the analyst, consciously and unconsciously what he may be doing wrong.

This same theme is explored in depth by Dr. Robert Langs, who examines the interaction between patient and analyst in *The Therapeutic Interaction, The Listening Process* and *The Bipersonal Field.* He says, "the relationship between analyst and patient has become too static, the analyst too often has been excluding many of his unconscious reactions, such as expression of anger, sexual fantasies and manipulativeness, from his awareness." He calls his approach "adaptive-interactional" because it takes into account in particular "the unconscious communicative interaction between patient and therapist and also the intrapsychic processes within both participants."

Langs found that patients' fantasies could be evoked by the analyst's words or fantasies, just as a dream is sparked by something experienced the day before, what Freud called "the day residue," and to which, Langs says, Freud did not assign enough importance.

When Langs started to examine "the adaptive context" within psychoanalysis and psychotherapy, he discovered, "much to my amazement that the significant contexts always involve the analyst's interventions or failure to intervene. More than that, I found that, based on criteria I developed, often these interventions were in error. I then discovered that the patient, quite unconsciously, was exquisitely sensitive to the unconscious implications of the therapist's interventions, including the countertransferences reflected in incorrect interventions. On that basis, I began to study the patient's unconscious perceptions and introjections of the analyst's difficulties and developed a far more balanced view of the patient than had existed previously."

The patient is "unconsciously perceptive far more often than he unconsciously distorts." As a rule, the valid perceptions are eventually worked over in terms of their soundness and additional distortions based on the patient's fantasies. Langs also found that, in response to "errors and sensed pathology" in the analyst, the patient often, though virtually unconsciously, engages in curative efforts directed at the analyst. "By stressing therapy as a bipersonal interaction and taking place in a bipersonal field, I was able to demonstrate the ground rules of treatment and their consistent maintenance," he says. "The bipersonal field concept calls for an explanation of contributions from both therapist and patient for every experience that takes place within the field or inside of either participant. The analyst's contributions are consistently under scrutiny, especially those related to the unconscious communicative interaction. Resistances and symptoms within the patient are viewed in terms of contributions from both participants. In this light, many unnoticed pathological contributions from the analyst to disturbances in the patients can be identified."

It is also possible to identify "unconscious misalliances between patient and therapist" and to identify "misalliance cures that take place without insight and through shared defenses and pathological gratification." What Langs calls framework cures "develop from unnecessary deviations in the frame which can provide temporary symptom relief for the patient but do not solve the underlying conflicts."

He identifies two communicative styles in patients. The first is "symbolic, illusory and involves a valid search for understanding." There is true regression, then growth at a considerable cost. This requires an analyst who can maintain "a secure frame" and interpret to the patient at the proper time. Langs describes this as "truth therapy."

He calls the second communicative style "lie therapy." This is based on an effort to destroy understanding and relatedness. Unconsciously, patients try to erect barriers to the truth about their inner disturbances and those they unconsciously perceive in the analyst. Langs says this kind of therapy is "by far in the majority," used by "lie" patients and "lie" therapists. "Such therapy is designed to create barriers that seal off the disturbing parts of the personalities of both participants and to generate falsifications that cover over these truths. There is an absence of meaningful communication and a presence of flat and empty barriers . . . Clichés are common. Both patient and analyst are trying to rid their psyches of accretions of inner tensions, to evacuate inner disturbances and dump them on each other."

It is important for the analyst to have a thorough understanding of his countertransference at all times so he may "never exploit the patient," warned Dr. Clara Thompson. She added, "I am convinced that the kindness and interest shown have to be genuine, or the patient will recognize the insincerity."

This highly important issue of countertransference will no doubt continue to be studied for years. Psychoanalysts constitute one group of physicians who are interested in "healing" themselves. They know how vital it is to be aware of what lies in the unconscious that may lead to ineffective treatment of the patient, disagreements among themselves that are not valid or schisms within the psychoanalytic movement.

As Freud once wrote to Dr. Georg Groddeck, a pioneer in psychosomatic medicine to whom Freud said he owed the word "id": "It is difficult to practice psychoanalysis in isolation; it is an exquisitely sociable enterprise. It would be so much nicer if we all roared or howled in chorus and in the same rhythm, instead of each one growling to himself in the corner."

But out of the "growling" often has come reflective thought that benefits both psychoanalyst and patient. Psychoanalytic research in many areas has given marked impetus to the understanding of the human mind so that today, more and more troubled persons with varying depths of mental illness, once given up as hopeless, are being treated and helped.

Still, in spite of all the valid knowledge, there has been an outburst of non-valid, ridiculous therapies, which have sprung up like weeds, making Freud's prediction of "dilution" and "distortion" of psychoanalysis in America, unhappily, come true.

Why has there been this proliferation of superficial, "pop" therapies? And how dangerous are they to the mental health of those who do not choose wisely in seeking to ease their unhappiness?

12

Of Sex Therapists and Swindlers

The idea Freud stimulated, that you do not have to remain unhappy if you feel troubled, has created a large demand for psychological help. To meet this demand, new ways of helping have appeared, some valid, some dubious, to put it mildly.

Many forms of therapy are not analytic, the therapist does not pretend to be an analyst but offers reassurance and help in a supportive way. Such help may be all that is needed or that can be financed and is better than no help at all.

But a degraded form of therapy occurs when men and women who pretend to be qualified therapists try to manipulate a troubled person or promise more than they can deliver. The goals range from eliminating a single symptom to claims of changing attitudes and behavior.

The professionally untrained of the mental health field are legion. It is alarming to learn how many of those doling out "advice" or "guidance" for high fees possess little or no training, much less wisdom.

Kipling wrote:

"If you can bear to hear the truth you've spoken
Twisted by knaves, to make a trap for fools . . ."

This has happened, in some degree, to Freud in America. In his fear of what this country would do to psychoanalysis, he did not imagine how many psychic gunmen would run rampant over the territory he so carefully explored and for which he devised a complicated, delicate technique. Calling themselves "psychoanalysts." Imposing their values on patients. Using "inspirational" harangues. Scolding, persuading, coercing, punishing, "implosiving." Treating patients with contempt. Playing Russian roulette with the repressed emotions of those in mental pain.

"We do analysis for two reasons: to understand the unconscious and to make a living," Freud told Theodor Reik. There clearly is nothing reprehensible about the need to make a living—but there *is* about so-called therapists who offer false promises, who have little or no conviction about genuine psychological help. Who do not understand the unconscious in themselves or anyone else. Who foolishly rush in where the experienced fear to tread, ignoring such basics as resistance and transference and become enraged when a patient does not promptly "obey" or change.

The relationship between patient and therapist as Freud envisioned it is ignored or distorted. The therapeutic interaction is treated as if it were nonexistent. "This approach to the therapeutic relationship with the focus exclusively on the surface of the patient's daily life serves the blatant denial and defense of both patient and therapist. It serves as a barrier for all that is transpiring unconsciously between patient and therapist," Dr. Robert Langs says, and adds, "there are qualities to these interactions that are so blatantly destructive and seductive that any observer could not fail to recognize their presence. Only the patient and therapist, bound up in a kind of unconscious conspiracy, could fail to do so . . . The creation of such massive barriers to painful inner truths on which symptoms are actually based serves as a defense against insight and understanding . . . Many patients and therapists strongly prefer to find a way of passing all of that by. While there is only one avenue to these truths of psychoanalysis, there are countless approaches to their avoidance."

There are two extreme types of pseudo-healer. One has no understanding of what Freud was talking about. The other chips off a theory or two of Freud's and publicizes the plagiarized "crumb from the psychoanalytic table," as Dr. Charles Fisher puts it, as a startling new "cure." Perhaps he adds a soupçon of his own high-sounding but meaningless verbiage.

Such a "therapist" steals from psychoanalysis a few pieces of jargon and makes them the basis of a system that purports to explain the whole person. "Ours seems to be the age of the simplifiers and the reductionists," says Dr. Francis McLaughlin, past president of the American Psychoanalytic Association. "We have an abundance of evidence that much of the present turmoil in our society is directly related to the search for magical and simplistic answers. We hardly need to be reminded of the prevalent wish to control man's mind and behavior, and also of the wishes for immediate relief from and escape from the complexities and uncertainties of life."

Some therapists give lip service to psychoanalysis even as they discard its basic premises—as was predicted by Freud, who once said to Dr. Franz Alexander as the latter left Vienna for America, "I know from my own experiences in the States that masterful way of giving lip service."

A warning that the "breadth of the spread" of Freud "must not vitiate the purity and clarity of . . . that which is uniquely priceless in psychoanalysis" was sounded by Dr. John Milne Murray at the twenty-fifth anniversary ceremonies of the Boston Psychoanalytic Institute on November 30, 1958: "The most valuable achievements of analysis as a research tool for the good of man will have the greatest influence upon mankind when they are used in the broader areas, but this very fact involves a danger that its broad use may minimize the importance of the purity and the uniquely valuable 'something' which is at the core of psychoanalytic research endeavor."

The current president of the American Psychoanalytic Association, Dr. Rebecca Z. Solomon, in her welcoming address to the Thirty-First International Congress, pointed out that some of the most vocal critics of psychoanalysis "have appropriated various aspects of analytic theory and applied them in distorted form to what is referred to as the 'newer therapies'." She added that the "title of psychoanalyst is coveted by many who adopt it even though their training and experience is questionable."

One of the major tasks of analysts is to "maintain as clear a definition of psychoanalysis as possible—to define its scope, nature of its practice and the clinical and theoretical concepts which make it effective," she said. "While encouraging diversity, innovation and originality, we want also to encourage a perspective which maintains and conserves the principles which are basic to the practice and theory of psychoanalysis."

Dr. Karl Menninger deplores what he calls "the commercialization of psychoanalysis, indulged in by those attracted to the field of mental health less by any humane dogma than by the dollar." Menninger, who has done more than anyone in this country to popularize the understanding of psychoanalysis through *The Human Mind, Man Against Himself, The Technique of Psychoanalysis* and *Love Against Hate,* recently told this writer: "I'm afraid that psychoanalysis is being ruined by avarice and materialism, in spite of its high ideals and great usefulness. The way this curious epidemic of therapeutizing people has spread is alarming. I recently talked with a group of people all claiming to be psychotherapists but all without adequate training. What is often called 'psychotherapy' represents an exploitation of the process. Many so-called 'therapists' consider patients experimental subjects. A therapist has no right to experiment with a patient. This means he feels no responsibility for that patient's welfare. Commercialism is wrong in any medical treatment. Perhaps it is all right for massage parlors and mineral baths, but doctors—real doctors—should not be tradesmen."

Freud wrote Oberndorf in 1919, ". . . the popularity of the term psychoanalysis in America is not evidence of a friendly attitude toward the subject, of a particularly broad dissemination of, or profound understand of its teachings." He predicted psychoanalysis would "suffer a great deal from being watered down." He also saw "many abuses" that had no relation to psychoanalysis finding "a cover under its name."

He expressed the fear that in America there would be aborted versions of his theories, that the "pure gold" of psychoanalysis would be debased into a copper alloy. Commenting on Otto Rank's "warm-hearted" reception on his first visit to New York, he wrote: "What is called 'a nine days' wonder' has a particular significance for Americans . . . [America] promises him a rich dollar harvest. But I am not sure how things will go when his new position is subjected to the full light of day."

Rank focused on the trauma of birth as the cause of neurosis. "Primal scream" therapy has followed in Rank's wake. It has taken one small facet of psychoanalysis and blown it up into an entire therapy. Transactional therapy is another "Freudian crumb," using the concept of id, ego and superego on a superficial level without concern for the underlying defenses or dynamics.

Psychoanalysis is not easy. It is an arduous, long-term process. For Freud there was no other way to face the inner self but hard work, discipline, refusal to give up in the face of high odds and inner suffering.

But there seems to be another way for today's would-be therapists—the way of avarice, charlatanism and deception of the public. This is the way of the second type of "wild" therapist, who does not even pretend to be associated with Freud in any way. He mocks Freud, calls him old-fashioned. He tries only to treat the symptoms, not the causes of distress. Though the symptoms may disappear temporarily, they often return or erupt in other ways. With psychotics or so-called "borderline" cases, not even the symptoms are apt to disappear, and such persons may become suicidal. The underlying conflicts of psychotics cannot usually be reached except through long-term, intensive therapy by highly qualified, gifted psychoanalysts.

Ignored by the horde of pseudo-therapists is one of the most important truths Freud discovered—mental torment cannot be eased by methods tried over the centuries: exhortation, threat of punishment, rest cures or good old "simple common sense."

Freud told Dr. Joseph Wortis, "A person who professes to believe in common-sense psychology and who thinks psychoanalysis is 'far-fetched' can certainly have no understanding of it, for it is common sense which produces all the ills we have to cure."

The easing of torment has to come from *within* the person, not from anything done *to* him. It comes from his ability slowly to gain emotional strength through a relationship of trust with a therapist who helps him face conflicts around which whirl the buried emotions he believes dangerous to his self-esteem.

This truth is thrown to the winds by therapists who promise get-well-quick panaceas for emotional suffering. Unfortunately, belief in gimmick solutions dies hard, and each year hundreds of thousands of unhappy men and women flock to charismatic charlatans, wasting millions of dollars on "therapy" that is useless and ineffective, sometimes dangerous.

There are many who believe that medical researchers will find or invent a new drug to "cure" mental anguish. Chemotherapy is "in." But as Freud said, "It is grossly to undervalue both the origin and the practical significance of the psychoneuroses to suppose that these disorders are to be removed by pottering about with a few harmless remedies . . . strictly regular unmodified psychoanalysis, which is not afraid to handle the most dangerous forces in the mind and set them to work for the benefit of the patient, will be found indispensible."

Those who seek a chemical balm to

> . . . *minister to a mind diseased,*
> *Pluck from the memory a rooted sorrow,*
> *Raze out the written troubles of the brain,*
> *And with some sweet oblivious antidote,*
> *Cleanse the stuffed bosom of the perilous stuff*
> *Which weighs upon the heart*

would do well to remember the comment of MacBeth's physician: "Therein the patient must minister to himself." Unless he is willing to undergo therapy based on psychoanalytic insights, one might just as well, like the Thane of Glamis, "throw physic to the dogs."

The fantasies in the unconscious have taken many years to form and become entrenched, and our defenses against becoming aware of them are extremely powerful. By fantasizing that some drug or "brief" therapy will help us swiftly face our hidden self, we continue to dwell in the magical world of childhood.

Whatever the latest fad, it is often heralded enthusiastically as "the" answer. Crude, naïve and sometimes harmful therapeutic concoctions constitute the raft of makeshift therapies offered the public. They are sometimes described as "breakthroughs in mental healing." To believe that a weekend of sex or a few sessions of angry screaming or attacking the defenses of other troubled people or to sit in an "orgone box" is of value is the ultimate in wishful thinking. At the very worst, these therapies may inflict so much damage on weak egos that a very depressed person, realizing his last resort has not worked, may well give up all hope.

Some of the "pop" therapies encourage wanton sexual acting out with other patients or between patient and therapist, hypocritically hailing this as "treatment." Male therapists may convince lesbian patients to have sex with them to "cure" their "perversion." This is flagrant abuse of Freud's warning that the psychoanalyst must never lay a hand on a patient. It is also in defiance of the Hippocratic oath to which a physician must swear, promising he will "remain free . . . of all mischief, and, in particular, of sexual relations with both female and male persons."

The "brief encounter" in therapy is equated in the unconscious of both therapist and patient with the wanton sexual affair that so often becomes a reality. Sex therapy has enjoyed a vogue as inhibited men and women seek sexual release, believing this will cure all their problems.

Actually, sex therapy represents "a regression, with emphasis primarily on the pre-genital phases of sexual development—the touching, looking, feeling, and other early expressions of sexuality," says Dr. Lawrence J. Friedman. "This here-and-now therapy encourages in the adult his infant inability to tolerate tension and seek gratification. This runs parallel to the general regressive state of our society."

The struggle "for a sense of self cannot be accomplished by sexual therapy, nor mutual love gained by sexual 'exercises', else all we have is the manufacture of a plastic person for a plastic world," warned Max Rosenbaum, a clinical psychologist, speaking at the annual meeting of the American Academy of Psychoanalysis in Atlanta, May, 1978. He urged psychoanalysts to "declare our opposition to the new worship of Eros and the fruitless nature of that pursuit. It is our responsibility to point out the illusory quality of the 'new' sexual mores." Sex therapy represents "a worship of Eros as the substance of life," which is not a new philosophy but one appearing in many past civilizations, he points out. "What is really new about the 'new' sexual mores? Aren't they really the same appeal to narcissism that Freud cautioned us about? Aren't we still engaged in observing the struggle of the child to rebel against the parent? Have we psychoanalysts abdicated our responsibility to consistently point out the self-destructive nature of sexual exercises which avoid the anxiety of developing healthy mutualism in love?"

Sex therapy does not promote intimacy but is related to a "preoccupation with achievement," he says. "Under the guise of sexual freedom people are locked into a different type of treadmill —how to perform." Sex therapy offers no new "freedom." The one who becomes the "sex object" is not accepted in mutual love but "seen as a part-object—the nourishing breast or the vagina—to prove one's masculinity. Or the man's penis is to prove the woman's femininity so that instead of frigidity we can now observe young men who are impotent because they cannot satisfy women."

Learning to master sophisticated sexual techniques does not lead to love. "Only when the individual has insight and control over his feelings is he in a position to love. He or she loves, as opposed to 'falling in love', akin to falling from a precipice. People move in stages as they love, from admiration to attachment to sexual enjoyment and finally intimacy, concern, devotion and mutualism. Intimacy is not groping for another person's body but the sharing of dreams, hopes and memories . . . Life demands a sense of morality, invoking Freud's belief that civilization depends on the sublimation of instinctual drives."

Rosenbaum also criticizes sex therapy for the tendency to cloak itself "in the confusion of violence and sensuality." He cites therapists who use "creative aggression" training exercises to treat couples who have sexual difficulties, and sex therapists who recommend fantasy rape scenes as part of sex therapy. This has little to do with the sense of self-esteem that leads to mutualism in sex, he says: "Sadism is not an expression of sexual freedom."

The therapist who has sex with a patient knows the patient is "transferring" on him the erotic feelings for the parent of child-hood infatuation. For a therapist to have sex with a patient is comparable to committing the tabooed act of incest, which is what it becomes in both the patient's and the therapist's unconscious. The libidinous therapist is inflicting further psychic damage on the patient.

In some cases this has resulted in serious mental breakdowns in women who have had affairs with therapists. To claim the patient plays his part in such an illicit affair is to misunderstand the nature of therapy. It is the therapist's responsibility, *and his alone,* to make certain there is no physical contact between the patient and himself.

One of the latest fads is called—can one get more modish?—"mind-jogging," which aims at "exercising" the personality as the body is exercised in jogging. The program of "Psychological Fitness," according to its two innovators, clinical psychologists, who describe themselves as "down-to-earth counselors," deals with "simple problems such as how to face your boss, how to really tell your wife how you feel." They protest that "the last thing we want to do is have people go around psychoanalyzing themselves. What we try to do is strengthen your personality . . . to function more effectively in those areas that are seen as weaknesses."

This philosophy hurls out the door all of Freud's findings about what will bring relief to inner suffering. Troubled souls pay hard-earned money for this double-talk and feel disillusioned when no lasting results occur, not understanding why they have been bilked.

The missing element in the various types of "pop" therapy is integrity on the part of the therapist. This shows in the little insults (which are always "big" insults) that the patient endures. A young lawyer, paying seventy-five dollars an hour to a psychologist who holds sessions in his loft in lower New York, received a phone call at his office one day from the therapist, who asked, "Did we have an appointment this afternoon? I forgot." *Forgot!* This is one of the deepest injuries a therapist can inflict on a patient; it tells the patient his therapist does not think enough of him even to remember an appointment. There is no excuse for such an act of contempt on the part of a therapist.

Among the questionable new therapies, at least as measured against the established integrity of psychoanalysis, are: behavior modification, rational-emotive, implosive, existential, encounter, primal scream, transactional, marathon (with or without nudity), est, sensitivity-training and scientology.

In their despair, their hunger for a magical cure and their general resistance to acknowledging the power of the unconscious, many are apt to accept any therapist holding out promise of quick and easy help. A week is better than a month. A weekend is better than a week. Ten hours is better than a weekend.

The public should seriously question:

1. Therapy that denies or ignores the unconscious or tries to reach it by quickie devices that have been shown to be at best ephemeral in their effect.

2. Therapy that ignores resistance or transference.

3. Therapy that over-focuses on a partial aspect of psychoanalysis—aggression, sexuality, narcissism—while ignoring the whole.

4. Therapy that encourages "acting out" of sexual or aggressive desires by the patient or the therapist.

5. Therapy that promises "cure" or fast relief.

6. Therapy that relies on the use of "will power" to bring about change: "Just get your act together," or "Chin up, kid."

7. Therapy that believes mental pain is inherited or organic.

8. Therapy that uses drugs or pills as a lasting way of combatting misery.

9. Therapy that is based on "simple common sense" or some equivalent bromide.

An increasing number of therapists are practicing without training or accreditation by *any* recognized national organization. The practice of "psychotherapy" is not controlled by national law but by state law. Some states have no laws, anyone can claim to be a psychotherapist. Or a psychoanalyst, as there is no law licensing psychoanalysts.

The accredited therapist practices under regulatory bodies. These include 1) The state agency sponsoring his certificate or license 2) The ethics committee of the profession of which he is a member 3) The judicial system through which legal action may be brought against him. These three sources of control do not exist for the nonaccredited therapist. While credentials do not always insure a competent therapist, they do at least offer some protection to the patient and possible recourse from psychic abuse.

Thus the title "psychotherapist" gives no indication of training or competence. Though qualified practitioners sometimes use it as an adjunct to their professional title of psychiatrist or psychologist, the term "psychotherapist" is widely used by those without any qualifications.

There are hundreds of marriage counselors or marriage therapists. Their work "covers a multitude of practitioners and approaches," as Miriam and Otto Ehrenberg write in *The Psychotherapy Maze*. Though anyone can call himself a marriage counselor, the American Association of Marriage Counselors sets minimum standards for its members.

Family counselor, or family therapist, are terms that also have no legal standing, nor does child psychotherapist. The terms "counselor," "guidance counselor" and "vocational counselor" are not controlled by law and can be used by anyone. The term sex therapist is also open to use by anyone—only a small minority of such people have credentials. "Sex therapy" has become a major area of abuse and unethical practices.

A few psychiatrists have indulged in unethical behavior—such as sexual intimacy or addicting patients to drugs. The American Psychiatric Association expells such offenders from its membership ranks whenever charges have been proven. When a therapist does *not* belong to a national organization, he is apt to go scot free if he is guilty of unethical practices.

The pressure for federal reimbursement for psychotherapy caused Dr. Gerald L. Klerman, director of the National Alcohol, Drug Abuse and Mental Health Administration, to call, in the fall of 1978, for controlled clinical trials of the sort used in drug-testing to develop "clear and compelling" evidence of the effectiveness of psychotherapies. He asked whether America needed an "FDA [Federal Drug Administration] for psychotherapy," saying, "there is the temptation for a government agency to become the arbitrator [of issues of effectiveness] when the profession itself has not, in order to respond to an unmet social need." The failure to generate "evidence of efficacy over the past few decades is now hindering the mental health field in its attempts to strengthen its position in the mainstream of health policy and programs."

This raises some pertinent questions about the many therapies offered today as valid and seeking federal reimbursement.

Consider the history of "behavioral therapy." It is based on the belief that attitudes may be changed by exhortation, pleading, suggesting and demanding—a throwback to the days before Freud's discoveries. It was tried in a number of private and public mental hospitals, most of which are now disillusioned about its values. "The bloom is off behavior modification—it's been recognized as just another gadget," says Thomas Dolgoff, organization and management consultant for the Center of Applied Behavioral Sciences of the Menninger Foundation.

The buyer must beware—and beware and beware—in the purchase of mental health. Andreas-Salomé was a prophet when she wrote Freud: ". . . all true revolutions are subject to abuse, but from its very nature Freudian psychoanalysis calls forth this abuse in a completely new fashion . . . For the truths of psychoanalysis lie hidden behind a series of resistances (in all of us!) . . ."

Psychoanalysis has proved itself no fad. It will outlast every "pop" therapy that blooms briefly in a fertile soil nourished by illusion, denial of the unconscious, demand for magic and inability to work for or withstand the frustration of waiting for inner change.

As Brill said: "I feel that both in theory and practice they [all other forms of therapy] are insignificant in comparison to Freud's psychoanalysis. Some are retrogressive confusions. Some are downright swindles."

He added, "It does not take much time to put a plaster on a painful area, but to find the source of the pain often takes a long time."

The useless or harmful therapies offer no *real* challenge to psychoanalysis. But psychoanalysis faces other, more realistic and legitimate challenges as it heads into the future. What is the nature of these challenges?

13

Challenge of the Future

Historically speaking, psychoanalysis is relatively young. Though its fundamentals are set, the years ahead will no doubt see important developments and changes.

Increasingly psychoanalysis will be used as a research tool into the development of personality and in its application to the fabric of society. Each of these areas has been expanding steadily and may be expected to continue to expand.

Freud looked into the years ahead as he spoke before the psychoanalysts of the world gathered in Budapest in September, 1918, at the Fifth International Psychoanalytical Congress. Pointing out that "we are but a handful of people, and even by working hard each one of us can deal in a year with only a small number of persons," he said that "against the vast amount of neurotic misery which is in the world, and perhaps need not be, the quantity we can do away with is almost negligible."

He predicted that perhaps someday "clinics and consultation-departments will be built to which analytically trained physicians will be appointed to help those who could not afford analysis." Then analysts will have "to adapt our technique to the new conditions . . . But whatever form this psychotherapy for the people may take, whatever the elements out of which it is compounded, its most effective and most important ingredients will assuredly remain those borrowed from strict psycho-analysis . . ."

A man of great compassion as well as insight, Freud hoped that psychoanalytic therapy would eventually be available to all who need and want it, rich or poor. In connection with this, at another time he warned, prophetically, *"If the patient's free choice of doctor were to be abrogated it would signify the removal of an important condition for mentally influencing the patient"* (italics Freud's).

How do some of today's psychoanalysts forecast the future? Dr. George H. Pollock predicts. "I can foresee a greater emphasis on prediction, prevention and early intervention. I can foresee applications to and from other fields, especially the social, political, and humanistic disciplines. I can foresee a greater emphasis on the study of all phases of the life course and their deviations. I can foresee a new alignment of specialties, health care facilities, and an increasing emphasis on quality-of-life issues. I can foresee different educational models and paths. I can foresee alternative therapeutic applications and treatment modalities where there is the simultaneous combination and application of different therapies, and can see a greater understanding and integration of biological and sociological approaches and data with those of psychoanalysis."

There are many indications that psychoanalysis is entering a period of new growth, according to Dr. Arnold M. Cooper, incoming president of the American Psychoanalytic Association. With Dr. Robert Michels he has written the chapter "Psychoanalysis and Future Growth" in the book *American Psychoanalysis: Origins and Development,* edited by Dr. Jacques M. Quen and Dr. Eric T. Carlson.

More candidates are applying to psychoanalytic institutes, new institutes are being formed and "there is an extraordinary burgeoning of theoretical ideas." This is due "to data generated by the experiences of psychoanalysts with new patient populations—severe character disorders, psychoses, perversions—from the stimulation of theoretical developments and new findings in related disciplines, as well as studies of young children and experiments with technical modifications." Cooper and Michels predict that "the integration of non-analytic treatment methods with psychoanalysis, without destroying the essence of the psychoanalytic process, will be a challenge to the skill of analysts in the future." Which was what Freud suggested.

This is one challenge. Another is the issue of whether those who are not medically trained will be accepted in greater numbers to the institutes accredited by the American Psychoanalytic Association, which introduced psychoanalysis to America and has fought for the maintenance of high standards in training. Psychoanalysis in America started within the medical profession. This differed from its origin in Vienna, where the medical profession rejected Freud's theories and his closest colleagues included not only M.D.s but lay analysts—educators, writers, a minister, a lawyer and several women who had not attended medical school. In America psychoanalysis has remained mostly within the province of medicine. The American Psychoanalytic Association is one of the Medical Specialty Organizations of the American Medical Association. The American Psychoanalytic Association considers psychoanalysis a sub-specialty of psychiatry. Psychoanalytic theory is incorporated into medical training as the dynamics of psychiatry.

In the past candidates for psychoanalytic training had to possess a medical degree. But now almost all institutes take in a few gifted applicants whose background lies in another field.

Strict limitation on training was one of the reasons Freud disliked what was happening to psychoanalysis in America. Dr. Clarence Oberndorf reports a telling moment when, seven years after his analysis with Freud he went to visit him late in August of 1929 in Berchtesgaden, where Freud was spending the summer. Freud walked slowly down a path in the woods near his summer home to meet Oberndorf. After a few friendly words of greeting, Freud's first question was, "And tell me, what do you really have against lay analysis?" According to Oberndorf, this was uttered "in a tone of annoyance and impatience."

Oberndorf explained the laws of New York State since 1926 (supposedly on Brill's instigation) discouraged the practice of psychoanalysis by the non-medically trained. More important, that the members of the American Psychoanalytic Association believed a knowledge of organic illness necessary before starting a patient's treatment, to rule out bodily ills, since "especially in America, quacks and impostors, extremely ignorant of the elements of psychoanalysis, presumed to hold themselves out as analysts."

Freud waved aside these explanations with an abrupt, "I know all that," turned, and walked slowly toward his house.

Thirteen years later, in 1939, the last year of his life, Freud wrote Jelliffe in New York: "A remark of yours saying that psychoanalysis has spread in the U.S. more widely than deeply struck me as particularly true. I am by no means happy to see that analysis has become the handmaiden of psychiatry in America and nothing else. I am reminded of the parallelism in the fate of our Vienna ladies, who by exile have been turned into housemaids serving in English households."

The Question of Lay Analysis was written by Freud in 1927 as reaction to an attempt made by Viennese authorities to keep Theodor Reik from practicing because he lacked a medical degree. Freud said he did not believe medical training should be a prerequisite for the psychoanalyst, that the personal psychoanalysis of the candidates was "the best means of forming an opinion of their personal aptitude for carrying out their exacting occupation." He added, "They must learn to understand analysis in the only way that is possible—by themselves undergoing an analysis."

He called it "unjust and expedient" to try to compel someone "who wants to set someone else free from the torment of a phobia or an obsession to take the roundabout road of the medical curriculum." He said, "The great mass of what is taught in medical schools is of no use to him for his purposes . . . What is known as medical education appears to me to be an arduous and circuitous way of approaching the profession of analysis."

Freud raised the question: "If it is impossible to prevent the lay analysts from pursuing their activities and if the public does not support the campaign against them, would it not be more expedient to recognize the fact of their existence by offering them opportunities for training? Might it not be possible in this way to gain some influence over them?"

Though he never said so publicly, Freud wanted psychoanalysis to become an independent profession, divorced from psychiatry and medicine, according to Jones. Freud believed his discoveries applied to a wide area outside of medicine. He saw them as a foundation for a new dynamic psychology that would lead to a more profound understanding of human nature. He envisioned psychoanalytic contributions as applied to many fields, including the bringing up of children, sociology, religion and perhaps even in government to promote more harmonious relations between nations. He foresaw all this as lost if psychoanalysis were to remain a small division of psychiatry.

Freud disapproved of what he called a "wild analyst"—his term for either a layman or physician who "pretended to practice" psychoanalysis without learning its theories or technique.

In the United States a few prominent psychoanalysts have fought the medical restriction established by the American Psychoanalytic Association—the American is the only regional member of the International Psychoanalytical Association to have this restriction. In Dr. Kurt Eissler's book in behalf of lay analysis, *Medical Orthodoxy and the Future of Psychoanalysis,* he wrote: "There is no kind of pre-analytic training that will guarantee the adequacy of the future analyst. Everything depends on innate talents, personal analysis, and the theoretical as well as practical training of the candidate in psychoanalysis proper. Yet I still insist that a realistic appraisal must lead to the conclusion that, if the preanalytic training of later candidates is uniform—that is to say, if only physicians or lawyers or historians or social workers become psychoanalysts—then psychoanalysis must take a lopsided course of development. Psychoanalysis would be best served, would in fact become a kind of academy of the science of man, only if the widest possible spectrum of experts were represented among the fully trained and practicing psychoanalysts."

Dr. Lawrence J. Friedman, past president of the Los Angeles Psychoanalytic Society and former dean of its training institute, has gone on record stating that restricting psychoanalytic training to doctors "eliminates a great number of creative, gifted, sensitive, psychologically-minded men, and especially women, because they are not attracted to long years of medical training and have great difficulty in being accepted by medical schools." He pointed out that some of the major contributions to the theory and practice of psychoanalysis have been and still are being made by lay analysts both in this country and abroad. He remarked that Anna Freud has neither an M.D. nor a Ph.D., though a few years ago she received an honorary M.D. from the University of Vienna. Others not medically trained included Erik Erikson, Ernst Kris and Robert Waelder.

A proposal was made to permit a psychoanalytic institute to train a group of non-medical students in 1974 when Pollock, at that time president-elect of the American Psychoanalytic Association, submitted for endorsement the Chicago Proposal. This document asked for a blanket waiver to cover eighteen students in a pilot program at the Chicago Institute for Psychoanalysis. The Chicago Institute, working with a select committee of the Association, planned to spend two years designing the program, setting criteria for selection and discussing problems that might arise. These "experimental students," all with the minimum of a master's degree, would come from a variety of fields. The project's goal was to determine whether the acquisition of psychoanalytic competence for treating troubled men and women was dependent on a medical background. The students, on graduation, would receive a doctorate in psychoanalysis.

In appealing for the passage of the Chicago Proposal, Pollock pointed out that since the research graduates for whom the twenty-six institutes had granted waivers were not supposed to practice analysis except as it directly related to their research, "this means that at the present time no individual other than a psychiatrist can be trained for the clinical practice of psychoanalysis." Therefore, he said, he thought endorsement of the Chicago Proposal was important—eighteen students trained by the Chicago Institute would not "precipitously convert us into a nonmedical Association."

He warned that at the present time "anybody can practice psychoanalysis and psychotherapy without a license. Anybody can go ahead and set up an institute for psychoanalysis, out of our control and where we cannot regulate standards. Anybody can practice psychoanalysis and the reason for that is that we are not a profession. Since organized medicine and psychiatry have not seen fit to say that one must have a medical degree and appropriate certification in order to be known as a psychoanalyst, we are faced with all these liabilities and, I believe, much danger to psychoanalysis."

The Chicago Proposal was turned down by the Board on Professional Standards and the Executive Council of the Association. In his post-presidential address given the following year, on December 20, 1975, at the annual meeting of the American, Pollock pointedly spoke out: "We must recognize we cannot rest on Freud's laurels . . . Our future depends upon welcoming new ideas, new people, new fields . . . Change is inevitable. If we plan for it, are not threatened by it, if we do not react fearfully or angrily to it, we can direct, lead, benefit, and become agencies of change. If we resist, become frozen and incapable of leaving what is past, what is gone, what is no longer utilitarian or realistic, we will survive —but perhaps as merely a paragraph in the history books. We must not act like the Viennese neurological hierarchy and possibly either stifle originality in the younger or in those who come from different intellectual lands. If we do, we may force the potential creators to go elsewhere. Our organization can and should welcome, accept, encourage, support and help in the testing of new findings, concepts, applications and in the education of the promising, the competent, the serious, and the creative."

Dr. Gerald L. Klerman, himself a psychoanalyst and director of the Alcohol, Drug Abuse and Mental Health Administration, urged the psychoanalysts attending the Thirty-First Congress "to contribute to an improved dialogue [with the federal government] that will lead to a better understanding that will reflect psychoanalytic advances, and to examine common steps and joint endeavors with the government so there will be a more prominent place for psychoanalysis in America and the patient sector can benefit from what psychoanalysts can offer." The attitude the federal government shows toward psychoanalysis is "inconsistent and ambivalent" because the government does not have "a clear understanding today of the best and proper role of psychoanalysis in the large American scene," Klerman said.

The burning question today in psychoanalysis seems to be: Who will speak for Freud?

There is a lively and continuing argument among several groups about whether psychoanalysis belongs in a medical framework, or whether eligibility for training should not be conducted on a broader basis so those with a background in psychology, social work, the humanities, anthropology and other fields may be admitted to institutes.

Actually, lay analysis is a fact. A growing number of psychoanalysts outside the medical profession, trained in institutes chartered by states throughout the country during the last few decades, are represented by the National Accreditation Association for Psychoanalysis, of which Phyllis Meadow, Ph.D. is president. She is also president of the Center for Modern Psychoanalytic Studies in New York and editor-in-chief of the *Journal of Modern Psychoanalysis*. The NAAP has led the movement to establish a nationwide accrediting agency for psychoanalysis outside the province of psychiatry, and to make psychoanalysis a profession in its own right.

An increasing number of psychologists in the American Psychological Association are also working to establish psychoanalysis as a profession. A new Division of Psychoanalysis, with 1,100 members, was created at the Association's 1979 convention in New York, traditionally held over the Labor Day weekend. The Association has a Division of Clinical Psychology and a larger Division of Psychotherapy.

The first president of the Division of Psychoanalysis, Reuben Fine, says, "This is an historic step in the annals of psychoanalysis. It marks the first official recognition by psychology that psychoanalysis is an important part of it. It combats the propagandistic statement by the medical psychoanalysts that psychoanalysis is part of medicine, inspired by purely economic and social reasons."

There is also conflict between the psychiatrists and psychologists over Blue Cross and Blue Shield benefits, each winning court cases in different states. In 1954 the American Psychiatric Association, the American Psychoanalytic Association and the American Medical Association issued a joint resolution opposing any laws that would allow other professional groups to practice psychotherapy without supervision by a psychiatrist. The resolution did little good. By 1977, after lobbying state legislatures with remarkable success, psychologists were licensed in all fifty states and the District of Columbia. Psychiatrists are now trying to block "freedom-of-choice" laws that allow professionals other than psychiatrists to be reimbursed directly by insurance companies for providing mental health services.

In New York state there has been an effort by the New York State Psychological Association to introduce legislation providing that anyone who wants to practice psychoanalysis or psychotherapy (other than medical analysts and psychotherapists) must have a Ph.D. in psychology (there is already a law in the state to prevent anyone from calling himself a psychologist who does not have a Ph.D. in psychology). This would extend the domain of psychology over all mental health professionals except psychiatrists and social workers.

Harold L. Davis, a former physicist, now a psychoanalyst and vice president of the NAAP, has been a leader in opposing this legislation. He believes that graduate training in psychology, which usually does not include a personal analysis, is not adequate preparation for a psychoanalyst or psychotherapist. He says that if mental health professions, including psychoanalysts without medical degrees, psychotherapists, marriage counselors and other practicing therapists, come under the aegis of psychology, this will set back the therapeutic movement. What happens in New York State is important, he adds, because such a large number of psychoanalysts and psychologists—not to mention other mental health workers—live in New York and also because the state is the traditional leader in legislation for the rest of the nation. Of the nation's 49,000 psychologists, about ten percent are clinical psychologists, who may or may not have had a personal analysis. Their certification as a psychologist does not guarantee that as therapists they understand the nature of the unconscious or human behavior in depth and this would "encourage the licensing of persons who are professionally unqualified," Davis says.

A new term, "mental health professional," includes everyone working in the mental health field, which has been expanding due to increasing third-party coverage and to larger numbers of persons seeking help. The term refers to anyone from the highly trained psychiatrist to the semi-trained or virtually untrained worker. In 1947, there were almost 5,000 psychiatrists and 23,000 other mental health professionals. By 1977, this had risen to 22,000 psychiatrists and 121,000 other mental health professionals, many working in the community mental health centers.

A pilot venture in the training of mental health professionals is being undertaken by the Department of Psychiatry of University of California School of Medicine under the direction of Dr. Robert S. Wallerstein, past president of the American Psychoanalytic Association and currently a vice-president of the International Psychoanalytic Association. This "Doctorate of Mental Health" program is an experiment in professional education in the mental health field. It consists of a five-year post-college professional degree program, including two pre-clinical years "with a *relatively equal mix* of biological science, psychological science, and social science, followed by three years of applied clinical experiences in the variety of settings in which mental health professionals are trained," says Wallerstein. Its curriculum includes biological, psychological, and social science courses, selected for their relevance to an understanding of the clinical issues in mental health. "The Doctor of Mental Health program differs from the training programs of each of the traditional mental health professional disciplines—clinical psychiatry, clinical psychology and psychiatric social work," according to Wallerstein. "The ways in which the graduates will be better or less well-trained than their colleagues in other disciplines to deal with the phenomena of mental health and disease is the focus of an intense ongoing process of evaluation, which has been in effect since the inception of this pilot venture. We hope that the graduates of the program will fill needed service roles, primarily in the public sector."

There are some fairly clear trends in psychoanalysis. One is the variety in the type of person coming for analysis. There is, for example, increasing occupational diversity among patients. Dr. Earl C. Witenberg, author of *Contemporary Thought in Psychoanalysis* and director of the William Alanson White Institute in New York, reports that within a six-month period he treated a sixty-six-year-old academician, a sixty-four-year-old investment banker and a fifty-six-year-old housewife, all progressing well in their first analytic therapy. He also said that more ethnic groups and more lifestyles "are represented by today's patients." Out of ten recent consultations, two patients were Orientals, one Irish Roman-Catholic, and one East Indian: "As the indications for treatment by a psychoanalyst have broadened, so has the patient base. I suspect this will be a continuing trend."

The age-range of patients entering psychoanalysis has also broadened considerably over the years. Once only the patient below age forty was encouraged to enter treatment, in line with Freud's own view, stated in 1918 in the "Wolfman" case: ". . . the mobility of the mental cathexes is a quality which shows striking diminution with the advance of age. This has given us one of the indications of the limits within which psychoanalytic treatment is effective. There are some people, however, who retain this mental plasticity far beyond the usual age-limit, and others who lose it very prematurely."

So Freud did grant that individuals vary greatly, no matter what their age.

During the Thirty-First International Congress, Pearl King of London reported that many middle-aged and older persons were being analyzed today. She described the chief problems of the middle-aged and elderly as: fear of the diminution or loss of sexual potency and the impact on relationships; threat of displacement in work roles by younger people and the possible failure of the effectiveness of their professional skills, linked with the fear they will not be able to cope with retirement and will lose their sense of identity; anxieties arising in marital relationships after children have left home and parents can no longer use their children to mask problems arising in their relationship with each other; awareness of aging, possibly illness and consequent dependence on others, and the anxiety this arouses; inevitability of their own death and the realization they may not be able to achieve the goals set for themselves, and that what they can achieve and enjoy in life may be limited, with consequent feelings of depression or deprivation.

The relative scarcity of literature concerning emotional illness in the aged, the comparative lack of interest in doing psychotherapy with elderly patients and the marked difficulties encountered in the attempts to enact legislation in their behalf are reflective, among other motivations, of man's wish "to deny this period of life which is all too reminiscent of the 'theme of loss'—loss of genital function, loss of occupation, loss of loved ones and familiar surroundings, loss of perceptual acuity, loss of physical health and loss of life itself," says Dr. Gerald V. Freiman, who has seen many elderly patients in his private practice.

Dr. Martin Berezin of Boston has been a staunch advocate of psychoanalytic therapy for the elderly. He was instrumental in the formation, in 1960, of the Boston Society for Gerontologic Psychiatry, which has served as a model for the establishment of a national organization, the American Association for Geriatric Psychiatry.

Another trend is that of longer treatment. A reporter once asked Jones—when he visited this country in May, 1956 to speak at the Freud Centennial celebration in Chicago—whether he believed analysis could be shortened without altering its effectiveness. Jones replied, "The more we know about the human mind, the longer analysis will take."

This seems true: analysis now takes between three and five years on the average (Freud said he treated one or two patients daily for ten years). But the number of days per week spent in analysis has decreased. Freud insisted on seeing patients six days a week; analysts today will see patients three or four times a week. This means in some instances the analytic process will be spread over a longer period of time.

Freud commented on what he called "the preposterous expectations on the part of patients, as well as doctors, concerning the supposed length of treatment." He ascribed those expectations "to the prevailing ignorance of the strength and depth of mental forces and the total obscurity surrounding a neurotic affliction." He compared this to the "maiden from afar"—no one knows where she came from and so they anticipate an equally mysterious departure. That a psychoanalysis is necessarily long, Freud said, was due not only to its "inherent difficulty" but also to the "timelessness" of the unconscious and the slowness with which deep changes can be brought about. Similarly, it is unreasonable to demand that only certain symptoms should be analyzed, he added, and the rest left to operate destructively.

Perhaps in the future, as Freud predicted, there will be some kind of treatment, based on psychoanalytic principles, that will be far briefer than psychoanalysis. There is today, for example, what is called "supportive therapy," which does not attempt to reach unconscious conflicts but tides the patient over difficult periods.

The high cost of analysis usually enters any discussion of it. With costs of all else rising, it is unlikely the analytic fee will decrease from its current scale of between forty and seventy-five dollars per session. Even so—contrary to popular belief—the income of analysts is far less than that of most medical specialists. A study conducted by the American Psychoanalytic Association shows that one-third of all psychoanalytic fees are covered by insurance companies.

It will be many years before psychoanalysis will be covered by any national health insurance plan, Dr. Robert Michels has pointed out. "We are going to see psychoanalysis covered last," he says. "We are going to have to live with it out of the system but we have to prepare for it being in the system eventually. It will be a long process, not a single event that is going to happen or not happen."

A study undertaken in 1966 under the direction of Dr. Burness Moore, past president of the American Psychoanalytic Association, revealed that a change has developed in the patterns of the practice of psychoanalysts in that an appreciable number were shifting from full-time practice to part-time or salaried positions in hospitals or teaching in medical schools. Some have even served as directors of state mental health departments.

The study also revealed that geographical distribution of analysts is unequal. Over two-fifths practice in the northeast, where about one-fourth of the national population is located. More than one-fifth practice in the west, where about a sixth of the population resides. The south and the north-central regions contain between a sixth and fifth of the analysts but almost one-third of the population. If psychoanalysts were to be distributed evenly per 100,000 population, eight states—New York, California, Pennsylvania, Massachusetts, Connecticut, New Jersey, Maryland and Illinois—and the District of Columbia would appear to be saturated relative to their populations, whereas some states have not a single analyst.

On the current mailing list of the American Psychoanalytic Association nineteen psychoanalysts are scattered over twenty states in the New England, the east south-central and west south-central regions. The problem this poses in relation to access to psychoanalytic and psychotherapeutic care under any national health financing is a major one.

An increasing number of women have become psychoanalysts. Since Freud welcomed women from the start, no feminist revolution was needed in the field of psychoanalysis. Women are also entering psychiatry, psychology and social work in larger numbers. "We may see women outnumber men as therapists in the years to come," predicts Dr. Henriette Klein, a training psychoanalyst and clinical professor at Columbia University College of Physicians and Surgeons.

Another change is the decrease in stigma attached to receiving psychological help. Twenty-five years ago people kept this secret. Today even public figures are no longer so reticent about revealing they are in therapy. In 1972 Senator Thomas Eagleton reported he had undergone psychiatric treatment, though it cost him the vice-presidential nomination when Presidential candidate George McGovern decided it would be inexpedient to keep Eagleton as his running mate.

Another development is a closer link between analysts and medicine. The newly created post of liaison officer between the American Psychoanalytic Association and the American Psychiatric Association is held by Dr. Lewis L. Robbins, vice president of the psychiatric association and former secretary of the psychoanalytic association. Dr. Karl Menninger was the first psychiatrist to receive the American Medical Association's Sheen award, in 1978, for scientific accomplishment. He said, on receiving $10,000 and a commemorative plaque, that this was emblematic of the acceptance of psychiatry into the fold of medical science.

Still another trend is analysts leaving their ivory towers and reaching out into the community. Dr. Gerald V. Freiman is chairman of the Committee on Affiliate Societies of the American Psychoanalytic Association, which is encouraging analysts to "use their expertise to educate community and government agencies."

Freiman says, "In the early days of the Association, emphasis was on maintaining high standards of training and this still remains one of the main functions of the Board on Professional Standards. But today analysts no longer tend to confuse anonymity behind the couch with anonymity in the world outside, and one of the other main functions of the Association and its affiliates is to educate the public as to what analysis is all about, exactly as Freud did."

According to Freiman the practice of analysis is "flourishing" in places where analysts have taken a more active role in community activities. He cites as example Chicago, where courses are given to business executives on "the psychoanalysis of management," and St. Louis, where, for instance, analysts hold seminars with firemen and police on the psychology of catastrophes.

Psychoanalysts are also serving as advisers to social agencies, prisons, the courts, colleges, juvenile delinquency centers. Some conduct group therapy in mental hospitals—Dr. Martin Grotjahn, author of *The Art and Technique of Analytic Group Therapy*, believes group therapy could bring on "a quiet revolution" if used more extensively in mental hospitals. Dr. Walter A. Stewart, who delivered the 1979 Brill Memorial Lecture, "Building a Clinical Theory: The Science of our Art", spends time at the Morristown Memorial Hospital helping doctors and surgeons understand the psyche of the patient who becomes angry and fearful when he enters a hospital.

In recent years there has been a closer relationship between analysts and the fourth estate. Dr. Karl Menninger, along with his brother, the late Dr. William Menninger, has helped bring about better relations between reporters and psychoanalysts, as did Dr. Robert E. Knight and Dr. Ives Hendrick during their presidencies of the American Psychoanalytic Association. At first analysts were understandably reluctant to talk to reporters and magazine writers because their theories were so often distorted in print. But over the years more and more analysts, encouraged by Robert L. Robinson, information officer for the American Psychiatric Association, who also ran the press room for the analysts at their annual conventions, have freely given interviews.

The insights of psychoanalysis have been and are still being widely used by writers. In the theater, Eugene O'Neill was among the first playwrights to use Freud's theories. In *Strange Interlude* characters speak not only the traditional dialogue but then, in asides, freely associate to their hidden thoughts. The late Moss Hart in the play *Lady in the Dark* eloquently presented not only the essence of psychoanalysis as the heroine says, in a sudden insight, "I never dreamed that the desperate desires of childhood could govern grown-up behavior," but also showed how analytic treatment could change a woman's life for the better. In the movie *Citizen Kane,* sensitively written, acted and directed by Orson Welles, the effect of a boy's premature separation from his mother was poignantly portrayed in the symbol of the sleigh, *Rosebud.* And in Alfred Hitchcock's *Spellbound* the interpretation of a dream led to the apprehension of a killer.

Novelists have long used psychoanalytic insights—notably Henry James, brother of psychologist William James. In his novella *The Turn of the Screw* James dealt with infantile sexual desires—critical interpretations differ as to whether there was actual seduction of the boy and girl by the former valet and governess or whether it was a fantasy of the young, sexually repressed narrator. Two of James' novels, *Washington Square* and *The Golden Bowl,* show the tragic effects of unresolved Electra complexes, while his *The Wings of the Dove* is, among other things, a moving depiction of psychosomatic illness.

Jones in his biography of Freud delightfully describes Freud's influence on the James brothers: "If William James wrote textbooks of psychology as if they were novels and his brother Henry wrote novels as if they were textbooks on psychology, Freud may be said to have combined the two aims in an enchanting degree."

In more recent times Sherwood Anderson wrote, in *Dark Laughter,* "If there is anything you do not understand in human life, consult the works of Dr. Freud." And novelist Theodore Dreiser said of Freud after he had read several of his books: "Every paragraph came as a revelation to me—a strong, revealing light thrown on some of the darkest problems that haunted and troubled me and my work. And reading him has helped me in my studies of life and men . . . he reminded me of a conqueror who has taken a city, entered its age-old, hoary prisons and there generously proceeded to release from their gloomy and rusted cells the prisoners of formulae, faiths and illusions which have racked and worn man for hundreds and thousands of years. The light that he has thrown on the human mind! Its vagaries and destructive delusions and their cure! It is to me at once colossal and beautiful!"

In the mystery field a number of writers have used Freudian concepts, including Stanley Ellin in *Mirror, Mirror on the Wall,* a look into the tormented mind of a man, and Robert Bloch in *Psycho,* a young man's psychic possession by his mother. Jacqueline Wein in *Roommate,* describes how the sexual aberrations of an inhibited young woman lead to murder.

Freud's impact on society is evident today in almost all areas. His discoveries have become a pervasive and integral part of pop culture. A comic strip by Parker and Hart is called "The Wizard of Id"; on the television program *The Cross-Wits,* on October 25, 1978, Jack Clark gave as clue to the unknown word in the puzzle, "The emotional type is not always visible." The word was "scar." And the engagement of Susan Ford, daughter of the former President of the United States, to Charles Frederick Vance, a divorced Secret Service agent assigned to guard the Fords in 1977, prompted Jerry Devine, secretary of the Wackenhut Corporation, which numbers many famous persons among its bodyguarded clientele, to say, "Bodyguards represent a combined mother-father-big brother image. These women are under extreme pressure, and when someone is there to protect them, they often come as the White Knight."

Freud's impact on modern life goes far deeper than this absorption of Freudianism into the popular consciousness. On a more fundamental level, there seems to be a new "right" added to man's inherent rights—the right to mental health. A young man in Oregon, for example, who spent time in a mental hospital, is suing his mother and father because they did not provide adequate emotional nurturing for him as a child. Such an act would have been considered absurd a few years ago.

The mental health rights of young people are being protected in more conventional ways. For example, the North Shore Mental Health Association–Irene Josselyn Clinic in Chicago, where Dr. Mary Griffin is currently medical director, invited representatives of the professional staffs of forty-four high schools and junior high schools in the area to take part in a workshop on "Consciousness Raising about Teenage Suicide," a national problem that is being increasingly recognized.

Psychological help based on psychoanalytic theory is being given to other groups never before considered in need. Under the auspices of the Clinical Services of the William Alanson White Institute, Dr. Miltiades Saphiropoulos and Dr. Leopold Caligor started the treatment of men in the United Automobile Workers Union—the Union Therapy Project—to show that psychoanalytic therapy was not just for the wealthy few. This service was recently extended to wives and children as well.

Programs to reach the "batterers" of wives and children are being developed by the American Psychological Association, such as the in-patient Domestic Assault Program at the American Lake Veterans Hospital in Tacoma, Washington. Lance A. Harris and Anne L. Ganley of the Tacoma program report: "Men who assault family members come from all races, socio-economic classes, and occupations . . . Men who batter seem either to have been battered as children or to have witnessed physical abuse in their families. Our own limited research sample indicates that sixty-three percent had that experience." They also found the wife batterers had "intense dependent relationships with their victims."

Psychiatric care and consultation is being given to remote Indian villages in Ontario by the department of psychiatry of the University of Toronto, which received a Gold Achievement Award from the American Psychiatric Association. Fifteen psychiatrists cross a myriad of cultural and language barriers each time they fly 1,300 miles northwest to offer care and consultation to the Cree and Ojibway Indians.

A number of children labeled "retarded," who were confined to institutions for life and denied any chance to be normal, now recognized as "autistic" and suffering from early emotional deprivation, have been given help that has restored them to normal. Other children suffering from emotional conflicts are being given "a second chance" at such places as the Center for Preventive Psychiatry in White Plains, New York, where Dr. Gilbert Kliman is director. In addition to early detection and treatment of childhood mental illness, the Center provides preventive services, programs in community education and psychological first aid in mass disasters.

The Reiss-Davis Clinic for Child Guidance of Los Angeles started in 1950 in a converted warehouse. A building fund campaign, with Frank Sinatra as honorary chairman, resulted in a new two-story modern clinic to house the expanding program of what has become the largest facility of its kind in the West.

A program for confused, disoriented, depressed elderly persons is offered by the I.C.D. Rehabilitation and Research Center in New York, whose director, Dr. James C. Folsom, a graduate of the Menninger School of Psychiatry, uses "attitude therapy," devised by Dr. Karl Menninger as an approach to helping the mentally and physically failing old person. It is based on psychoanalytic concepts.

"Prejudices which anticipate that mental decline is a normal part of the aging process serve as a very great barrier in the treatment of elderly persons with mental disease," Dr. Monica Blumenthal, program director of Geriatric Psychiatry at the Western Psychiatric Institute and Clinic of the University of Pittsburgh, told a conference on aging. The depression appearing in the elderly "is not naturally a part of old age" but "hallmarks of illness, most of which are amenable to treatment and to cure," she said. The "old," slightly less than eleven percent of the population, commit twenty-five percent of the known suicides, she pointed out, many of which could be prevented if treatment were given.

Psychoanalysts are currently being employed by business concerns and other large organizations, including even baseball clubs. The Chicago Cubs were among the first to use an analyst to help players with their personal problems. General Mills is conducting a study of how America's fifty-five million families view some of the crucial questions affecting physical and mental well-being. Law enforcement officers throughout the state of California are being given training courses in "Law Enforcement and the Mentally Disordered Individual," designed to prepare policemen to deal more effectively with the mental health responsibilities that occur in their duties. The California Psychiatric Association, the State Department of Mental Health and the California Peace Officers Association cooperated in producing the training programs.

Psychoanalysis is very much a part of the thinking of philosophers. In a lecture, "Freud and Philosophy," Donald Brady, philosophy professor at Cheney State College in Cheney, Pennsylvania, told the faculty and students of St. John's College in Annapolis, Maryland:

"Some ethical philosophers preoccupied with thinking—indeed debauched with thinking—appear to believe that logic and exegesis rule the world. Freud knew better; love and hunger rule the world. In the deepest heart of all of us, beyond the aristocratic desire to contemplate universal and necessary theorems, is a great restlessness that would be cured. There Freud plunged and found the hurly-burly of human fact, a fierce confusion of ambivalent man, ever contradictory, ever Faustian, ever aware that he is an amphibian—never at home, always yearning—wanting what he does not choose, choosing (like Phaedra and all of us) what he does not want."

Freud has made it possible for more men and women to choose what they *do* want. In *The Future of an Illusion* he expressed the hope that the science of psychoanalysis would replace the "illusion" of religion.

Today, four decades after Freud's death and one hundred years since Dr. Josef Breuer first treated Bertha Pappenheim, out of which came the "talking cure" that stimulated Freud to explore the unconscious, psychoanalysis has indeed proved more than an illusion—both in the treatment of the individual and the approaches it has given all mankind by which to achieve a more humane society.

Psychoanalysis seems well on its way to achieving the dynamic place in reality for which Freud hoped—in spite of those who would misuse and misrepresent it—because of the strength and resiliency of its proven truth.

Sources and Acknowledgments

Dr. Karl Abraham, *Clinical Papers and Essays on Psychoanalysis.* 1955. Basic Books, Inc. New York.

W. H. Auden, "In Memory of Sigmund Freud," *Collected Shorter Poems* (1927–1957). Copyright © 1964, W. H. Auden. 1966, Random House, Inc.

Dr. Charles Brenner, *An Elementary Textbook of Psychoanalysis.* 1955, International Universities Press. New York.

Dorothy Bloch, *So The Witch Won't Eat Me.* Copyright © 1978 Dorothy Bloch. Houghton-Mifflin. Boston. Reprinted by permission of the author.

Dr. Harold Blum, "The Prototype of Preoedipal Reconstruction". *Journal of the American Psychoanalytic Association,* Vol. 25, No. 4, 1977.

Dr. Arnold Cooper and Dr. Robert Michels, "Psychoanalysis and Future Growth," chapter in *American Psychoanalysis: Origins and Development.* Edited by Dr. Jacques M. Quen and Dr. Eric T. Carlson. 1978, Brunner/Mazel, Inc. New York.

Theodore Dreiser, "Dreiser on Freud". Reprinted from *The Psychoanalytic Review,* Vol. 18, No. 3, 1931, through the courtesy of the Editors and the Publisher, National Psychological Association for Psychoanalysis, New York.

Dr. Kurt Eissler, *Medical Orthodoxy and The Future of Psychoanalysis.* 1965, International Universities Press. New York.

Anna Freud, *The Ego And The Mechanisms Of Defense.* 1937, The Hogarth Press, Ltd., London.

Dr. Sigmund Freud, *The Basic Writings of Sigmund Freud,* translated and edited, with an introduction by Dr. A. A. Brill. 1934, The Modern Library, Random House. New York.

Dr. Sigmund Freud, *Beyond The Pleasure Principle.* 1942, The Hogarth Press, Ltd. London.

Dr. Sigmund Freud, *Civilization And Its Discontents.* 1958, Doubleday Anchor Books. New York.

Dr. Sigmund Freud, *The Ego And The Id.* 1957, The Hogarth Press, Ltd. London.

Dr. Sigmund Freud, *Inhibitions, Symptoms And Anxiety.* 1949, The Hogarth Press, Ltd. London.

Dr. Sigmund Freud, *Studies on Hysteria,* with Dr. Josef Breuer. 1957, Basic Books, Inc. New York.

Dr. Lawrence J. Friedman, *Psy'cho-a-nal'-y-sis.* 1968, Paul S. Eriksson. Middlebury, Vermont.

Dr. Frieda Fromm-Reichmann, *Principles of Intensive Psychotherapy*. 1950, The University of Chicago Press. Chicago.

Dr. Ralph R. Greenson, *Explorations in Psychoanalysis*. 1978, International Universities Press. New York.

Dr. Martin Grotjahn, *The Art And Technique of Analytic Group Therapy*. 1977, Jason Aronson, Inc. New York.

Calvin Hall, "Sigmund Freud—Founder of Psychoanalysis". May, 1957, *Wisdom* magazine. Beverly Hills, California.

Dr. Ernest Jones, *The Life And Work of Sigmund Freud*. Volumes 1, 2, 3. Copyright © 1953, 1955, 1957 by Ernest Jones, M. D. Basic Books, Inc., Publishers. New York.

Dr. A. Kardiner, *My Analysis With Freud, Reminiscences*. Copyright © 1977 by A. Kardiner. W. W. Norton & Company, Inc. New York.

Dr. Robert Langs, *The Listening Process*. 1978. Jason Aronson, Inc., New York.

Helen Liegner and Ronda Motycka, "James Joyce's Ulysses Revisited: Matricide and the Search for the Mother". To appear in a forthcoming issue of the *Psychoanalytic Review*. Through the courtesy of the Editors and the Publisher, National Psychological Association for Psychoanalysis, New York, N. Y.

Dr. Hans W. Loewald, "Instinct Theory, Object Relations, and Psychic-Structure Formation." *Journal of the American PsychoAnalytic Association*, Vol. 26, No. 3, 1979.

Dr. Karl Menninger, *The Human Mind*. Copyright © 1930 by Alfred A. Knopf, Inc. New York.

Maria W. Piers, *Infanticide; Past And Present*. 1978, W. W. Norton & Company. New York.

Dr. George H. Pollock, "Anniversary Reactions, Trauma and Mourning". *The Psychoanalytic Quarterly.* Vol. XXXIX, No. 3, 1970.

Theodor Reik, *From Thirty Years With Freud.* 1940, Farrar, Rinehart. New York.

Paul Ricoeur, "The Question of Proof in Freud's Psychoanalytic Writings". *Journal of the American Psychoanalytic Association,* Volume 25, No. 4, 1977.

Dr. Gregory Rochlin, *Griefs and Discontents: The Forces of Change.* Copyright © 1965, Little, Brown & Company. Boston. Reprinted by permission of the publisher.

Hanns Sachs, *Freud, Master And Friend.* 1946, Harvard University Press. Boston.

Dr. Calvin F. Settlage, "The Psychoanalytic Understanding of Narcissistic and Borderline Personality Disorders: Advances in Developmental Theory". *Journal of the American Psychoanalytic Association,* Vol. 25, No. 4, 1977.

Dr. Charles Socarides, *Beyond Sexual Freedom.* 1975, Quadrangle, New York *Times* Books. New York.

Dr. Rene Spitz, *First Year of Life.* 1965, International Universities Press, New York.

Dr. Hyman Spotnitz, *Psychotherapy of Preoedipal Conditions.* 1976, Jason Aronson, Inc., New York.

Dr. Walter A. Stewart and Lucy Freeman, *The Secret Of Dreams.* Copyright © 1972 by Dr. Walter Stewart and Lucy Freeman. 1972, The Macmillan Company. New York.

Dr. Robert Stoller, "Boyhood Gender Aberrations: Treatment Issues". *Journal of the American Psychoanalytic Association,* Vol. 26, No. 3, 1978.

Robert Waelder, *The Living Thoughts Of Freud,* edited by Alfred O. Mendel. Copyright © 1941, 1969 by David McKay Co., Inc. Reprinted by permission of The David McKay Company, Inc.

Dr. Joseph Wortis, "Fragments of a Freudian Analysis", *American Journal of Orthopsychiatry,* Vol. X, No. 4, October, 1940.

Index